365 DAYS
in
God's
Presence

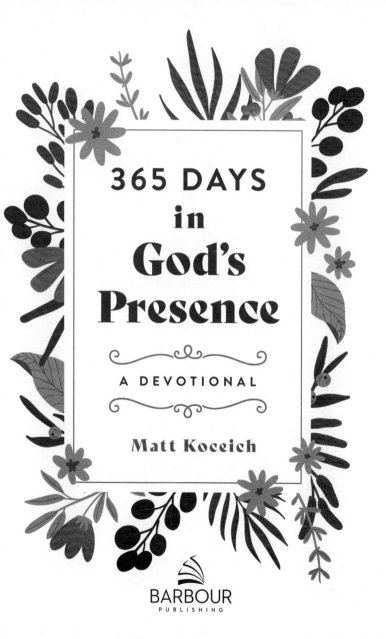

365 DAYS
in
God's Presence

A DEVOTIONAL

Matt Koceich

BARBOUR
PUBLISHING

Member of the
Evangelical Christian
Publishers Association

January 1

Precious child,

You are so beautiful.

Holding you makes Me smile. You are perfect in every way. Please know how much you mean to Me. I want you to know that I am ever-lasting, and what I feel for you right now will be the same tomorrow and a million tomorrows after that. I have searched you. I know you and am with you through every part of your day. Whether you are up or down, I know what you are going through. I perceive your thoughts and am here to help you sort them out. I won't let you be alone.

Holding you brings Me glory because you have been fearfully and wonderfully made. Don't ever doubt My love for you. You are My treasure. I am filled with infinite joy when I think of you. I go before you and I come after you. I lay My hand on you. My Spirit and presence are with you no matter where you go. My hands guide you and hold you. Even though the world tries to cover you in darkness, My light shines over you, making the deepest nights like day.

I am giving you an intimate gift of days to cherish. I have ordained the hours of this new year for you to love others like I love you. This gift is so much more than the breath I've breathed into your lungs. Your life is also meant to shine. I know there are times when you might believe otherwise, but those are not from My heart. The enemy tries to pull you away from Me. Don't focus on the world's hatred. Don't let the evil mock your heart.

You are so important. Never forget this. I have wonderful plans for you that you cannot imagine, and nothing can take you away from Me. I am leading you. Let Me search your heart and remove the anxious thoughts. You are Mine, and I love you.

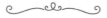

Psalm 139

Precious child,

You are now forever free from the burden of sin. I have given you this freedom to love Me and each other. I know this doesn't always mean an easy, carefree experience. There will be days when you are tempted to question My sovereignty—days when you wonder if I'm really here. But remember how I asked Abraham to offer his only son, Isaac, as a sacrifice? He not only obeyed Me, but also called it worship.

Years later, a famine came, and I commanded Isaac to stay where he was and be blessed. He trusted Me and planted his crop. When he reaped a hundredfold, the Philistines grew jealous of Isaac's prosperity and forced him to move. I came to Isaac in his time of need and told him not to fear. Both Abraham and Isaac were obedient to the service that I had called them to.

I saved you to take away your fears so that you too might bring Me glory. You may not feel like a king, but My grace is not about how you feel. My grace is how I feel about you! You are My child, not a failure. You are a reflection of Me, not a picture of despair. You are royalty in My eyes, not an unnoticed, unappreciated servant. Simply put, you are priceless to Me.

The enemy tries hard to see that you follow your own desires. He hopes the emptiness of accumulating material things will fill you up and make you believe that you no longer need Me. He tries to enslave you to false promises and fool's gold. The enemy makes it easy for you to serve yourself.

But, when you serve Me in the ways I choose, you are truly free to live life the way I meant for you to live it. Go through this day renewed by My mighty power. Without fear, in complete obedience, let Me be your freedom.

Genesis 22:5; Psalm 8:4–5; 116:16; Romans 8:21

January 3

Precious child,

As I shed new mercies over you today, please walk knowing that I am making your path straight. This doesn't mean everything will be perfectly filled with clear skies and happiness, but it does mean that every one of your days is secure in Me. Nothing the enemy throws at you ever catches Me off guard. You are safe in Me. Even when the world makes you believe that you are on your own, I want you to know that our relationship is unbreakable.

Tell Me everything. Your questions don't make Me mad at you. That's the enemy's game. Not only do I want to hear what you have to say, but I promise to answer you. I always hear your cries for mercy, and My presence is your strength and shield. Let My mercy become tangible as you receive My power to endure hardships. Feel My protection cover you from potentially harmful situations. Remember, it wasn't your might but My mercy that saved you. And My mercy sews patience in your heart so that others around you will see Jesus there.

My mercy helps you from the time you get up until the time you go to sleep. I love on you even when you're unaware and dreaming. Mercy teaches you that you have overcome the problems of this life. By My mercy, I want you to see trials as opportunities that will bring Me glory. The enemy works hard at making you feel defeated, but please know that you are righteous in My eyes, and I have delivered you from his dark clutches.

Mercy, which Jesus made possible on the cross, means you will never again drown in sin. It means I save you, forgive you, keep you on solid ground, answer you, give you strength and protect you, help you, and promise to take away your stress. You are worth all these things and more to Me!

Psalm 34:19; Daniel 9:9; 1 Timothy 1:16; Titus 3:5

January 4

Precious child,

Jesus said, "I am the resurrection and the life. The one who believes in me will live, even though they die." He spoke those words to a woman named Martha from the town of Bethany. Martha's brother, Lazarus, had been very sick and eventually died. Martha's heart was torn. She was devastated because she had sent for the Lord days earlier, knowing that He would be the only one able to help. It seemed as if Jesus had ignored her pleas for mercy. These are the times when the enemy wants you to quit. He'll try to tell you that I'm not real, but know that he is a liar.

When Jesus first received word that Lazarus was ill, He stayed where He was for two days. Child, when it feels like I'm not listening or answering your prayer, please remember that I'm still on My throne. My reason for waiting to help Martha was so that My Son would be glorified. Real living, surrendered to My will and promises for you, glorifies Me by glorifying Jesus.

Jesus shared another truth about the gift of life He offers while he was in Bethany: "Lazarus is dead, and for your sake I am glad I was not there, so that you may believe." Living your life each day for Jesus creates an opportunity for others to believe. Just before raising Lazarus, Jesus looked up to Me and thanked Me, saying, "I knew that you always hear me, but I said this for the benefit of the people standing here, that they may believe that you sent me."

My gift of days isn't about suffering through the week and barely feeling renewed on Sunday. It's about accepting that My love for you is unfailing and My timing is perfect. I am your sovereign Creator. Wait for Me and live the real life that brings Me and My Son glory. Live the life that leads other people back home to My heart. And never forget how much you matter to Me.

Isaiah 64:4; John 11:14–15, 25, 42; 1 Corinthians 2:9

January 5

Precious child,

Jesus said, "I no longer call you servants, because a servant does not know his master's business. Instead, I have called you friends." The Savior of the world is for you. The Holy One desires to treat you as a friend. The Lord Almighty seeks out your life and loves to know how your day is going. And when the world tells you that your life is meaningless, or that you don't matter, Jesus calls you friend. When anyone says you aren't good enough, Jesus says you are His prized possession! This is why you are a new creation. Before, you were lost in your sins, but now you are saved completely.

"Greater love has no one than this: to lay down one's life for one's friends." Jesus said this to His disciples, and when you open the Bible and read the same words, a powerful truth appears. You are such a true friend of Jesus that there is no greater love that anyone will ever be able to give you. He loves you more than anything, and He proved it when He gave up His life on the cross!

Jesus spoke to the people He did life with in this way: "I tell you, my friends, do not be afraid of those who kill the body and after that can do no more." By position, you are no longer a slave to the world or anything it has to offer. You are My adopted child. You have been redeemed to be a light in the darkness. The enemy's plan is to destroy your walk with Me. But real friends don't keep a record of wrongs, just as I don't hold on to even one of your sins. I have removed your transgressions from you as far as the east is from the west. Friendship with Jesus is the only bond that will help you know how much I love and forgive you!

Psalm 103:12; Luke 12:4; John 15:13–15

January 6

Precious child,

Breathe. It's going to be okay. I am blessing you today with My courage. I want you to think about the time Jesus walked on water. The disciples were in a boat on the Sea of Galilee as a strong wind whipped the water into threatening waves. Terrified, the disciples saw Jesus walking on the water and were filled with fear.

"Come," Jesus said. And Peter got out of the boat, kept his eyes on Jesus, and walked on the water. Jesus gives you this same courage. When you need to step out in faith but are afraid of the unknown, My courage will take you to the places I am calling you to. When you let life become a distraction and take your eyes off Jesus, you will start to sink. But Jesus will save you just like He saved Peter.

Moses spoke these words to his successor, Joshua: "Be strong and courageous. Do not be afraid or terrified because of them, for the LORD your God goes with you; he will never leave you nor forsake you." King David said almost the exact same thing when he spoke to his son Solomon about building the temple: "Be strong and courageous, and do the work. Do not be afraid or discouraged, for the LORD God, my God, is with you. He will not fail you or forsake you until all the work for the service of the temple of the LORD is finished."

Like Peter, Joshua, and Solomon, you will also do the work I have planned for you, and you will do it with the courage of your Savior! Today I am calling you to get out of a different boat called fear and step out onto the water of My will. It's all going to be okay because I love you.

Deuteronomy 31:6; 1 Chronicles 28:20; Matthew 14:28–30

January 7

Precious child,

Jesus loves you so much He chose to leave heaven and take on the burden of flesh and bone. My servant Paul wrote, "In your relationships with one another, have the same mindset as Christ Jesus: who, being in very nature God, did not consider equality with God something to be used to his own advantage; rather, he made himself nothing by taking the very nature of a servant, being made in human likeness. And being found in appearance as a man, he humbled himself by becoming obedient to death—even death on a cross!"

During the Last Supper, before Jesus was handed over to be crucified, He wiped the dirt from His disciples' feet onto the towel around His waist. Jesus told His friends, "Unless I wash you, you have no part with me." When you apply this gift of the Lord's humility, you show the people around you the love of Christ that they won't see anywhere else. Becoming humble means you let Jesus "wash you." You let Him take away the dirt in your life and praise Him for the forgiveness only He can give!

As you go today, remember how Jesus humbled Himself for you. He was stripped of His clothes. Pierced with a crown of thorns. Torn by the centurion's whip. Felt the soldiers' spit. Carried the cross. Was nailed to it. Shouldered the weight of your sin. . .

Jesus went through all that just for you! He went through it so you could be with us forever. Precious one, find ways to lift others up so they may see the real Jesus. The hard times of this day don't have a hold on you because the one who beat death lives in you! In humility, serve. The enemy will try to distract you with stress and confusion, but I am with you forever!

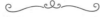

John 1:14; 13:8; Philippians 2:3–8; Hebrews 9:28

January 8

Precious child,

The book of Hebrews says, "Without the shedding of blood there is no forgiveness." The blood of Christ, shed on the cross, is the only atonement needed to cover sin. The beautiful gift of My forgiveness to save you from all your sins comes by crying out to the Savior and surrendering your life to Him. Paul told the Roman church, "If you declare with your mouth, 'Jesus is Lord,' and believe in your heart that God raised him from the dead, you will be saved."

A Samaritan woman Jesus met had five former husbands, but she finally found true love with Christ. After her time spent drinking the living water that Jesus offers, the woman was free to serve the Lord by proclaiming His glory. She had felt His forgiveness, and it opened her eyes to look past herself to people who didn't know Him. The result of her new mission was changed lives: "Many of the Samaritans from that town believed in him because of the woman's testimony."

A paralytic man was carried by friends to Jesus in hopes of being healed. Jesus turned to the sick man and said, "Friend, your sins are forgiven." Before Jesus fixed the man, He fixed his heart! Jesus healed the paralytic man and told him to take his mat and go. All the way home, he praised God, so much so we read that everyone who saw him also praised God.

Be transparent with Jesus. Tell Him what's on your heart and confess your sins. Remember He died for you so that His forgiveness can heal the wounds of your deepest sin. Keep your life right and praise Him. Today, the broken ones will see your worship and turn their eyes to heaven. My child, your life literally means the world to Me!

Luke 5:19–20; John 4:39; Romans 10:9;
Ephesians 2:8–9; Hebrews 9:22

Precious child,

I know you are exhausted. I know you are distraught. Today, hear My gentle whisper remind you that only Jesus can make your heart strong. The Bible says, "For the eyes of the LORD range throughout the earth to strengthen those whose hearts are fully committed to him." The enemy has clouded the world's vision, making people think that somehow they can discipline themselves long and hard enough to be strong for whatever life throws their way.

But you realize this and seek to love Me, the one who gave you life. I have filled you with the same strength that made the galaxies and the mountains and even raised Jesus from the dead! You are a light in the dark world so that the broken may see Me.

My servant Nehemiah undertook a very strenuous task of rebuilding the city wall around Jerusalem. He had a lot of detractors. Many people hoped he'd quit. His spirit for the project was weak. In the middle of it all, Nehemiah prayed: "Now strengthen my hands." Nehemiah used his hands to love Me, and through the answering of his prayer, I filled him with My supernatural power to complete the task! Job declared the same truth: "You have strengthened feeble hands." Both knew that the only way they could live life was by letting Me be their only source.

Abide in Me through faith and feel Me be your strength. As you receive this powerful gift, you also acknowledge that you cannot do anything of eternal worth on your own. I will guide you always and remind you that I will satisfy your needs and strengthen you. I am faithful, and I will strengthen and protect you from the evil one. My strength in you isn't earthly power but rather a miraculous chance to move mountains in love for My glory!

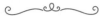

2 Chronicles 16:9; Nehemiah 6:9; Job 4:3;
Romans 4:20; 2 Thessalonians 3:3

Precious child,

Always and abundantly your sweet Savior, Jesus, provides. For everything you need in life, only His provision satisfies. In Christ, you will find your greatest and richest prize.

Jesus was invited to a wedding in Cana, and during the celebration the host ran out of wine. Mary asked Jesus for help and then gathered the servants around and said, "Do whatever he tells you." My child, let the meaning of those words become part of your daily heart song. Not only does Jesus provide more than you ask for, but His provision is the best. What Jesus has to offer is always better than what you can make on your own. The master of the wedding banquet commented on the new wine that Jesus made: "Everyone brings out the choice wine first. . .but you have saved the best till now."

Another time, Jesus provided for a gathering of more than five thousand hungry souls. When the crowd was satisfied, the disciples collected twelve basketfuls of leftovers. Jesus provides for your daily needs no matter how big or small, and He does so abundantly. The enemy tries to keep you satisfied with a "five loaves and two fish" life, but Jesus loves you so much that only He can transform it into a miraculous provision of grace. You will never have a need that Jesus can't fill.

After Jesus rose from the grave, He appeared to His disciples who had been spending the night fishing on the Sea of Tiberius. Jesus met them on the shore and asked if they had caught anything. They hadn't. Jesus told them to go back out and guaranteed that they would find some. They obeyed. The disciples caught so many fish that they couldn't haul in the net. When you let Jesus guide your daily steps down the path He has charted for you, you will be abundantly blessed.

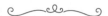

Matthew 14:18–21; Mark 8:8; John 2:1–10; 21:1–14

January 11

Precious child,

Have confidence in My promises and watch faith unlock all the doors the world closes. Remember that Jesus endured the cross and scorned its shame so your faith would be perfectly complete. The apostle Paul told the Galatians, "I live by faith in the Son of God, who loved me and gave himself for me." Faith is the spiritual air your soul breathes. It tethers you to Me and reminds you that your hope of eternal life is not in vain.

By My strength, rise above the pains and burdens, and press on in faith knowing that doing My will brings Me glory and honor. My servant Noah had faith in Me and not his circumstances. He endured the world's ridicule and obeyed Me by building the ark. Child, I'm calling you to build a life that points the world back to Me. Even though they may laugh and call you crazy, your constant obedience and love for Me have an eternal purpose.

Like Moses, who chose to be mistreated rather than enjoy Egypt's money and material things, I want you to regard Jesus as of greater worth than anything the broken world has to offer. Have the faith of Moses to look past your current struggles to your eternal reward with Me. Say no to the enemy who tempts you with a life that makes you feel good only for the moment.

Through faithful living, Noah and Moses did amazing things. Trust completely in Me and know that My promises don't go unfulfilled. Even though you sometimes face challenges that seem insurmountable, through faith you will overcome these obstacles and give Me glory. Your life has become a testimony to the richness of living life through faith in Me. I love you and can't tell you enough how proud I am of you.

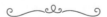

Galatians 2:20; Hebrews 12:2; 2 Peter 1:1

January 12

Precious child,

Today, as your Sovereign Lord, I am filling you with confidence so you can be certain that I Am. I want you to take this gift and have hope in the words and promises of My Son, Jesus Christ. In Him and through Him you can approach Me with freedom. The enemy will try to tell you that your mistakes make Me ashamed of you, because he doesn't want you talking to Me. But remember he lies, so don't let your heart be turned by his temptations.

Be certain that Jesus doesn't want you to be afraid and that He is always with you. I want your heart to proclaim with confidence that I am your helper. I don't want you to be afraid. What can man do to you when your life is securely in My hand? Be certain that I love you like a father loves his children and that I listen to you. Have confidence to approach Me with your burdens and fears. Ask anything according to My will. I am listening. I want to hear everything you have to say.

I have great plans for you. Be confident of this, that since I first created you in your mother's womb, I began a good work in you. I am here today to help you carry it on. People who are lost and hurting will be blessed by Me through you. Be certain that you have a special part to play in the sharing of My gospel message with the world! And be certain that one day you will see Jesus! My servant John wrote, "And now, dear children, continue in him, so that when he appears we may be confident and unashamed before him at his coming."

Precious child, take your confidence off the things you can see, and put it safely in the heart of the one who died for you. Be confident that Jesus is who He says He is and that He loves you!

2 Chronicles 32:8; Psalm 71:5; Jeremiah 17:7;
Ephesians 3:12; 1 John 2:28

January 13

Precious child,

I want salvation to be found by everyone. I want the world to know My truth. Today, I am calling you to be still long enough to look a little deeper into My heart. I am God, the one and only, and My Son, Jesus, is the only mediator between the world and heaven. No man can redeem the life of another man. No one but Jesus. When I saw the love He has for you poured out on the cross, I knew that your heart would sing His praises. His blood wrote the love song of your salvation!

Jesus left His throne to serve the world. He didn't want to be served. I love the world so much that I sent My precious Son to love them. He died to be their merciful ransom. This was part of My plan for Him. Part of My plan for you is that His blood purifies your heart from all your sins. Jesus had to be broken so you could be snatched out of eternal hopelessness. Jesus had to be sacrificed so you could be saved. You have been brought near to Me!

Jesus has made your eternal inheritance secure. His blood has washed you and set you free from all your sins. You are released forever to dance with Me and never again feel chained to regret. The enemy tries to sow seeds of fear in your mind and shame in your heart, but I hold your life in My hand. All your ways are with Me. I am the God of peace. Please share your doubts and every question you are holding on to with Me. The world has been built up around you in a way that makes Me seem distant sometimes, but I am with you. Hear Me call you loved!

Isaiah 52:10; Daniel 5:23; Mark 10:45;
1 Timothy 2:6; Revelation 1:5–6

January 14

Precious child,

The gift of grace that you have in Jesus is unique because out of all the things you desire, My grace is all you need. When you are at your lowest, rejoice, because that's when My power is perfected in you. I want it to free you to live the life I made for you. Let grace wipe the dust off your memories so that you may remember the darkness I saved you from. You are a brand-new creation, and I will take care of every need you ever have. Today will not pass without Me blessing and taking care of you.

Because of the cross, Jesus made a way for you to go from death to life. You can't work your way into heaven, and grace helps you know that Jesus was the only one who died for you. He died so that you may call Him Savior and holy. He died so that you wouldn't be separated from Me. Jesus died so that your sins and guilt would be cast away. Jesus endured your shame and rightful punishment all because of grace.

I need you to carry My grace to your family and to your coworkers. Bring it to the dirty beggars on street corners. You were in the exact same place before Jesus rescued you. Give them grace.

As you go, don't rely on the world's wisdom. Let grace teach you in quiet times spent reading My Word, listening to Me, and praying. These are your guides down the river of My grace, which carries you past the mountains and valleys to eternity with Jesus. The current of His love moves you on, through the highs and lows, as you focus on Him alone. Jesus is the great plan I have for you. Today let Him be the hope and horizon your heart longs for.

2 Corinthians 12:9; Ephesians 1:6; Hebrews 2:9; 2 Peter 1:2

January 15

Precious child,

Jesus said that heaven and earth will one day pass away, but His words never will. The enemy is full of false promises, but when Jesus gives you His word, I want you to be confident that He will do everything He says. He is the light that shines in the darkness, and the darkness cannot overcome it. Disappointments can no longer smother you, and heartaches will never again overwhelm you. The sweet words of Jesus heal and encourage. His word never fails.

I am truthful. I give you My word that in Jesus you have true life. Nothing can snatch you out of His hands. You are safe from the enemy's lies and misfortunes that try to take your attention away from Jesus, because He holds on to you and never lets go. You are not only protected but also empowered. As you go through today, boldly tell people about Jesus. Be encouraged from His words: "I tell you, whoever publicly acknowledges me before others, the Son of Man will also acknowledge before the angels of God."

The words of My Son create a beautiful symphony of love and praise between heaven and earth. Jesus speaks to His angels, and they hear your name, and I honor you as you serve like He served. Precious child, I haven't left you to wonder how it is you go about this service. As you head into this day, simply do the works Jesus did. Walk in Him as you go, because He is your light that guides you through this dark life.

Read all the things Jesus said. Soak up His teachings. The Lord's words are your only truth, and they last forever. Jesus won't go back on His Word or ever change His mind, because He loves you too much and gave His life to prove it!

Matthew 24:35; Luke 12:8; John 3:33

Precious child,

I want to remind you how special you are. Because you received Jesus and believed in His name, I have given you the right to become My child. You follow My Spirit and are no longer a slave to the enemy's darkness. I never want you to live in fear. My Spirit made the way for your adoption as My wonderful child. Now you call Me Abba.

As My child, you are also My heir and coheir with Jesus. Please believe how amazing you are to Me. I know that the day's sufferings can make you feel abandoned, but the exact opposite is true. Your trials allow you to share in the glory of Jesus. The Spirit also testifies that you are My child. All of heaven sees you and knows your name!

Call me Abba and be reminded of our intimate relationship. You call Me Father, and I call you My precious one. This is another reason why I don't want you to ever live in fear. I will do anything for you. The world reaps fear and uncertainty. As My child, you are free from all that because I am the protector and lover of your soul.

You are no longer a face in the crowd of millions, lost and alone. You are called, child, to live a life that glorifies Me and testifies to the riches of My grace. Jesus said, "Which of you, if your son asks for bread, will give him a stone? Or if he asks for a fish, will give him a snake? If you, then, though you are evil, know how to give good gifts to your children, how much more will your Father in heaven give good gifts to those who ask him!"

I love you. Receive My approval and blessing. You mean everything to Me.

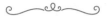

Matthew 7:9–11; John 1:12; Romans 8:14–17; Galatians 4:6

Precious child,

I am strong enough. I am able and will always protect you.

I know how hard it is to look past all the distractions that the enemy puts in your path. Books that promote quick fixes. Music that worships self. Television programs that show who the world worships. The enemy strives to make life easy. He longs to surround you with one pleasure after another and entices you to join him in his broad-road masquerade.

The enemy lives to drag you away from Me by shifting in the shadows. Just when you find his wicked handprint on your suffering, he pulls away to form a new attack. The enemy leaves you delirious and convinces you that you are outnumbered. He tricks your heart into believing that I can't save you. Keep your heart on the truth of My love. I am here for you, child. My precious Son loved you so much that He endured My will and took the narrow way.

Remember My servant Elisha. He spoke My truth to the man who looked out and saw that their city was surrounded by an army of horses and chariots. My faithful prophet told the man not to be afraid. "Those who are with us are more than those who are with them." And then Elisha prayed, "Open his eyes, Lord, so that he may see." Then I opened the servant's eyes, and he looked and saw the hills full of horses and chariots of fire.

When the city of your heart feels surrounded by wickedness and armies of dark suffering, don't fear. I am your strength, and I am with you. I look at the wonderful light you've become, and I am so proud of you. I am more than the one who is in the world, and I will never let anything happen to you!

2 Kings 6:16–17; Luke 22:42; James 1:17

Precious child,

I hear. I care. I answer.

Let your heart yearn for the blessings that prayer brings. The enemy is skilled at trying to fill your time. He strives to put things in your path that will complicate your schedule and leave you spent. At your lowest, he knows you will be tempted to see prayer as a choice rather than what I made it to be.

Isaac prayed to Me because his wife was barren. I answered him, and Rebekah became pregnant. Moses spread his hands in prayer to Me so Pharaoh would know I was in control and faithful. When you talk to Me, know that I listen. I want you to pray and feel My love spread throughout your being. Solomon prayed and pleaded with Me, and I answered him with My name, eyes, and heart. According to My will, I reminded My child Hezekiah that I heard his prayer, saw his tears, and would heal him.

Prayer is also your act of worship. Hannah prayed, "My heart rejoices in the LORD." Nehemiah said, "Lord, let your ear be attentive to the prayer of this your servant and to the prayer of your servants who delight in revering your name."

Prayer brings a supernatural power that stirs your soul and lets My love permeate your entire being. A man named Cornelius testified: "Three days ago I was in my house praying at this hour. . . . Suddenly a man in shining clothes stood before me and said, 'Cornelius, God has heard your prayer and remembered your gifts to the poor.' "

I am here to listen. Call out to Me because I am here to accept your prayer. I will never reject your prayers or withhold My love from you. Tell Me everything. I love you and will answer you.

Genesis 25:21; Exodus 9:29; 1 Samuel 2:1; 1 Kings 9:3;
2 Kings 20:5; Nehemiah 1:11; Psalm 66:20; Acts 10:30–31

January 19

Precious child,

Jesus is the gate. He stands between you and the world. On your heart side, you will always find rest in pastures of My everlasting righteousness. Through the gate, on the world's side, you will always find high, ominous walls that have been built for defense. Ironically, they invite nothing but destruction. See how the enemy stirs the people to compete with each other. Instead of Me, they desire their neighbor's possessions. For the world, it's never enough to be satisfied with only Me. This competition to have more than Me is a yoke of slavery that I have freed you from carrying.

My child, because Jesus is your gate, I want you to go through Him with everything. When you go to labor at your job, go through Jesus. Take every decision and every choice you make through Jesus. I promise I will provide for every one of your needs through My glorious riches in Him. The enemy wants you to be comfortable, but he doesn't know you. He didn't die for you! Jesus took the cross and suffered its shame so that you could freely live life in the pastures of My salvation.

I am calling you to go into the world and let people know that Jesus is standing at the doors of their hearts. Tell them their Savior is knocking. Be bold and explain that even though they might be comfortable, the yokes they bear aren't Mine. Show them the way back to Me. Lead them back to the narrow gate. Let them see Jesus. Show them how He cleaned your heart and provided the endless pastures you freely roam. Help them have strength to open their locked doors of pride. Help them let Jesus in and rejoice because today is the day of grace!

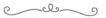

Proverbs 17:19; John 10:7; Philippians 4:19; Revelation 3:20

January 20

Precious child,

One of the many reasons I love you is your teachable heart. I have created this in you so every day you can yield more and more to My Spirit. The enemy wants you to yield to comfort and things the world deems good. But remember that every good thing you have is found only in Christ! I promise that as you share your faith, your understanding of this will deepen.

As you go about your day, remember Me. Walk in obedience to My commands. That is truly what love is all about. Because I love you so much and want you to be with Me in heaven, I sent Jesus. He loved you enough to take up the cross and allow the soldiers to nail Him to it. Jesus died and rose again so that one day you will do the same. Because of the love Jesus has for you, death no longer has a hold on you. One day in paradise, you will see Me face-to-face, and what a glorious day that will be!

Until then, continue to have a holy fear for Me. Not fear the way the world sells it. Holy fear means keeping My commandments and not being afraid. Don't worry about what the enemy is trying to put in your path. Don't worry about following the world. All you need to do today is seek Me with all your heart.

Remember Me, child. Remember that I love you and will never walk away from you. I will never leave you alone to face your struggles. Be bold and take a step toward sharing My love with someone you meet today—plant seeds of hope in their heart—just as Jesus did in yours.

Exodus 20:20; Ecclesiastes 12:13;
Amos 5:4; Philemon 1:6; 2 John 1:6

January 21

Precious child,

A great day is coming when all of your pain and stress will be washed away.

Yes, that great day is coming when you will sing and be free to spend eternity with Me. It will be a glorious and great day because you will also see Jesus face-to-face. His mercy for you will bring you home into eternal life. Rejoice because your sweet name is written in the Lamb's book of life and you will also see My face. Night will never fall over you again.

Don't let the world take these truths from your heart. Don't let the enemy steal your hope. Be strong and courageous because I am your God, and I am with you always. Don't let the people who don't believe in Me divide your heart. I have told you that I am proud of you for following Me with everything that's within you. The scoffers will try to make you doubt that I mean all of these words I am sending you. But they don't have the Spirit. Keep yourself in My love because the world sows seeds of self, and they will reap destruction.

Show mercy to the ones who doubt. Your life matters. I know that so many days seem like one defeat and heartache after another. But the truth is found in what you cannot see. Your faith and your merciful, compassionate heart are snatching souls from the fire. As you do this, know that I am keeping you from stumbling and that you are walking in the light of life. Continue to do good works and seek to honor Me, because these sow seeds pleasing to the Spirit. My radiance is shining on you and warming your wonderful heart now and forever.

*Psalm 56:13; Romans 2:7; Galatians 6:8; Jude 21;
Revelation 21:27; 22:4–5*

January 22

Precious child,

Don't let the enemy trick you into thinking you are one mistake away from losing Me. From the beginning, I formed you with grace. Before you took your first breath, I was with you and wrapped you in love. I have since saved you, and this had nothing to do with your good deeds but was because of My grace. So continue walking on the path of truth. Keep hoping in Me all day long. I am guiding you according to My will for your life. My words are truth. My love for you is the standard.

The enemy, who is in the world, roams in the darkest places, creating lies that are disguised as truth. The ones who listen to his twisted lessons cannot hear Me. They hear the world's song of hatred and join in its fearful chorus. The lyrics speak of a hopeless place of self where forgiveness and compassion are not wanted. This is the dark garden that I'm calling you to.

Don't be afraid. Go and be courageous by My power in you and share the gospel message. You matter, your song of truth will be heard, and the lost will turn to Me. Being obedient to My calling frees your soul to do all the things I created it to do.

Remember that true living isn't only surviving. Food and water have their place, and I provide those for you. But I want you to really live, and that comes from counting on every one of My words. And the words I am speaking over you today are the ones that remind you your life is hidden in Christ. The second you surrendered your life to Me, I forgave you. I marked you and sealed you with the Holy Spirit. I did this as a guarantee of your eternal inheritance. You are Mine. Forever!

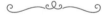

Psalm 25:5; Isaiah 45:19; John 8:44;
Ephesians 1:13–14; 2 Timothy 1:9; 3 John 1:3–4

January 23

Precious child,

Be strong because I am with you. Don't worry. At night and again during the day, let your soul desire Me above all things. Spend your time running after Me. With all of your heart and with all of your soul, want Me more than you want anything else. My heart is for you. I feel your love for Me, and I want you to feel Mine for you. Crave My truth. Long for the life that is in Me alone. Yearn to hear My voice over all the noise.

Out of all the things the world is offering you, let it be Me you desire most. Let it be My Word that you want and wait for more than anything. The world is the enemy's stage. The things your heart may desire are only temporary. They have no eternal worth, and to put all your energy into them is the same as saying you don't really need Me. But remember that I love you more than anything, and I am patient. I wait for you to seek Me. The world trudges on with hearts of stone, but I have given you a heart of flesh. You have been set free. Follow Me.

Your soul was made to need Me like dry land needs the rain. Run to Me, child. I am here, and because of Jesus you are abundantly pardoned. The enemy moves pieces of temptation around to distract you. He longs to keep your eyes on them and off Me. When your desire is on the world, it is not on Me, leaving you with a divided heart. This is the enemy's endgame. But I am faithful. Make Me the only thing your heart desires and I will teach you. Rely on Me.

Psalm 73:25; 86:11; Proverbs 8:17; Lamentations 3:25; Ezekiel 11:19

Precious child,

I am your one true God.

There's only Me. I am the one who made you. I am the one who loves you. I am the one who is with you forever. I am the sovereign king over heaven, earth, and most of all, your heart. Don't make room for anything else but Me. I have saved you, and now you are a new creation made for growing in knowledge of Me. Sweet child, My grace is free, so you don't have to worship empty gods with your time and money.

Since Eden, the enemy has been mastering the art of idol worship. He has used his experience to study the things that take people's eyes and minds off Me. He diligently creates these objects and skillfully builds them up for the world to see. After he has their attention, he shows them more and more—but it's never enough to completely satisfy their desires. The enemy doesn't love them. He only loves that they are so easily distracted. Because once they're distracted they begin to serve themselves.

The enemy didn't make you. He has no idea what's in your heart, and he surely doesn't care about it. He didn't die for you, and he never will. The enemy doesn't understand sacrifice. He is trying to raise his throne above the stars. He is trying to make himself like Me, but that will never happen. He is filled with sin and violence. He wants to see you suffer.

So don't let your heart get distracted. Be satisfied with Me and rest secure in My plan for your life. My words are true. I have kept My promises to you, and I'm not stopping now!

Isaiah 14:13–15; Ezekiel 28:14–16;
Colossians 3:10; 1 Thessalonians 1:9

January 25

Precious child,

Be still. I am your God, and you are My beloved child. This is the truth, and nothing the enemy tries to make you believe will ever change our relationship. Know that these are not just words I'm giving you, but promises that will forever remind you how much you mean to Me. Even if you feel sad and disconnected from My heart, remember the truth: I will never leave you defenseless.

Be still and feel My grace forgive you. Sweet Jesus is with you, and His love is grace added to the grace I've given you. And since He is with you forever, My grace for you has no end. Jesus said, "It is finished!" His sacrifice covered your sins for all time. You have been washed clean. Your mistakes do not define you! I define you. And I call you Mine.

Be still and let My mercy shower you with waters of compassion. Let it wash away the disappointments and stress. Child, please know that you are safe in My mighty hands. My great mercy covers you. I will never abandon you.

Be still and let My peace reign in your life. I know how busy you are and how worn out your spirit gets. Driving, working, going, doing. All I want you to be is My child and know that I am your God of peace. Breathe deep. Let out the worries. Jesus is with you, and He is your Prince of Peace. This is truth.

When I bless you, I bless you with grace, mercy, and peace. These are forever blessings. Take them and celebrate this new gift of today by raising your hands in worship. I've made this day for you to unwrap new gifts, not bear the burden of old regrets. Don't keep trying. Just be still and know that I've got you covered in never-ending grace, mercy, and peace.

*1 Chronicles 21:13; Nehemiah 9:31; Psalm 46:10;
2 Corinthians 13:11; 2 Timothy 1:2*

January 26

Precious child,

I help the powerless. I know the enemy conspires to wear you down. I know. . . . I am there to lift your tired arms. Don't be sad, because Jesus lives in you, and He has overcome the world. I will never hide My face from you. It is shining down and warming your soul. You are never alone. See Me, child. See Me heal your weariness. Watch Me help you enjoy abundant peace and security. Feel My power, which cast the stars and filled the oceans, flood your heart with love.

Today, I want you to know how important you are to Me. I sent Jesus to meet you where you were, lost in sin. He saw you wandering, chained to a debt you had no way of paying. Jesus heard your plea for forgiveness. He crossed from heaven to earth and healed you of your sins. Jesus poured out His blood for you. And He didn't stop there. He makes sure you are taken care of for all of your days. Jesus is holding your hand and leading you to new life.

Anyone who loves the world does not love Me, so don't ever let them tell you I don't understand suffering. Don't let them tell you My love for you is conditional. I am love, and I love you. In fact, humble yourself before Me and feel Me lift you up. Feel My presence come over you. Pray that My will is done, and know that you are right where I want you to be.

In Christlike humility, make My ways known. Run and tell the world that salvation is found in Me alone. I am lifting you higher, to the mountain of My love and grace. The enemy can't reach you here. Rest, child. I love you.

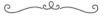

Job 26:2; Psalm 67:1–2; Jeremiah 33:5–6; Luke 10:33–35

Precious child,

I know your heart longs for answers. I know the pain from not understanding rises like a storm in your soul. Please let Me be the answer for all your questions. Let Me be the solution for every problem. I'm here. There is no fear in Me. Your life and all of your days are safe in Me. You can't undo My love for you. You can't stray outside the reach of My grace. I hear your cries for wisdom. I know you are spent from trying to figure out the reasons why.

Jesus cried. Jesus suffered. He called out to Me in the darkest night. My silence was His answer. In that dark garden, My sweet Son cried out to Me and asked if the pain could pass, a pain that overwhelmed His soul to the point of death. Even though I didn't answer His pleas the way He asked Me to, Jesus called out for My will to be done. For your soul, Jesus didn't let the darkness paralyze Him. He prayed that My will would be done, and with complete faith in My love, He got up and allowed Himself to be delivered into the hands of sinners.

In the world's darkness, the enemy strives to keep you stuck in your insecurities. He works hard to keep you rooted in the moment, hoping that your focus will be taken off Me. The evil one wants your eyes to see sin's injustice and believe that I am not who I say I am. While the world sleeps, you are burdened with a grief that only I understand. Use My strength to stand and face the day. Go, not waiting for answers, knowing that you are My child and I love you. I am faithful, and I will never stop loving you.

Job 42:3; Matthew 26:38; 1 Thessalonians 5:24

January 28

Precious child,

Make room for My voice. I have so much to tell you. When I created all, I didn't leave anything to chance. The beautiful things I have waiting for you are found in the sound of My words. I want you to hear them say, "I love you."

The enemy works hard at getting people to believe I don't talk to My children. The world has bought into the lie that I am too big to care about the little things. The sound of darkness says that I am too big to be a loving, personal Father. The enemy's songs are composed to keep your mind occupied with rhythms of independence. These are the anthems the world sings instead of listening to My words of grace.

Hear My song rise above the world's noise. Like a clear mountain stream, it flows from My heart to yours. The world is filled with yelling souls competing for attention and love. But what they find will never satisfy, because they have no room for Me. Hear My voice lead you to pastures of peace.

Hear My words remind you that I have saved you from the enemy's hands. You have been freed from the chains that once oppressed you. I have delivered you from the enemy's power. Today, hear Me tell you that My favor is on you. Hear Me encourage you. I am the helper of the helpless. Hear Me remind you that I am not far off and I do not hide Myself from you in troubled times.

I am listening to you too. Let's create a new song together. You sing about the things on your heart, and I'll reply that today is the day of salvation. Today is the day you will hear Me say, "I am proud of you!"

Deuteronomy 5:27; 1 Samuel 10:18;
Psalm 10:4; Isaiah 49:8; Malachi 1:2

January 29

Precious child,

I know you are hurt by the shards of the world's bitterness, but I want you to love your enemy. Do this by becoming more and more like your sweet Savior, Jesus. He became a living sacrifice for your sins. While you were still My enemy, Jesus hung and hurt and died on the cross in order to forgive you. His love brought Him to meet you where you were on the seas of darkness. He reached out and pulled you to the shores of mercy. His love forgave even when it hurt. Love the broken pieces.

I know you are busy and have very little time to spare, but I want you to love your neighbor. You are all they have. You are My light in their darkness. Your smile and generous heart will show them Jesus hasn't given up on them. Your constant kindness will remind them that His love lasts forever. So you could have salvation, the King of kings took on flesh and brought you His perfect love. The love that Jesus has given you hangs on through the tough times, not because it has to, but because it wants to. Reach out to souls around you and bring them My love. Love the ones in need.

I know you love Me, but today I want you to love Me more than anything else. Jesus knew you needed Him long before you ever knew there was a problem. He proved His unconditional love for you when He left His throne and came to earth to conquer sin and death. He came for you and died for you so you could be completely free to love Me with all that I created in you. Don't let the enemy trap you in selfishness. Praise Me and feel the weight of trying to please the world wash away. Love My perfect plans for you, and let your heart belong to Me alone.

Leviticus 19:18; Joshua 23:11; Matthew 5:44; 22:37; Romans 5:10

January 30

Precious child,

Let Me be your dwelling place.

I know that you try to get by, enduring the dark world's trials, and by day's end you are one step past exhausted. I want you to see a different path. I want you to trust Me when I say I have an answer. Let My strength enable you to tread on the heights of this day so you can walk far above the drudgery. Let My compassion go with you. Let My hands guide you across the hours. Feel My heart beat for you. Nothing can reach you here. Listen to My truth clear a path and lead you to quiet pastures of mercy.

Let Me be your refuge.

The world is not your safe place. I am your stronghold. The enemy has flooded the world with false teachers who plant heresies in the hearts of all who will listen. Crops of destruction grow wild. Rivers rage with greed. I know the path I have you on leads through these dangerous places, but walk on, My child. Don't fear. I command My angels to protect you. I send them to lift you up in their hands so the enemy's traps will not strike you.

Let Me be your shield.

Believe Me when I tell you that I am with you. I will rescue you from the trials. I will lift you up on eagle's wings so you may soar above the lawlessness and find rest on the mountain of My righteousness. Just as I saved Noah from the floodwaters, I saved your soul from the deadly wages of sin. Today, I have you in My arms, safe and free. The enemy will try to shout that you are alone and far from hope's reach. Child, you know My voice. Hear the whispers of mercy say you are Mine.

Psalm 91:9–12; Isaiah 40:31; Joel 3:16; Habakkuk 3:18–19; 2 Peter 2:9

Precious child,

I am your defender.

When it comes to you and your beautiful heart, I am jealous and avenging. I will protect you. When darkness is sent to cover your path, I pour out My wrath on the enemy. I am slow to anger, and I don't want anyone to perish. But I am just and great in power. When the Israelites cried out to be saved from their oppressors, I rescued them. When you were trapped and oppressed in your sins, I promised you Jesus. He conquered your enemy and rescued you from death.

Remember, the mountains of toil and hardship that rise far above you do not rise above Me. In fact, their rugged peaks melt away in My presence. I am the one who looks out for you and ensures your protection.

The world listens to the darkness. They move the pieces of the enemy's evil around you. They say and do hurtful things. In your weakness you are tempted to take the lies to heart. You feel swept away and forgotten. But child, My love for you dries up the rivers of anxiety and oceans of sorrow. My love for you is a firestorm that burns in a wall of protection to keep the hard-hearted ones from hurting you.

Stop fearing. I am for you! Let love be your sword against the world's army. Don't run away from Me, believing that you are okay on your own. Don't welcome the world. They don't love Jesus. They know His name, but they don't call Him Lord. They know He is wise, but they don't call Him teacher. They know He is good, but they don't call Him Savior. Jesus is the truth, and He lives in you. Let His words cover you. You are truly alive because you stand firm in Jesus!

Isaiah 19:20–21; Nahum 1:2–6; 1 Thessalonians 3:8; 2 John 1:9

February 1

Precious child,

I want you to take an important truth on the journey. Your enemy wants to convince you that you are walking the path of life alone. He works hard at getting you to doubt Me and My power to forgive you. His treacherous plan involves getting you to think you are a failure and that you have failed Me. Do not fear. I have never left your side, and I will never leave it. And when I see you, I see My child who is forever forgiven, whom I love, and who makes Me proud.

Remember that Jesus said, "I am the light of the world. Whoever follows me will never walk in darkness, but will have the light of life." I have given you Jesus so your path will never be shrouded in shadows of regret. I have given you My only Son so your days will be wrapped in His love.

Jesus in your heart gives you the ability to put on the armor of His light and avoid the enemy's dark schemes. Because you have Jesus, the enemy's lies can no longer blind you to My truth. The moment you surrendered your life to Him, Jesus began to guide you out of the land of doubt and has since kept you on the righteous path that leads far away from it.

The darkness of past mistakes isn't where I made you to live. I am giving you this new day, not to regret, but to rejoice. I know that some days it feels easier to stay where you are and feel a sense of comfort in the doubting. I know, and I'm not mad at you for feeling this way. But precious child, I want you to understand how important you are to Me. I made you very special. Come and follow. I won't let you down!

Isaiah 2:5; 60:19; Micah 7:8; John 8:12; 9:4–5

February 2

Precious child,

Rejoice!

You are Mine. Whatever you have been trying to gain, I want you to consider it a loss. I love you, and I want you to lose everything the world is giving you in exchange for knowing Jesus. This doesn't mean doing good things, but receiving righteousness from Me. This will help you live today in faith and be found in Jesus. Today is for you to understand My strength that raised Him from the dead. My strength will shape you into the humble servant I've called you to be. It is for you to breathe deep My mercy and to gently lift the heads of the needy so they may see Jesus.

These hours are for sharing in My Son's suffering by becoming unselfish and obeying Me even in the hard times. Noah understood this as he faithfully obeyed My instructions to build the ark. When the world ran after selfish desires, Noah had the faith to walk with Me. He had the courage to turn away from evil and devote his life to Me and My plans. Rahab also made the hard choice to obey unselfishly. She decided to hide the spies and risk worldly condemnation. She sacrificed her old ways by acknowledging Me. She obeyed in the difficult hour.

This day is also for you to become more like Jesus as you die to self. As you pray for My provision, listen to My words remind you that the world is ready for your heart. The enemy is calling out to you, telling you that doing what makes you feel satisfied and safe is good. The world is waiting to take care of all your needs. But I made your sweet heart. Let Me be the one to fill it with My perfect love. Let Me fill it with Jesus.

Genesis 6:22; Joshua 2:1–11; Philippians 3:7–10

February 3

Precious child,

I am just.

Today, I count you worthy of My kingdom. I see your perseverance and suffering, and I am here to bring you relief, not harm. Be with Me and let the worrying go. Allow Me to love you the way I made you to be loved. The enemy wants you to focus on the people who misunderstand you. He wants you to harbor anger at the ones who disrespect you. The world says that you should hold the desire for revenge close to your heart. But when Jesus returns in glorious splendor with His angels, those who sow evil will be repaid trouble for the trouble they gave.

I am good.

My love for you endures for all time. The enemy is trying to get your thoughts on the daily struggles. He wants you to believe that My compassion for you is conditional. In My eyes, you are more than the bad days. You are My precious child. No matter what, I am for you. You don't need to worry about getting the world's approval. I approve of you! You don't need to please people, because I see your heart is for Me. You serve Jesus, not the world, and for that I am pleased.

I am here for you.

As you face this new day, know that I am rising up before you. I am rising up to scatter the enemy's traps so you may pass unharmed. I am rising up to make the evil one flee from your path. Walk with Me. And when the day's end comes near, I am here to gently lay your head down and watch over you as you sleep. So be bold. Tell the world that My grace is still free. Tell them Jesus died for them too. I love you, My child.

Numbers 10:35; Ezra 3:11; Galatians 1:10; 2 Thessalonians 1:4–7

February 4

Precious child,

Don't quit.

I understand every ounce of pressure you feel. Continue on the path I have laid out for you, and ignore the enemy's ridicule. You mean so much more to Me than the gains you get or the mistakes you make. When the enemy says you are feeble and not capable, I declare you righteous in My sight. You are more than able. The world's insults and accusations are meaningless. Work with all your heart, and leave the results to Me.

Don't forget.

The world's darkness makes it hard to see your true worth. But when you continue on in faith, your light shines and the enemy flees, pulling the deep shadows with him. Following the demands of the world does not bring life. Jesus Christ gives life! In Him, you have been set free to be called My child. The enemy works to make you believe that the world is your guardian. He tries to convince you that if you continue to do good things and work hard for Me, you will be okay. But Jesus has made you more than okay. His blood has made you a coheir of My eternal kingdom!

Don't stop being the person I made you to be.

The world might deem you poor by its selfish standards, but in My eyes you are rich beyond imagination. The enemy judges, but I have mercy. Keep following My will and leave the world's opinions behind. I know the hardest part is not being able to see Me with your eyes. But know that I have not abandoned you. I will never do that. Ever! Close your eyes and feel Me holding your heart. Whether you suffer for the moment or sing for a day, I have blessed you to be the one who honors Jesus.

Nehemiah 4:1–6; Galatians 3:23–26; James 2:13; 1 Peter 3:14–15

February 5

Precious child,

Keep your heart on Me and the things of My kingdom. You are not alone in your struggles. I want you to be encouraged by the ones who have gone before you. Take My servant Esther. She lost her mother and father and grew up as an orphan. Along the way, she lived her life with integrity so that she found favor with everyone who knew her. Her lowly position, with all of its problems, did not dictate who she was as a person. As her life story played out, she was sent to a king's palace and eventually chosen to become queen.

I want you to see that the same is true of your life. When you were lost in an ocean of sin, the enemy had you alone in the dark without a heavenly home. Then Jesus, the King of kings, ransomed you! And now you too are royalty. Please don't forget this, child. Like Esther, continue to be the kind of person whom people find favor with. Today, I have you in a place of influence to turn the world's eyes back to Me. You are stronger than you know. Jesus is with you, to love you and help you be a courageous leader of My people.

I have given you all the tools you need for the job I've called you to do. I have enriched you with every spiritual blessing so you don't have to worry about not being good enough or strong enough or smart enough. Everything I am is enough, and I am with you. I am keeping you strong until the end because I am faithful. I have called you not to do a list of religious things, but to spend this gift of days in fellowship with Jesus! Let your time with Him overflow in grace to others. Pray and be thankful. Trust Me. You are loved!

Esther 2:15; 1 Corinthians 1:5–9; Colossians 4:2–6

February 6

Precious child,

Hear Me.

Many things clamor for your attention, and I know it's easy for you to get distracted. The world's song lures you away from My voice, filling your ears with seemingly sweet melodies. But at some point the sound fades, and you're left with an echo of empty promises. Just know that I am your God, and you are My child. From the rush of many waters to the gentle flow of whispers, My voice will reach you. You will hear the sounds of righteousness that will drown out the world's noise.

Accept what I say.

The enemy moves about trying to snatch My words from you. He loves to see people go about their day listening to the faulty wisdom of men. Not so with you, My child. You don't harden your heart against My commands, and for that I'm so proud of you. I know when you're in the middle of storms, the temptation is great to ignore My will. In the middle of suffering, the enemy's voice calls out for you to accept fast and easy ways to avoid the problem. But remember, you have Jesus, and He alone is the solution to every problem!

Bear fruit.

Today, I will help you make the work of your hands produce a crop one hundred times what was sown. Your life isn't hidden from Me in a world of billions. Your life is hidden *in* Me so you can reach billions for My glory. Remember, I want you to make your gift of days a labor of love, not a chain of grueling tasks. The enemy tries to twist your desires. He'd like nothing more than for you to make the world think you're a good person. But you are so much more than good. You are forgiven!

Deuteronomy 15:5; Jeremiah 7:23; Ezekiel 43:2;
Mark 4:20; Hebrews 3:15

February 7

Precious child,

Jesus is My wonderful Son of righteousness.

The rays of His unending love reach out to the farthest corners of the world. His warm light shines on all of My creation to heal the brokenness caused by the fall. Cold hearts, frozen by sin, will thaw and be loved because of Jesus! For the sake of His holy name, I want you to be an example of His mercy so the world will be moved to cast their eyes upon Me. I want them to hear what you have to say about Jesus. I want you to love everyone and send them on their way in a manner that honors Me.

Your life is crucial to reach the world for My glory. You are so important because I have given you a clean heart, filled with My light. The world doesn't love the light, because all they know is darkness. They don't understand that freedom is found in Me. The enemy has made them believe they are safe in the dark, but when the world sees you, your light will draw them out. When they come to you, show them grace and remember that you once hid in dark places. Don't judge. Just be a witness to My glory.

I am light. There is no darkness in Me. Take My words, all of them, and see My light radiate out from each letter of every word. Watch scripture unfold understanding in your heart as pinpricks of healing light burst forth and become a sunburst of love over your path. Every ounce of your being is saturated in My commands. My wisdom is with you to absorb truth. This is what it means to walk in the light. The world will never take you away from Me, so be strong and shine with Jesus!

Psalm 119:130; Malachi 4:2; John 3:19–20;
1 John 1:5–7; 3 John 1:6–7

February 8

Precious child,

I want Jesus to be the Lord of lords in your life. In every moment and over every desire, I want Jesus to keep His rightful position in your heart. He is the Savior of your soul. He rescued you from the grave so you could be with Us forever. His blood washed away your sins so you could be free. Jesus traded His glorious position on heaven's throne for a humiliating place on Calvary's cross. He chose to be hung up over the darkness, with all its pain and agony, so you could be saved.

Jesus doesn't show favoritism. When He died on the cross and suffered its shame, He died for everyone. He didn't just die for the pretty people or the people who make you feel good. He didn't just die for the ones who are fun to be around or the ones who are outwardly kind. Jesus died for the dirty ones. He died for the ones who are mean and full of anger. He died for those who mock your lifestyle. Jesus bore the heavy burden of the world's sin so everyone could have the chance to be saved.

Today, lift Him up with your life so that the people living in darkness around you will see and hear His name. Lift Jesus high by the way you speak and the way you love. Lift Jesus above everything you hold dear by the way you stop and listen to the ones the world has deemed unlovable. When you decide to lift Jesus high and call Him Lord of lords, the dying world around you will see, and many will be like the murderer and the soldier who realized that Jesus really was their Savior. Be a bold witness to My grace and watch dying hearts rise to new life.

I am for you, always, and My love for you will never end!

Deuteronomy 10:17; Psalm 136:3; 1 Timothy 6:15; Revelation 19:6

February 9

Precious child,

I am the Holy One. The world and everything in it is impure, but My will is that you become sanctified in spite of the immorality around you. The world has become mastered by selfishness and greed. But My great love for you has set you apart. Your days are for learning from Me. I call you to live a holy life. I teach you the best lessons for your life, and I direct you in the way you should go.

Jesus prayed for you. He lifted you up, long before you were born, and asked that you be protected from the enemy. He didn't want Me to take you out of the world, but to keep you in the world and your heart safe. Jesus asked Me to sanctify you, and that is what I'm doing. My words are true and full of grace. By them, you are being built up and becoming a strong servant for My kingdom purposes.

You have the Spirit who does a good sanctifying work in you. So today I am sending you out into the world, because just like Jesus, your life is not your own. Your Savior went into the world and redeemed you. Jesus gave His life so that you could have eternity. He took the nails so you could be set free.

My scriptures are truth and they sanctify you. As you read My words and let them guide your steps, your heart changes. I have set you apart from the world to be a holy light that shines bright in the darkness. By faith, you are becoming sanctified so you may tell people about Jesus and turn their eyes from darkness to light. Proclaim My gospel to them so they may hear My truth. Today, like yesterday and tomorrow, your life matters!

Isaiah 48:17; John 17:15–19; Acts 26:18; Romans 15:16

February 10

Precious child,

Pray. Talk to Me. Tell Me everything on your heart. Please don't see prayer as a formality. Don't see it as something you have to do. When you speak, I am listening. I don't want you to hang on to thoughts just because you feel like they might be too trivial. Tell Me. Call out even when you are burdened, because you are never a burden to Me. See prayer as a privilege.

Prayer keeps you strong. The enemy places one temptation after another along your path—even the temptation not to talk to Me. Life seems to conspire against your dreams. The enemy speaks lies, putting before you the idea that you are selfish if you ask for things. I know what you need, and the fact that you pray to Me for provision glorifies My name. And the enemy also tries to discourage you with the idea that since you can't see Me, your prayers are in vain.

You don't bore Me, child. The opposite is true. I love hearing your voice. I am near to you. Every time you pray, no matter how short or long, I listen. When you pray, I am near. And I want you to pray all the time because I never get tired of listening to you.

I created you to do amazing things for My kingdom. I know you don't always feel that, but today I am here to remind you that I don't make mistakes. Everything about you is important to Me. Everything. So be faithful in prayer. Pray when the sun shines, and pray in the storm. Pray when you are filled with hope, and pray when you are weighed down with afflictions. Whether with a smile or tears, pray. I love you!

Deuteronomy 9:19; Isaiah 38:5; Matthew 21:22;
Romans 12:12; 1 Thessalonians 5:17

February 11

Precious child,

I am the only Judge of all the earth. The world tries to take this from Me, but I am stronger than the world. I am almighty. So when people cast judgment on you, I want you to remember that their words hold no worth. When the enemy casts the verdict that you are not worthy of My grace, ignore him, because I have already called you Mine.

In mercy, I always rule in your favor. You have been made worthy by the sacrifice of Jesus. Because He is your Savior, you are free. Live out your gift of days, not by the world's assessment of your heart, but with Jesus protecting you by His loving heart.

As you go, understand that the evil one is also trying to get you to see yourself as a judge. If he can't tempt you into believing that his verdict about your worth is valid, he employs another tactic. He'll make you believe, through layers of excuses, that you have been appointed judge over others. But you know how it feels when someone says you aren't good enough. Stay away from the gavel and commit to spreading My love.

Everyone will stand before Me and give an account of their days. So I want you to see the world as a courtroom where you've been called, not to judge, but to testify to My lovingkindness. When Jesus went to the cross, He endured pain in your place. He died and rose for you. The powers of the world were destroyed. Therefore, the enemy's accusations aimed at your heart are the only things that are worthless about you. So go and share My truth. Be patient with people and be an encouragement to them. Love them as I love you!

Genesis 18:25; Romans 14:10; 2 Timothy 4:1–2; James 4:12

February 12

Precious child,

Fill your day with Jesus.

I know you need your job, but don't forget I am the one who provided it. I know you need to spend time pouring into others, but don't forget I am the one who meets their needs. I know. . . . The enemy gives you things to do, but I give you people to love. I give you grace, faith, and love abundantly. Take them and let your heart be satisfied. Take them and let your soul be at peace.

Jesus knows too. He didn't suffer so you would live your days in fear. He endured the agony of the cross so you would spend your hours in faith. Above the world that crucified Him, on the tree that held Him high for all to see, Jesus said, "It is finished." The problem of your sins was solved. But also your stress. Your worry. Your fear. All of it is finished.

The enemy works to see you consumed with earthly tasks to wear down your spirit. He wants you tired so you will be in a position to accept doubt as truth. But the riches of Christ are limitless. His love covers you even when you feel like it doesn't. His love fills you and erases doubt. I give you My word that nothing will ever push us apart. My love for you in Jesus will never be taken from you no matter how hard the enemy works at making you feel otherwise.

You have been chosen and made holy, and you are deeply loved! Let this truth open your eyes so you can see yourself the way I see you. I don't see you consumed by fear, but fearless. I don't see you consumed by worry. I see you filled with confidence. I don't see you consumed by stress, but strong. I love you!

John 19:30; Romans 8:39; Ephesians 3:8; Colossians 3:12

February 13

Precious child,

By My voice, I made everything from warm sun rays and cool spring breezes to the strong shade trees and the sound of children playing. From birds chirping their staccato symphonies to the stars like grains of sand across the heavens, all creation bears the sound of My voice. My eternal power and My divine nature have been clearly revealed. Close your eyes, rest your head, and listen to the rhythms of My work.

The enemy tries to mar the beautiful world I created. From his very first assault in Eden's paradise to today, his mark continues to spread. Slavery. Hatred. Abuse. It all stands against the plans I have for you. What I created wonderful, the enemy tries to stain, twist, and corrupt. Everything that the world creates is nothing more than breathless idols.

But have hope! This is not the end. You are My creation, and you are filled with the breath of life. A new day is coming when My Son will rise and return. He hasn't forgotten about you. You will see your inheritance that has been prepared for you from the beginning. He waits, though, because I do not wish that anyone should perish. Oh, how beautiful it would be if everyone repented.

In the same way I thought about everything I made, I thought about you. I thought about how I would knit you together and about the loving person I wanted you to be in Jesus. Let Him warm your heart. Let Him sing over your days in a chorus of infinite blessing. Let Him be the shade that allows you relief from the heat of conflict. Let Jesus be the only one you worship. Let the world see what He means to you. Before I made anything, I chose you in Jesus to be sanctified. Please see how special you are to Me!

Habakkuk 2:18; Romans 1:20; Ephesians 1:4; 2 Peter 3:9

February 14

Precious child,

I am calling you to love like Jesus. He left heaven because He loves you. He died for you because He loves you. He rose and is your Savior because He loves you. Jesus has a special place in His heart just for you!

With this in mind, love everyone. And when you are talking to someone the world deems unlovable, they will hear a symphony of compassion. They will hear My Son's heartwarming voice call to them in the sound of yours. Live by loving like Jesus. Help the ones whom the world has passed by. Through the work of your hands, they will see His hands move away their mountains of guilt and sadness. Give to those whom the world has forgotten, and they will see the storehouses of heaven open and know that only Jesus is ready to provide for all their needs.

But I need you to show the broken ones patience. Show kindness to the ones who look at you with accusing eyes. It's not about you. It's all about Jesus! Don't be envious of anyone, because you have all you need in Me. Leave your pride behind and go into the world boasting of the cross. Humble yourself so you can honor others. Seek the outcast and show them the real love of Jesus.

The enemy harvests anger but sells it to the world as a needful desire. I harvest love. Find Me in the good, and reject the enemy's offers that are always rooted in evil. As you love the least of the world's people, show them how to rejoice in truth. Protect the helpless ones, and trust Me to be your God at all times. Keep your hope in Me, and help others do the same. Persevere. My love for you never fails!

1 Corinthians 13

February 15

Precious child,

Shout out to Jesus! Tell Him everything. He lives to listen to you. Don't worry when the world rebukes you for turning to Jesus as your first resort instead of your last. They don't have any idea. Don't listen when they try to quiet you. Throw your burdens aside and run to Jesus, because He is the one who cares. Like the blind man Bartimaeus, who was begging by the roadside, don't let the size of your stress keep you from Jesus. When the world told Bartimaeus to be quiet, he cried out to Jesus even louder.

Jesus loves you. The world tries to drown out your prayers, but your Savior is bigger than the world. He hears every word you say. Like the Canaanite woman whose daughter was suffering from demon possession, call out to Jesus. She cried out for Jesus to have mercy on her, but it appeared that He wasn't listening. His disciples came up to Him and urged Jesus to send the woman away. But the woman edged closer to Jesus and fell to her knees before Him. She asked for help a second time. He praised her great faith and healed her daughter.

There was also a royal official from Capernaum whose son was very sick. When the man got the news that Jesus was close by, he went and begged Him to heal his boy. Jesus stated that people wouldn't believe unless they saw miracles happen. The official pressed closer to Jesus with all his heart. He asked Jesus a second time to heal his son. The official had to travel back home and didn't get the word until a day later that his son had been healed.

All of these people had patient faith! They didn't look to the world for solutions. They looked to Jesus! Today, I'm calling you to do the same. Be bold for Jesus. Be patient. And press close to Him with all your heart. He lives to listen to you.

Matthew 15:21–28; Luke 18:35–42; John 4:46–53

February 16

Precious child,

I want you to lead a quiet life. Tend to your own business so that the world will see a difference when they see you. They will stop using My name in vain and start using it in holy praise! They will know that the thing they've been searching for isn't found in the world, but in your heart. They will ask, and you will tell them! Then they will call out to Me, and I will save them.

The strength I give you comes from being quiet and trusting Me with everything. Use the quiet moments to read My Word and pray. Use the quiet moments to listen. Let Me tell you things you do not know! My peace that reigns over every hour of your days always brings confidence and quietness so you will be able to discern the enemy's false promises from My lovingkindness.

The world is loud. The enemy uses his armies to transmit messages of self and pride. These messages are the ones that tell you to defend yourself in anger. But I am your defender, and I love you. Remain quiet and let the enemy's song of lies be nothing more than clanging gongs. Find rest in the quiet places. A gentle and quiet spirit is of great worth in My sight. I am here to fight for you. All you have to do is be still.

The enemy tries to fill your day with different sounds. He wants you to have a hard time focusing on Me. Turn off the noise. I have saved you to be still and learn My plans for your life. My love for you endures forever. Trust Me. By quiet waters, walk along the way of My will. Follow the sound of My voice and know that you are right where I want you to be!

Exodus 14:14; Psalm 131:2; Isaiah 32:17;
Lamentations 3:26; 1 Thessalonians 4:11–12

February 17

Precious child,

Today is for you and Me to love each other. It's also for you to know Me more and to grow in your faith. Today when you go about your routine, think about the power you have in Me. The words you say, the way you act, the way you love. All of these qualities about you are being seen. I am calling you to be an example so the world will be drawn to Jesus! Through your holy living, broken hearts will be brought to My Son and He will make them new.

Your speech should persuade people to think about Jesus. When the world is talking about prideful things, let them hear a different sound as you talk about My grace. Let the words that pass over your lips stir the world to come back to Me.

Your behavior should convince the world that Jesus loves them. Conduct yourself with integrity. Pray that whatever you do, whether it's for one person or many, it would open the eyes of those who think I've left My throne.

Your heart should show the world that My arms are mighty enough to hold them too. Carry the love that I've shown you into the world and let them feel real compassion.

Your faith should push back the enemy's schemes so that the hurting ones look at you and see Jesus. I want the ones who are seeking a Savior to look at your faith in Me and realize that Jesus is who they've been looking for. I want them to understand that salvation isn't a hope but a fact.

Be pure. I know that the world doesn't know what this means. And to the ones who do, purity is just an idea. But you know that when you live each hour according to My words, your heart remains strong. I do love you, and I'm so proud to call you Mine.

Psalm 119:9; 1 Timothy 4:10; Hebrews 11:1

February 18

Precious child,

Act in a way that is worthy of the gospel. Just as Jesus died on the cross for you, I'm calling you to die to self. Use My strength to bury your pride so you can preach the message of salvation to the dying world. Give My grace to everyone. Don't save it for the people who are easy to look at and listen to. Give My grace to the ones the world has labeled unattractive and the ones they've stopped listening to. Give grace to both the beggar and the one who disagrees with you. Give grace to the needy as well as the one who belittles you.

I want you to be the one to show people who I really am. I want yours to be the life the world hears about, and after they hear, have their lives changed because of Me. Let the world look at you and the way you live and let them see a sinner saved by My grace.

I want you to stand firm by the power of the Holy Spirit. Don't trade the Spirit for the world. The enemy's playground has enough sinful ways to make you feel strong, but I'm calling you to stand against them and rise above the world by the strength of My loving arms.

You can't do this alone. Just as I am with you, I need you to stay connected to other believers. Together, I want all My precious children to strive to teach the world about the good news of Jesus.

Don't be afraid when people roll their eyes at you because of Me. Don't be discouraged when people treat you like a child because you aren't ashamed to tell them that Jesus died for them. Don't worry when people close to you mock you for caring more about Me than them. I am alive in you, and your heart means everything to Me!

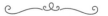

Genesis 26:24; John 17:22–23; Acts 15:11; Philippians 1:27–28

February 19

Precious child,

The enemy tempts you to ask why. He wants you to ask questions like "Why did this happen to me?" He is relentless in convincing you that you are forgotten. "Why am I being treated this way?" That is what the enemy would love for you to spend your time asking. He'd like you to use your hours thinking, "Why am I still in this bleak place of fruitless labor?" He wants you to feel as if you have been sent where you cannot be blessed. The enemy wants you to feel vindictive.

When the struggles of life get overwhelming, I want you to ask *who*: "Who died for me?" Jesus is relentless too! He took the nails so you would know you're forgiven. Spend your time considering "Why was Jesus treated that way?" Or think about this: "Who feeds the hungry?" Remember, when the world tries to send you away, Jesus shows you compassion and promises to meet your needs. He blesses you in abundance so you will have blessings left over. Jesus wants you to feel victorious.

My voice resounds in marvelous ways. Just as I spoke the world into existence, I spoke life into your heart. The things I do are beyond your understanding, but that doesn't mean I leave you unloved. Spend this day thinking about Me and all the ways I have protected and am protecting you from the unseen powers of darkness. Be with Me today and let Me teach you more about My commands. Let your life take root in My plans. Let My love happen to you. Let Me treat you with everlasting compassion. Let Me bless the work of your hands so you will be fruitful in the day of drought. I am your God who turns curses into blessings!

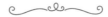

Nehemiah 13:2; Job 37:5; Psalm 1:2–3; Mark 6:34–43

February 20

Precious child,

Everything I say is true. I do not lie. Before the world was formed, I gave you a blessed eternal hope in Jesus. So believe Me. I take up the cause of truth because with Me there are no secrets. The world keeps what's true at a distance, and even if some truth should draw near, the enemy causes honesty to stumble in order to keep the world in dark shadows. The enemy's rebellion leads the world to throw My words away, but I'm calling you to pick them up and hold them close to your heart. As you acknowledge Me, your life helps break this wicked cycle.

The world has also discarded humility. Show them who I am by lifting others higher than yourself. Make it your ambition to share the love of Jesus with the ones still trapped in darkness. Lift Me higher than anything you value in the world, so they can see Me above the war of self that rages on. You find favor with Me when you use My wisdom to seek humility. Go into this day expecting to find lost souls who have been seeking something different. Find them and share the good news that Jesus humbled Himself to die for them.

Be careful not to keep justice from the stranger, the fatherless, and the widow. Instead, care more about treating these people with respect and dignity than anything the world is trying to distract you with. The enemy has gotten good at pushing these weary ones to the margins. His desire is that they would be left there and forgotten. He has led them to a place without hope. Go and tell them I am their defender! Show the world truth. Show them humility. Show them justice. And most of all, let your life show them Jesus!

Deuteronomy 27:19; Psalm 45:4; Isaiah 59:14; Titus 1:2; 1 Peter 5:5

February 21

Precious child,

Everybody makes mistakes. No one is perfect, and everyone stumbles. As you rest in My promises and seek to glorify Me, I want you to think about other people. I created them in My likeness, and I love them too. Remember your heart that praises Me is the same heart that can quickly grow cold toward others who are different from you. Your hands you raise to worship Me are the same hands that can be kept from helping the ones who don't agree with you. I'm not upset. I love you! I just want you to know that I have so much more in store for your life.

Follow wisdom that comes from heaven. Use it to be humble. I'm not telling you these things just for you to be obedient. I'm giving you My wisdom so you will know Me more. The enemy has built temptations around you, knowing that if he can distract you long enough, you will spend your time in fear and worry. If you live like that, your focus is not on Me and My plans for your life. Resist the world's calling. Call out to Me, and I will answer you. My words are true and will keep your heart pure.

Child, I made you to love peace. I am doing a good work in you so that My peace will fill your heart and then overflow into the world. I made you to worship Me, but also to consider others. Let My love for you be your guide. Let My truth help you be submissive to the wonderful things I made for you to experience. Be full of mercy for the lost and for each other. Bear good fruit by not taking sides. Have a sincere heart and don't forget how much I love you.

Zechariah 7:9; Ephesians 1:17; James 3:9–17

February 22

Precious child,

Think about everything I have reminded you of and everything I have done for you. Let thoughts of Me flood your mind. Let them fill you with the knowledge of mercy and teach you that following rules doesn't make you perfect. That's the enemy's scheme. He wants the world to ignore the fact that Jesus is their hope. My only Son is the guarantee of a heart saved by grace. Take the same mercy I have given you and bring it to the world so they will experience Jesus.

He saves completely! There's no more "almost good enough." You are completely forgiven. When you make mistakes today, I see you through the work Jesus did on the cross. He conquered death and made a way to save you from your sins. The devil hopes that when you slip, you will feel that you've let Me down. But you can't let Me down because I am higher than the heavens. With Me there is forgiveness, because I love you at your best and I love you at your worst. I love you all the time, and at all times Jesus lives to intercede for you.

He gave Himself as a sacrifice to cover all your sins, once and for all time. He gave His best. He gave His all so that you could call on Him and receive the gift of salvation. Use this day for His holy name. Open your eyes and see the people who smile when the world is looking but who are hurting on the inside. Let them hear about the love of Jesus that will turn their sorrow into songs of praise. Open your eyes and find the ones who act confident when the world is watching but who are lost and feel like their lives don't matter. Tell them about Jesus, and praise Him as He turns their darkness into light!

Numbers 14:19; Psalm 130:4; Acts 26:18; Hebrews 7:19–28

February 23

Precious child,

I make the sun shine in warm rays to bring light to the darkness, but also to remind you that Jesus is the light of the world who has saved your soul. When the enemy tries to shed darkness over your hope, let My only Son shine His love over your life. I remind you that your life matters because the enemy has thrown a shroud over the minds of unbelievers. I want you to go to them in the love and mercy and compassion and grace of Jesus! Go to them, and by the light of the gospel, help them see His glory.

I cause the wind to blow across the land for comfort, but also to remind you that My Spirit is your counselor. When the world has left you drained, the Holy Spirit will teach you everything and remind you of My words. Remember that Jesus said the gospel must be preached to all the nations. My child, be a beautiful part of this sending and don't worry about what you will say. When the time comes for you to tell the world about Jesus, the Holy Spirit will speak through you. All you have to do is go.

I send the rain in drops of falling water to refresh the earth, but also to remind you that Jesus is the living water who restores your soul. When the heat of life's struggles comes and parches you, let Jesus reign. Don't just honor Him as king over the areas of life you need help with. Hail Jesus as king over all of you. I also want you to have hope in your eternal inheritance. One day, you will be with Me in heaven, and Jesus will lead you to streams of living water and I will wipe away all your tears! I love you.

Mark 13:10–11; John 14:26; 2 Corinthians 4:4; Revelation 7:17

February 24

Precious child,

Take My hand. I have rest for you and a plan to help you learn more about My heart and how to be free of your burdens. As you read My words, allow yourself to listen. Let Me in. Knowing more about who I am will help you walk faithfully with Me through all your days.

Whatever is oppressing you, I am stronger, and I will set you free. Just as I delivered the Israelites out of bondage in Egypt and brought them into the Promised Land, I am mighty enough to deliver you! Focus on the truth that I am the one who delivers. You aren't strong enough, but that's not a bad thing. The enemy wants you to believe it's a sign of weakness, but submitting to My power is a sign of worship. By doing that, you show the world that I am worthy of their praise.

I am faithful. I do not lie, and I never say one thing and do something else. When I say I love you, it is forever. When I say you are My precious child, you are Mine forever. I am also your holy God who acts. I don't just command things to be done. I speak to you and act for you. I say I love you, and I show you love. I make promises to you, and I keep them.

The world and all of the enemy's plans will not consume you. People and their hurtful words and actions will not overwhelm you because of My great compassion for you. You cannot make enough mistakes to use up My love for you, because My compassions for you never fail. They are new every morning! I do not get tired or worn out by your requests. You don't make Me mad, and you certainly don't disappoint Me. Drop your burdens and take My hand. Let Me show you how special you are!

Exodus 13:3; Numbers 23:19; Lamentations 3:22–23; Hebrews 10:39

February 25

Precious child,

Your well-being pleases Me. I don't want to see you swallowed up in sadness. The enemy is a master of deception and wants you to believe that your actions determine your peace. He would have you believe that you get what you deserve. Oh, hear Me when I say that it's the actions of Jesus that determine your peace! He suffered on the cross so that death could be swallowed up. Jesus rose from the grave so that your mourning would be turned into gladness. Your king has ransomed you! Rejoice!

I am here for you. The world is filled with sorrow, but I am the God of all comfort. When misery tries to take hold of your heart, I am there to bring you peace. Find joy in My promises that I will never leave you and that My love for you never ends. Find joy in worshipping Me and also find joy in life's trials. This goes against logic, but child, My ways are higher than yours. I made you for so many good things, and finding joy in the struggles helps you persevere and strengthens your faith. In this way, you will lack nothing.

Don't forget that I am the one who sent My only Son for you. The world and all its temptations hasn't sacrificed a thing for your benefit. The enemy is prideful and can't be concerned with you. He tries to keep your thoughts on fearful things so you will feel empty and scared. But I care about you, and you will be filled with My blessings. Where the world gives you sin and heartache, I have given you Jesus. When the world leaves you feeling rejected, know that I have chosen you. Today, let Me show you just how much you mean to Me!

*Psalm 35:27; Jeremiah 31:13–14;
2 Corinthians 1:3–4; James 1:2; Revelation 21:4*

February 26

Precious child,

Today I want you to think about an important truth. In Jesus, all things are held together. Your hard work and hopes are not strong enough to turn darkness into light. Your good intentions are not strong enough to save people. Your will, no matter how strong, isn't mighty enough to heal the hurting. Only Jesus can do all these things and more, because in everything, Jesus has supremacy. In Him your days will make sense, and in Him your life will show the world that He is Lord of all creation.

Because of Jesus, I look at you and see a beautiful person. In My eyes, you are holy, without blemish, and free from all accusation. All because of Jesus. The enemy makes you believe that in the broken world, you have to defend yourself. He makes you think that if you don't try to solve your own problems, you are somehow unworthy and weak. But in truth, Jesus is your defender. He is before all things, and I created you for Jesus. I made your life to be lived through Him and be kept in Him. Let Jesus take over and be your problem solver.

Come to Me humbly in prayer and let Me tell you more about Jesus. Give Me your teachable spirit so I can show you more about Jesus. Life lived without Him unravels and leaves you running to pick up the pieces. The enemy has mastered the art of convincing you that you are alone and that your life is your own. He desires this lie to consume you so you'll be defeated. Feel Me open your eyes to truth. Look and see that your life is in Jesus. Take this new day and hand it to your Savior. He won't let you down!

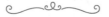

John 1:3–4; Acts 10:36; 1 Corinthians 8:6; Colossians 1:17–22

February 27

Precious child,

Jesus traded His throne for a manger because you were worth it. Jesus took on flesh so that you would know without a doubt that He knows what you're going through.

After He was baptized, Jesus followed the Spirit into the wilderness where the enemy tempted him for forty days. Hear Me say that you are not alone. My Son, your Savior, is always with you. Unlike anyone else, He understands your situation because He has been there.

Jesus ate nothing during his long desert journey, and by the end He was starving. He wanted relief from the pain. This was the moment when the devil came and tempted Jesus to turn stones into bread. The enemy didn't care about Jesus, and he certainly doesn't care about you. Resist his lies. Jesus did. He said, "It is written: 'Man shall not live on bread alone.' " He was referring to the time I provided manna for the Israelites who had been wandering in their own wilderness for forty years. Live on every one of My words.

The enemy tries to find new ways to make you stumble and feel unworthy of My love. He led Jesus up a mountain and offered Him all the kingdoms of the world if He'd only worship him. Jesus answered, "It is written: 'Worship the Lord your God and serve him only.' " You can't serve two masters. Even in your struggles, don't fall for the lie that things of the world will solve your problems.

Finally, the enemy took Jesus to the highest point of the temple and said to throw Himself down and let My angels rescue Him. Jesus answered, "It is said: 'Do not put the Lord your God to the test.' " Child, I know your needs. Don't spend time wishing I'd answer your prayers in one way or another. Let Me take care of you. I want more for you than you can ever imagine!

Deuteronomy 6:13–16; 8:3; Luke 4:1–12

Precious child,

I know there are times when the words of others hurt you. They speak to you, whether in word or deed, in ways that burn your heart. They leave you to wonder, Why would they speak that way? Why do they cut down instead of encourage? I made your life to be a blessing to the world so that they might see a better way. My servant Paul said, "When we are cursed, we bless." I remind you of this truth because Jesus became a curse to redeem you!

I know you are persecuted too. Whether an outright attack or a negative attitude, these actions hurt. Even being misunderstood or feeling like no one cares is enough to bring pain. Paul also said, "When we are persecuted, we endure it." And Jesus said, " 'A servant is not greater than his master.' If they persecuted me, they will persecute you also."

The enemy wants you to question Me. He wants you to stay hidden behind your pride so you can remain part of the problem. But child, I have called you to be part of the solution. In order for the world to see Jesus, they need to see a difference. Paul finished his teaching by saying, "When we are slandered, we answer kindly." All of this is so My name will not be disrespected.

Remember that your worth isn't in people's words. Your worth is in the Word, My precious Son, Jesus. In Him, your life is secure. In Him, you have the strength to bless others no matter what they say. In Him, you have courage to endure trials so that your faith may be multiplied. And in Him, you have the power to offer kind words to those who slander, so they will ask why you act the way you do. Then you will have the chance to tell them about Jesus!

John 15:20; 1 Corinthians 4:12–13; Galatians 3:13; 1 Timothy 6:1

March 1

Precious child,

Please be content with what you have. In every situation that you experience, be content that I am your sovereign God who made you and loves you. Remember to live each hour of each of your days through Me. I will help you be content in all circumstances. Whether you are satisfied or hungry for more, whether you're living in plenty or in need, you can do and endure all things through Me because I am the strength giver.

I have told you that I will never leave you. Don't worry about the things you don't have, because you have Me. Don't fall in love with things of the world, because you already have My love. Be content with where I have you and what I've given you. Because of My grace, the blood of Jesus has saved you. When your life was lost in sin and you didn't even know you needed a Savior, Jesus reached out and hugged you. He loved on you and whispered that He forgave all of your sins. Jesus lifted you up and wiped away all your tears.

I have also told you that I will never forsake you. When I created you, it was simply My heart making yours. That is why My Word says you brought nothing into the world. You were born by My hand because I am all you need. And when your gift of days is over and you come to be with Me forever, you won't bring anything. As you serve Me and obey My commands, contentment will cover you. You will be untouched by the enemy's lies that tempt you to want more and desire what you don't have.

Be satisfied with just My grace. It was enough to save you and will surely be enough to satisfy you today.

Proverbs 19:23; Philippians 4:11–13; 1 Timothy 6:6–8; Hebrews 13:5

Precious child,

I want you to be encouraged by how similar your life is to Jesus'. I gave these words about Him to the prophet Isaiah: "Here is My servant, whom I uphold, my chosen one in whom I delight." You serve because you've been saved. Continue serving knowing Jesus left heaven to do the same. I also chose you! I love you and oh, how I delight in you. Your life is so amazing and so connected to Jesus that I want you to start stepping out in faith like He did.

I put My Spirit on Jesus and He proclaimed justice to the nations. Oh sweet child, please know that I'm calling you to do the same. Use your days to be the hands and feet of Jesus and share justice with the world. The enemy has sown so many seeds of injustice that the lost can't fathom how I could be just. They say how could I be God if I allow so much pain and suffering. But you'll be there to remind them that I allowed Jesus to endure pain and suffering so that the world might call out to Him and find salvation.

Live like Jesus by not arguing or crying out to be heard. Be kind to everyone. Let humility cover you, both in word and in deed. Isaiah continued his prophecy of Jesus, saying, "He will not shout or cry out, or raise his voice in the streets." Child, I know that most days you feel like you're doing the same thing with the same results. You wake up, do your job, go to sleep. Wake up. Repeat. But your life is so much more than what you feel or see. The dying world is watching you! Trust Me when I say they're listening. Tell them that their hope is found in one name alone. Tell them that Jesus is their justice and their Savior.

I love you.

Psalm 18:19; Isaiah 42:1–4; Ephesians 1:11; 2 Timothy 2:24

Precious child,

I give you My word that to live is to live for Christ. This new day is here for you to fall deeper in love with Jesus. Pray to Him. Listen to Him. Follow Him to places you've never been. Ask Jesus to teach you and explain things you struggle with. Let Him show you how special you are. This doesn't mean you head out on your own and think about Jesus while you go about your routine. This means commit each breath to Him. Commit each thought and desire to Him. Commit each heartbeat to your Savior.

The enemy would love for you to focus on the stress. He would love for you to keep your eyes on all the problems that don't have answers. He wants you to live in fear of life and death so your confidence in My Word will never be secure. But I am giving you My strength to resist these wicked ways because your days are wrapped in Jesus. Between living each day for Him and considering your eternal inheritance that He has prepared for you in heaven, don't doubt My plans for your life.

To die is gain. You are an heir of eternal life! One day, you will be with Us in heaven. Jesus has come to prepare a place in My house for you. And while this eternal inheritance is guaranteed, I also want you to remember that Jesus died for you so that you would die to sin and live today in righteousness. This means that you should leave selfishness behind and lay down your life for a brother or sister in need. Let My love flow through you as you care for them. Let your choices show the world that Jesus is worth it all!

Philippians 1:21; Titus 3:7; 1 Peter 2:24; 1 John 3:16–17

Precious child,

Grow in the grace of Jesus. I want you to study His words and through My strength live out His teachings. Growing takes time, but even a small amount of grace given to others changes hearts. Jesus gave costly grace. He taught His disciples to bless people who cursed them and to pray for those that brought them harm. Jesus showed you real grace long before you were even born as He stood and allowed His enemies to crucify Him. Your Savior gave His life so you could receive His grace.

Darkness holds temptations that the enemy has created for you. He places things in your path for you to follow so when the time comes for grace, you are too occupied to give it. The enemy is also skilled at making you think you're different from everybody else. He works on keeping your thoughts fixed inward so that pride can take hold. In that way, he has you in a place where you keep score. Yes, I made you very special, but you were saved by the same grace I'm calling you to give. The world is full of scorekeepers. I have saved you to be a grace giver.

Grow in your understanding of who Jesus really is. Plant My words deep in your heart and meditate on them. I want you to know more about Jesus so that your heart will bring Him honor and not just your lips. Learning more about the heart of Jesus helps you to stand with Him through life's trials. Knowing more about Jesus helps you live in such a way that you help gather people to His cross instead of scattering them away from it. Let the grace I gave you in Jesus pour out of you today in amazing ways. Know His love for you is unfailing!

Matthew 12:30; Mark 7:6; Luke 6:27–31; 2 Peter 3:18

March 5

Precious child,

The world has no fear of Me. They don't even know I'm here. They keep their eyes on their own reflections and cannot even see their own sins. Trapped behind mirrors of pride, they flatter and serve only themselves.

My faithful servant Joshua reminded the Israelites to throw away the gods their ancestors worshipped and serve Me. He kept My words in his heart too. At the right time, Joshua issued a challenge to the people he dearly loved. He told them a decision had to be made. He asked them to decide who they were going to serve. The beautiful part about this is that Joshua didn't leave his people with the challenge. He finished by boldly proclaiming to all who could hear, "But as for me and my household, we will serve the LORD."

Stay humble. You too were once in darkness and had no fear of Me. You didn't know where I was. Like Adam in the garden, you hid behind your sins. But also like Adam, I didn't leave you in that helpless, dark place. I sought you and made a way to save you from your prideful hiding place.

So keep My message in your heart. My truths remain wrapped in My priceless love for you. There is no place you can go and find yourself outside of My love and instruction for your life. Your humble fear of Me is what holds you in the shadow of My mighty arms. Today is My gift not only of life for you, but of salvation and freedom for the people who are still trapped behind their own reflections. Today, I am calling you to be brave like Joshua and take a stand. Let the world see that I am more important than anything to you. Love them like I love you so they may finally see who I really am.

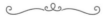

Joshua 24:15; Psalm 36:1–4; Romans 3:10–11; 1 Timothy 2:4

Precious child,

Live today to keep My name glorified. Don't get so distracted by the things of everyday living that you take your heart away from worshipping Me. With all that I have for you, and everything I've given, make this day about Me. Live in a way that helps people see I am for them.

Jesus took up His cross for you, and He gave His life to set you free. Your Savior destroyed the powers of darkness so you would be able to live life untethered to your mistakes. The devil knew this was coming, so he intercepted Jesus at the start of My Son's ministry. The enemy tried to tempt Jesus to give up His life, not for you, but for evil. But even today, all the enemy can do is try. Jesus defeated him, so the devil will never defeat you.

Live today in My will, not yours. Beware, the enemy is trying to outwit you by making you believe you shouldn't forgive the ones who grieve you. He wants you to focus on the hurt rather than on My help. Know without a doubt that I will provide everything you need. In light of My mercy, forgive the ones who sin against you. As hard as this is, forgiving others causes My love and light to shine brighter across the world's darkness.

I promise you that I am leading you away from temptation and delivering you from the enemy. I am building you up so that no matter what you do, you can do it all for My glory. Don't be afraid to take a stand. I have called you to be an important part of sharing Jesus with the world so that when His name is spoken, everyone will bow down and every voice will confess that He is Lord of everything. I am with you, and I love you.

*Matthew 6:9–13; 1 Corinthians 10:31;
2 Corinthians 2:11; Philippians 2:10–11*

Precious child,

Consider the heart of My servant Hezekiah. As king of Judah, he did what was right in My eyes. He trusted Me, held fast to Me, and obeyed all My commands. Hezekiah didn't stop following after Me. He lifted a prayer that I want you to take blessing from today.

"LORD, the God of Israel, enthroned between the cherubim, you alone are God over all the kingdoms of the earth." I want you to remember who I really am. I love you more than anything, and I am the God over everything. I am on My throne surrounded by My guardian angels whom I send to protect you. The enemy is toiling to keep your eyes on life's problems. He wants to put a different image of Me in your heart.

"You have made heaven and earth. Give ear, LORD, and hear; open your eyes, LORD, and see." I want you to remember who you really are. You are My forgiven child who can tell Me anything. I listen to you, and I see everything that happens to you. I didn't create you to claw your way through life's struggles on your own. I filled your lungs with My breath, and I filled your soul with My hope.

"Now, LORD our God, deliver us from his hand, so that all the kingdoms of the earth may know that You alone, LORD, are God." I want you to remember what your life is really all about. Take time today to look back to the moment I delivered you from the pit of destruction. Look back to that time I saved you from the enemy's clutches. I put a story in your heart that I want you to share with the world. I want you to be the one who proclaims My glory so they will know that I alone am God.

2 Kings 19:15–19; Micah 7:7; Romans 7:25; 1 John 5:14

March 8

Precious child,

You are not who the world says you should be, and you are certainly not what you feel. You are who I say you are! When Jesus saved you and you were baptized in Him, sin was dethroned in your life forever. The enemy once smiled at the fact that sin had been your ruler, but now a new day has come. You are free. And the enemy tries desperately to distract you from the truth that when you were baptized into Christ, you were also baptized into His death. And through all of this you were raised to new life. Jesus defeated death for you, forever!

Own these truths today. They have been in your heart, but the enemy has tried to distract you from them so you might think sin is still your master. The passions and desires that once directed you in sin have been crucified so that now My Spirit leads your steps. Now your heart's passions and desires are for Me. Your heart is alive because Jesus has cut away the darkness that once lived there.

Remember, the evil one wants you to forget this. He wants you to believe that you are dead to Me. He tries to fan the fire of your bad days and let you feel overcome by the flames of regret and disgrace.

Jesus saved you. You are made new, created to be like Me in righteous holiness. The enemy wants nothing more than for you to feel that your sin problem still hasn't been solved. He whispers that you should keep putting Jesus back on the cross. But Jesus bore all of your sins that day on Calvary's cross so the power of sin would be dead in you. I have hidden your life in Him. Bring Me glory by trusting that you are truly forgiven.

Acts 2:24; Romans 6:6–7; Galatians 5:24; Colossians 3:3

Precious child,

Know that you are not alone. Today isn't another set of hours for you to endure by trying to be someone I didn't create you to be. I have given you this day to explore more of who I am.

Jesus is standing by your side and will give you strength today so you will be able to find Me in places you cannot reach on your own. Being with Him is more important than anything. He is your Savior, and letting Him lead you is My will for your life. I love you so much that I sent Jesus to die for you, and now that you have been saved, I want you to live for Him.

Jesus is by your side to rescue you from evil attacks the enemy will throw your way. I know life has many struggles, but I want you to always obey Me, not man. Don't find your solutions in the world. Jesus is your answer! And don't forget you are My chosen child who has been washed clean by the blood of the Lamb. He is with you in the storms. Don't forget Jesus saved you from the biggest battle of your life when He saved you from your sins. You were lost with no way out when My precious Son left His throne and rescued you.

Jesus will bring you safely into His heavenly kingdom. You don't have to worry, because Jesus will never let go of your hand. Even when you have finished the race, Jesus will guide you into paradise.

I tell you these things so you will lay down your worries. Then, with empty hands, reach out and hold on to Jesus. Let Him show you how to love and give and hope and pray so your heart will overflow with more of Me!

Psalm 34:17; Acts 5:29; 2 Timothy 4:17–18

Precious child,

My grace has come and offers salvation to all people. This is why you are so important. Your life is a picture of My grace that saved you. I sent this grace to you through Jesus, and I'm sending you into this new day to bring My grace to others. If the person you meet already knows My name, then the grace you give them will be added to the grace already in their hearts. You will be a blessing and reminder that I love and care for them always. If the strangers you show grace to don't know Me, then My grace will begin to soften their hearts and turn their eyes away from the darkness.

My grace is powerful in you so you may boldly testify to the resurrection of Jesus. The enemy has tricked the world into thinking that My Son was a good man and a teacher who lived a holy life and who eventually died a horrible death. The enemy has made the world believe that Jesus is still dead. Your testimony that Jesus rose and is alive in you will help people understand the truth.

You are so special to Me. Be grace where there isn't any. Be love where hate has harmed. Let My grace pour out of your heart onto the ones who have believed the lies. When you show grace, the needy will soon be satisfied.

I know that in darkness sin increases, but as you love others in humility, grace grows even more! So many who are still lost in the enemy's lies deny Jesus as their sovereign king. They twist grace into a license for immoral living. Oh, how they need to meet you and experience real grace. They need to know that salvation comes from knowing the real king. They need to know Jesus. Meet them where they are and show them the grace that has set you free.

Acts 4:34; Romans 5:20; Titus 2:11; Jude 4

March 11

Precious child,

Make all of today about Me. In the quiet time of morning, proclaim My love. Let your prayers rise up in songs of joy. As you do this, be reminded of your amazing worth to Me. Remember that I didn't just create you and set you on your way, but in love I have given you life. I am here loving you so your day may be rich in My mercy and grace. My goodness for you is great. I didn't create you to feel alone and stressed. You are such a treasure to Me, and I want to remind you that you are a treasure to the world. Your life story and your heart for Me are exactly what the world needs!

During the middle hours be glad as you remember all the things I have done for you. I know as the day moves on, you begin to feel tired. Your mind gets distracted, and your body needs rest. Through it all, don't forget that I am with you. I work everything out for good because I have called you according to My purpose. I am for you! Don't be confused about this, My child. No matter what you feel, I am for you. The mistakes you make don't define the amount of grace you will receive from Me.

In the stillness of night, proclaim My faithfulness. Think back to the ways I carried you past the enemy's tempting traps. Think back to the ways I led you down the paths of righteousness. Even though the world is faithless, I am true. The enemy works to get you stuck thinking about that one thing you've asked of Me that I haven't answered. He wants you to believe that I am not loving enough to answer that particular request, but remember I am faithful. In My perfect time, I will answer you, because I love you!

2 Chronicles 6:41; Nehemiah 9:25; Psalm 92:1–5; Romans 8:28

Precious child,

I am your majesty who reigns over everything. I am over every minute of all your days. Take comfort that I am from all eternity. I was God over all the earth long before this day ever came to pass, and I will be God over everything long after these hours are gone. But you will be with Me forever, secure in My promises. I am robed in majesty and armed with strength. Since you are My child, I clothe you in the same way. Don't listen to the enemy's lies that you are poor in spirit and powerless.

I am the mighty one who loves and cares for you. Even the mighty oceans lift up their thunderous voices and declare My power. I am bigger than the greatest waters of the earth and mightier than their crashing waves. I bring down the proud and lift up the humble. Let Me raise you above the pressures of the day so you will be able to spend time realizing how blessed you are. You don't have to try harder or waste time forcing things to go a certain way. I've got every one of your concerns, worries, and fears covered.

My ways are sure. My commands stand firm. As you grow closer to Me, let My holiness replace your weariness. The enemy says you can have an intimate relationship with Me and the world at the same time. Your heart beats by My command. You breathe by My command. By My words you were made. Live in Me and by My words. Your heart has been washed clean. The commands of My heart are for you to experience all that I have for you. They are not to restrict or lessen your joy. As you keep My commands, you walk away from the world and remain living in Me.

Psalm 93; Hebrews 1:3; 1 John 3:24

March 13

Precious child,

Remember that faith in Jesus breaks the chains of weakness. My servant Peter kept this in mind one day as he went to pray. Just outside the temple gate called Beautiful there was a man who was lame from birth. Every day the man had people carry him to the gate so he could ask for money. When the beggar asked Peter for help, the man's life changed both physically and spiritually. Peter gave the man something much better than money. He gave him Jesus! After the man was healed of his affliction, Peter boldly proclaimed that Jesus is the author of life and that faith in Him makes people truly alive.

Remember that the love of Jesus breaks the chains of isolation. When Jesus encountered the Samaritan woman at the well, he knew she felt alone. She had been married five times, and when Jesus met her, the woman was with a sixth man. Jesus gave the woman true love. He gave her all of Himself. Her life was never the same. I want you to live your life the same way. You'll meet people who are very different from you. They won't talk like you. They won't care about Me like you do. They'll act like they don't want to hear about Jesus. Don't worry about any of those things. Just love them like Jesus loves them.

Remember that keeping your hope in Jesus breaks the chains of regret. Pray to Me. Lift up the work of your hands so that you remain in My plans for your life. Let everything you do be done in love. Please continue on the path I've called you to. Even when the enemy arrives and tells you that you're wasting your time and nothing fruitful will come of your labor, resist his lies. I am giving you all the strength you need to endure and be inspired as you keep your hope in Jesus.

John 4:6-26; Acts 3:1–16; Colossians 1:5; 1 Thessalonians 1:3

March 14

Precious child,

Jesus left His throne for sinners. I want you to leave what's comfortable and go to someone who doesn't know who I am. Jesus was ridiculed because He ate with people whom society had deemed unworthy. My Son shook hands and lived life with the lonely ones. Jesus didn't just share a few words about Himself and My glory to people who were downtrodden. He gave all of His time to sit down and talk with the ones who made bad choices. Jesus reached out and showed compassion to strangers who wouldn't have acknowledged Him otherwise.

Jesus left His throne for the lost. Even on that dark day outside Jerusalem's walls, when the enemy thought he had finally won the battle, Jesus reached out and loved the broken ones. On the cross, lifted up between two criminals, Jesus continued to pour out forgiveness. As the crowd below shouted insults for Jesus to save Himself, He still loved on the lost. Using His last breaths, with arms opened wide, Jesus listened to one of the criminals proclaim My Son's innocence. In return, Jesus promised him paradise.

Jesus left His throne for you. He promised that in Him, you will have life abundantly. Let your Savior be the answer to every one of your prayers. Let Jesus be in the middle of everything you desire. Let Him be your reason for all that you do. There was a day when you were under the same sentence as the criminals on either side of Jesus. You were a stranger lost and alone in the darkness of My enemy's world. Your life had made a mockery of righteousness as bad decisions reigned in your heart. Then came that glorious day I appointed when Jesus led your heart to His cross, and like the criminal, you surrendered your life to Him.

Rejoice in what I have done for you. Leave your life behind and bring Jesus to the burdened ones!

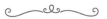

Mark 2:17; Luke 23:32–43; John 10:10; 1 Peter 2:21

March 15

Precious child,

Live each day in thanksgiving for all that I've done. In every situation, remember that Jesus is with you. My will for you is that you give thanks at all times. This keeps your heart tender and tuned in to the Spirit. It also is a powerful witness to the world when they see your grateful attitude. Many will wonder where the source of your strength is, and you will tell them. Being thankful doesn't mean ignoring the pain and the hurt. Being thankful to Me means knowing that I am using everything for your benefit.

I am good. Giving Jesus to you was the highlight of My goodness. The broken world is full of darkness. Bad things happen every day that cause many to question My existence. But remember that I am alive and on My throne. I am sovereign, and I will never allow you to be outside of My goodness. Even Jesus felt pain wrapped in deepest darkness. In His sacrifice, My goodness has been poured over your life forever, and the enemy cannot take it away.

My love for you endures forever. From the first moment I breathed life into you, I loved you. Through every day since, I have loved you with an eternal love. I don't have limitations. My heart for you is unlimited. The enemy tries hard to mask this truth by using things of the world to hide your eyes from My love. He throws conflict and anger over you in hopes that you will take your focus off Me. He tries to heap coals of insecurity over your days in hopes that you will question My timing.

Just know I am for you. Be thankful for the goodness I have given you in Jesus, and let My love be enough.

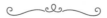

1 Chronicles 16:34; 2 Chronicles 7:3; Psalm 106:1; 1 Thessalonians 5:18

March 16

Precious child,

    I have given you a special gift of days to live your life in Me. But much greater than this is Jesus. He is My greatest gift. My holy Son, your Savior, is for you. He wants to be the light of your world and the hope of your heart. Jesus wants to be your friend. Today, let Him be worth more than fear of not measuring up. Let Jesus, your Messiah, be worth more than your shame. Let Him be worth more than carrying your burdens alone. Let Jesus be everything you desire because I sent Him to be my complete gift of wonderful grace.

    What the enemy wants you to do is work hard for sin. I know this sounds unusual, but the truth is you are part of a world that doesn't recognize their real king. All around you, people toil for prideful gain. They labor long and hard out of love for themselves and try with all their hearts to bring attention to the work of their hands. The enemy knows that the wages of sin is death, but My gift of Jesus is eternal life. Jesus did the hard work on the cross for sin to be conquered forever.

    I sent Jesus into the world, and He overcame it. He destroyed the veil of lies the enemy tried to keep over you. Your life is secure now in Jesus. You are no longer a servant to misunderstanding. Keep your eyes on the truth that I love you and care about everything you are feeling. Spend your time testifying to My Son's great name. Dedicate your days to letting the world know what grace is. Show others how My Son broke through the darkness and rescued you from selfish pride. Help people see that Jesus is for real and that He is for them too!

John 4:10; Acts 20:24; Romans 6:23; 1 John 5:20

March 17

Precious child,

Give Me your heart. Give Me all that you hold hidden in it. Let Me create purity there. Let Me renew your spirit and make it steadfast within you. I will never push you away. I want you to know that I will never cast you out of My presence. My will is to restore joy in your life so you will be able to remember the joy you felt on the day salvation came to you. Feel Me sustain you so you will have the overflow of strength to sustain others.

Please don't be too proud or ashamed to ask for forgiveness. The enemy loves darkness. He loves it when you justify your actions. He wants nothing more than for you to ignore My commands. He has an infinite number of excuses waiting for you to use to avoid humbling yourself before Me. He also loves the times you believe the lies and feel so much shame that you don't run to Me. Selfish pride will keep your heart from seeing My kindness. Letting shame rule will keep you from experiencing My healing hands of mercy. Giving Me your heart means knocking down the walls so I can heal you and so the world can see the beautiful person I made you to be.

Living from a humble heart brings wisdom. It helps you understand that being with Me through all of life's trials and triumphs is more important than carrying your pride through even one day on your own. Giving Me your whole heart restores all of My mercy and grace within you. Everything I made you to be, I made from Me. Let Me bring you back to the kindness and goodness I have for your life. Put your dear heart in My hands and feel My strength wipe away your mistakes. I will never let you down. I love you.

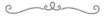

2 Chronicles 32:25; Psalm 51:10–17; Proverb 11:2; Lamentations 5:21

March 18

Precious child,

Wait for Me. Be patient and know that I hear your prayers. Wait for Me because My timing is perfect. I hear your songs of praise and your cries for help. Wait for Me because I will answer and I will provide. Don't doubt My love, and please remember where it was that I first found you. Trapped in the deep pit of sin, covered with layers and layers of guilt and shame, you called out to Me. I reached down and pulled you out of the darkness. I set your life on the rock of sweet Jesus and gave you a place to stand, far away from and free of the enemy's grasp.

I have given you a new song of forgiveness to sing over the dying world. As you live each day for Me, your conversation with others about Jesus becomes a new song of praise to Me. Because of your humble heart and your courageous desire to honor Me above all things, many souls will be added to My kingdom. They will see Me and stop trusting in the world. They will be blessed because, like you, they will keep their eyes on Me. They will turn from the world's temptations and put all their hope securely in My hands.

Remember that nothing compares to all the wonderful things I have planned for you. Nothing in the world compares to Me. The gifts and plans I have for you are without end. You don't need to earn My love and provision. All you have to do is have faith that I am faithful. Make your greatest desire be to live in My will for your life. As you do this, keep My words hidden in your heart. Don't forget that My love is a shield of protection that keeps you safe from the enemy's schemes. You are My sweet child, and I love you.

Psalm 40; Isaiah 25:1; 1 John 4:7

March 19

Precious child,

Desire Jesus. Concentrate on your relationship with Him today. He is worthy to be the center of your thoughts. Let Him captivate your heart. Let Jesus be the object of all you want. This will keep you from wandering away from My truth. Staying focused on Jesus keeps your eyes open to the way I have mapped out for your life. The enemy wants you to get caught up thinking about your past mistakes. He wants you to own a stagnant faith so you won't press on toward Jesus and all the wonderful things I have for you in Him.

I am at work in you. Don't let your dreams include everything but My grace. Don't let your heart be satisfied with anything less than My love. The life of righteousness I have called you to is only possible because Jesus became your sacrifice. Don't let His death be for nothing by giving in to the enemy's lies that you're helpless. Don't believe the lies that you're trapped in a battle I cannot rescue you from. I am so much bigger than your past, and I'm certainly bigger than the enemy's desire to keep you from living free in Jesus.

I don't want you to put your trust in things of the world. Trust Jesus because He made you priceless in My eyes. Boast in His holy name! Put all your hope and confidence in Him. No matter what, pursue Jesus in faith, never forgetting that I am with you always. In all situations, My protection covers you. Jesus took hold of your life so that you might take hold of Him. Let go of the world's treasures you still cling to. They have no worth now and only serve to take your attention off living and working for My kingdom. Live what you're worth!

Psalm 95:10; Galatians 2:21; Philippians 3:12–14; Hebrews 3:1

March 20

Precious child,

Since I created the world and everything in it, I want you to remember that I do not live in temples built by human hands. I am not defined by the will of man. The skills and talents of the world did not knit Me together. I want to remind you of this so you don't limit your view of My almighty power. Live life in Me through humbly submitting to the truth that I am mightier than you can ever imagine. I am stronger than you will ever know. Seek My will today. Take a stand for My kingdom and My righteous name.

The enemy has twisted the world's expectations by convincing them that they can talk back to Me. The world looks up at the sky and with pointed fingers accuses Me of being absent and unreachable. Child, listen to Me. Although it is true that I am sovereign and there is nothing you can give Me, I desire your heart, and I want to love you with a love like no other. I want you to move through today by My strength. Reach out and hold Me. I want to satisfy your soul. Let the world see you as My humble servant, forgiven and set free by My grace.

I give everyone life and breath. Make the choices that keep your life anchored in Me. Rest in My Word. Take comfort in My commands so you will find Me. Let My great love for you shape your heart for My purposes. Don't worry about spending your time in ways that make the world see a certain version of you. The world needs to see who I made you to be, because I made you wonderful. They need to know that you are made in My image. Celebrate today all that I've done for you. Make all of today all about Me.

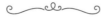

Jeremiah 18:6; Matthew 6:33; Acts 17:24–28; Romans 9:20–21

March 21

Precious child,

I want you to understand what My love for you means. First, My love for you is not some ideal that sounds inspirational. My love for you is a covenant between us. It's a bond that joins our hearts and keeps them that way for all time. I gave you the breath of life as a gift so you could experience My promise that your heart is held securely in My hands, and I will never put it down or set it aside. The enemy will never be able to steal this truth from you no matter how hard he tries.

I want you to see yourself like I see you. There isn't a perfect you somewhere down the line that you will discover through change. Yes, I am sanctifying you, but your heart has been cleaned. Sin holds no power over you anymore. Don't let the enemy persuade you to become somebody you're not. When I first formed you in My image, I didn't think I might love you one day if you were good enough or looked a certain way. My love is the very thing that knit you together, which means I am in love with who you are, not what you could become.

I want the world to know who I am through the love you show others. Love them like I have loved you. Love them so they will know that you care. Listen to what they say so they will know you are genuine. I know your time is given to many things, but walking in the way of My love means you are offering up your life as a sacrifice, just like Jesus did for you. Love others by giving them your time. Just as I gave you the breath of life, I want you to speak My hope into the life of another. I love you.

Deuteronomy 7:9; Nehemiah 1:5; John 13:34–35; Ephesians 5:2

March 22

Precious child,

Let your faith rest in My power. Declare My wisdom to the world by sharing the message of Jesus. Let His name resonate over all your words and deeds. Let Him be over every wish and dream you ponder. Let Jesus love you by allowing Him into the hidden places of your heart. Tell Jesus why you've been holding on to these fears. In that quiet place, give Jesus everything you've been hanging on to. Give it all to Jesus today; then embrace your precious king with your now empty hands.

You don't need to live an eloquent life, but rather a quiet one where you spend your time learning more about Jesus. In humble meekness, consider your Savior's crucifixion and how He chose death so you could receive life. Live this day understanding that Jesus is My Son and your Messiah who has set you free to live in peace. Don't just go through the hours knowing about Jesus. The enemy would love for you to waste time reading the Bible and not doing what it says. Use the gift of today to live like Jesus.

Focus on testifying to My love, and let My Spirit guide you through the day to people who are broken and seeking true love. Remind them that My mighty arms are not too short to save! Remind them that My ears are not too dull to hear their cries for mercy. Let your life testify to My goodness so they will understand that I am the answer to all of their prayers. Please know that your life is beautiful to Me. You are a song of worship to Me. Feel My blessings pour over you and be renewed. Let My grace wash away the pain. My love for you is everlasting.

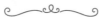

Psalm 37:11; Isaiah 59:1; John 1:34; 1 Corinthians 2:1–5; James 1:22

March 23

Precious child,

I hear your prayers. The enemy whispers that your prayers to Me don't matter, but you know the truth. You know that your life matters, and I am aware of every one of your needs. Unless I had helped you, your inheritance of sin would be death. Instead, by My grace you have inherited eternal life! I remind you of this truth because when you call out to Me, know I hear your voice and I listen to every word you say. I am for you. Tell Me everything and be confident that I am listening.

I have seen your tears. When your feet slipped over the enemy's traps, My love lifted and supported you. If I don't answer your prayers in the way you hoped I would, please don't take that as a sign of indifference. I care about you more than you will ever know. The world pretends to care, but don't get caught up trying to please people. They will always let you down. Spend your time thinking about how much you mean to Me. Understand that I see your beautiful face, and I know when you smile and I know when you cry. Know that I am answering you according to My perfect plan for your life.

I heal you. When anxiety filled your heart and threatened to hinder your walk with Me, I consoled you and brought your soul great joy. This is My desire for you today. I am at work to sanctify you. I am leading you in ways that will make you more like Jesus. Whether you are walking in a valley, experiencing the pain of life's sorrow, or climbing a mountain of life's delight, don't forget that I am with you. I am the one who comforts you. Trust Me to be mighty enough to take care of you. You are My child, and I love you.

2 Kings 20:5; Psalm 94:17–19

March 24

Precious child,

Decide to keep your heart on things above where Jesus is seated. Your life has been raised with Him out of the darkness, so let His love for you erase all of your doubts and fears. Think about things above, not earthly things. Look at the way Jesus thought about people and do the same. Go where He is calling you. The only thing that matters is that you express your faith by loving Me and loving others. Be brave and speak the name of Jesus to people who are blindly roaming through the world. They are lost and can't see. With your words and actions, give them hope. Give them Jesus.

Rest your heart on the truth that I am not only God of all creation, but also your heavenly Father. Continue to seek Me in all sincerity and allow your heart to thirst for My presence. Let everything that's in you long for Me. The enemy has convinced many that the world is filled with delightful things that bring true peace and contentment. Run after Me because you know the world is really a waterless desert of temptations.

Let your thoughts return to the fact that My love for you is greater than the life you're living. All day long, think on things that will bring Me glory. Let your life be a song of praise. Lift your hands high in worship so the world will know that I am worthy and that I am the one who satisfies. At night, remember all the ways I help you. Remember Me. Grab hold of Me because I am here to hold you. In My eyes you have been made righteous. Be encouraged, and remember that My home is in your heart. Use My power to glorify My holy name.

You make Me so proud. You are wonderful to Me.

Psalm 63:1–8; Mark 8:25; Romans 3:22;
Galatians 5:6; Colossians 3:1–2

March 25

Precious child,

Here I am, with you forever. Let your life tell My story to the world. Let them know of all the ways I've blessed you. Tell them about My power to heal and all the wonderful things I have done for you. I have made today for people to put their trust in Me and keep My commands. Let them know that I am your rich habit. Let them see how you always remember My plans for your life. Break the chains of injustice by giving the world My mighty name. Set the oppressed ones free by not being afraid to minister to the oppressor.

The world is consumed with rebellion. They refuse to have loyal hearts by putting their faith in each other. They love to test Me with faulty accusations and are content to doubt My strength. Their spirits ignore My great love and seek out worldly treasure. They forget that My provision flows in abundant streams. In the middle of this selfishness, proclaim My gift of salvation. Tell them how I saved you from the floodwaters of sin. Testify that when your heart was thirsty I gave you living water from the rock, My Son, Jesus.

Because of your faithfulness to Me, people will consider My love for their hearts. Then like a spring rain, I will shower them in mercy and forgive their sins. I will not abandon them. Tell them to follow Me to safety and that today is the day I will erase their fears. Break burdens by feeding the hungry and giving shelter to the wanderer. Don't turn your back on the lost. Open their eyes to see Me. Speak the name of Jesus so they can hear Me. Love the unlovable so they will understand that I am their God. Let your light shine in the darkest places. My glory is your guard.

Psalm 78; Isaiah 58:6–9; Matthew 13:15

March 26

Precious child,

Relive that moment you surrendered your life to Me. Oh, the sweet freedom that rained over you, unlocking the chains that sin had wrapped around your heart. My love banished the darkness that surrounded your soul and replaced it with the glorious light of Jesus. Let the memory of your salvation give you the strength to put today into perspective. Let the memory of Jesus coming into your life energize your spirit. You have been released from the burdens of your past, so you can see this new day as an opportunity to receive My love and give it away to the ones the world has forgotten.

As a new creation, your life has been saturated with My faithfulness. I hear your prayers and listen to the rhythm of your heart. Remember that I have saved you by My mighty name. I have justified you by My powerful hand. This is the new reality I have given you. Yes, the world will continue to attack your spirit. The enemy will plot ways to make you feel hopeless and alone, but I am the one who helps you. Use your freedom to be a comfort to those who cry out for help. Be the one who makes the broken ones feel beautiful again. Give them My gladness.

Today, put Me first. I lift your life up above the hurtful words people speak and above the ones who seek to make you feel unwanted. I know the world is full of strangers who are fueled by darkness. Their accusing glances try to stagnate your walk with Me. But this day is not about the hurt. It's about the healing. Sacrifice your heart's desires to Me and be filled by doing the work of My kingdom. I am calling you to bring good news to the poor and proclaim liberty to the captives. I have given you My power to open the prison doors of fear to those who are trapped by it. I am so proud of you!

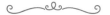

Psalm 54; Isaiah 61:1–3; Acts 13:38–39

Precious child,

Feel My grace pour over you today. Let it free you to live the life I made you to live. Hear My grace tell your guilt and shame to flee. Watch it keep your heart safe from the lies the world is selling. Lies that say you aren't really good enough and you're definitely not smart enough to be Mine. Let grace wipe the dust off your memory so you can remember where you came from and what I did for you.

Let grace help you remember that Jesus was the only one who died for you. He died so you can call Him Savior. He died so that you wouldn't be separated from Me. Jesus died so that your sin and guilt would be wiped away completely. Jesus endured your darkness and rightful punishment because of My grace.

The more you know Me and Jesus, the more you understand grace. And the more grace you receive, the more you must give. Today I am calling you to be a steward of grace. Jesus has overcome every bad day you will ever have. He has overcome every pain you will ever suffer. And best of all, Jesus has overcome death! So don't rely on worldly wisdom. Rely on My grace.

Quiet times spent with Me reading My Word, listening to Me, and praying are your guides down the river of grace. Life, formed as the mountains and valleys, is the land on the shores. Grace carries you through them all to eternity with Me in heaven. The current of My love moves you on, through the highs and lows, as you focus on Jesus alone. Because of grace, Jesus is both the horizon and the hope of your heart. So My child, don't forget that I go before you and I am with you. Nothing that will happen today will surprise Me. I will never leave you or turn My back on you!

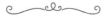

Deuteronomy 31:8; John 16:33; 2 Corinthians 1:12

March 28

Precious child,

Nothing can stand against Me, and since I hold your life securely in My hands, the same is true for you. No person, no word, no scheme of the world can stand against you either. The enemy lies to you so you might feel helpless and weak. No matter how small or massive the attack, you will not be overwhelmed because today you are under My protection and care. I am here to pour My strength into you and keep you safe.

The enemy has planted lies in the world. People believe that My power has limits. They have bought the deception that I set everything in motion and walked away. They try to tell you that if I was a good God I wouldn't allow evil. They shout from the mountaintops that I must be dead because all they see is evil. Where do they think I've gone? Why do they feel I don't care? The enemy stirs their doubts into storms of unbelief. He gets the world worked up and confused so all their time is spent questioning Me. He persuades them they've been appointed judge and have the right to accuse Me.

I created you beautiful. Your debt has been paid. You have been set free by the blood of Jesus. Through Him, I am calling you to uproot the devil's lies. By your faithfulness to My heart, show the world that My power is unlimited. Treat them like Jesus would so the deceptive veil will be lifted and they will know I haven't walked away. Shout from the mountaintops that I'm alive and that I have moved close to their hearts, ready to save. Help their unbelief by sharing My love with them. Let My power move you to reach out in peace to the judges and accusers. By your unselfish ways, give them Jesus!

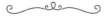

Numbers 11:23; Job 41:10; Isaiah 44:24; John 3:2

March 29

Precious child,

Let your life be a witness to My grace. The world is watching you. Even if you don't think people pay attention to your choices, they do. Their actions say they are not interested in Me because they are afraid to give up control. The world is afraid of letting go of their false sense of security. But they are watching. They see how you serve the needy. They see you love those who are suffering. When you give away grace, the world has to stop and ask why you would do such a thing. They listen when you give your answer.

As you testify to My holy name, let your life be an example of mercy. Keep yourself humble and know that I am exalting you. Give your life in service to the ones who can't pay you back. Let your days be a banquet of giving help to those who are blind, poor, lame, crippled, homeless, imprisoned, unloved, lonely, abandoned, and weak. I will pay you back at the resurrection of the righteous. The world spends time making excuses, but not you. I am proud of you because you sacrifice your time for others, knowing in your heart that it is really Me you are serving.

You are My disciple because you are not afraid to carry your cross. You are not ashamed to speak the name of Jesus. You are not proud. Don't hold on to anything except Jesus. As you live life for Me, remember to avoid judging others. Show them compassion. In doing so, you are being a trusted minister of My kindness, which is intended to lead people to repentance. If you need wisdom, ask and I will give it to you generously. Believe Me in all these things. Without doubting, give grace and know that I am your forever provider and protector. I love you!

Luke 14:1–27; Romans 2:1–4; James 1:5–6

March 30

Precious child,

I can accomplish all things, and no plan I have for you can ever be ruined. Today is the day you will learn more of who I am. My mighty arms are your eternal dwelling place. You are safe here. Watch and see how I will reveal My loving kindness over your life. I am the living God, and I will not let your day become worthless when the enemy tries to tell you that it doesn't matter. Through faith, push away all of your doubts and fears and yearn for Me. Let everything I made you to be cry out in praise, and let your song magnify My heart so the ones walking in darkness may see Me.

The closer you walk with Me, the more of My wonders you will uncover. My strength is for you. I don't want you to try to solve your problems on your own. Don't struggle and then turn to Me when you can't go any further. I pour out My blessing over you and set your heart safe in My hands. As you pass through valleys of stress and confusion, I promise to turn them into places of renewal. When the day feels like a long desert of turmoil, I promise to send healing rain.

Pray and know without a doubt that I am listening. It is better to be with Me today than anywhere else. Your chains are gone. The walls of sin that once imprisoned you have fallen! I am your light and your shield. I look on you with favor. I do not withhold good things from you. Continue to trust Me and receive My endless blessings. Sweet one, give Me everything. Don't hold on to what the world is offering. Reach out and know that I am for you. Hear Jesus telling you that everything is possible if you just believe.

Job 42:2; Psalm 84; Mark 9:23

Precious child,

I care about every part of you. I won't let your feet slip as you run the race I've marked out for you. I think about you, and I care about everything you go through. Don't worry about keeping up with other people as you go, because I keep you with Me. The plans that I have for you are different from the ones I have for everyone else, so the course you're on will take you to different places and experiences. When the terrain becomes hard to cross, I won't forget you. And as you navigate the hills, remember the cross.

I formed every part of you. Each of the trillions of cells in your body bears My fingerprint. I made you special and different from everyone else. Listen to Me, and be untouched by fear. Pace yourself with My words of truth. Let go of the sin that entangles your feet and hinders you from moving forward. Let My love saturate your life. Let it guide you through the wilderness and be like water as you move through the desert places. Obey My truth, and as you run, express your faith in Me by loving others along the way.

I lift up every part of you. The entire race is about Jesus. He is the start and the finish. He gave everything so you could be freed to participate. He is the water that quenches your soul. Remember the race is to glorify Him for all He has done for you. There are people in the crowd watching who don't know Jesus. They have heard His name, but they are caught on the outside of the barrier. Don't be ashamed. Slow down and look for them. Go to them and explain what they're watching. Share the good news that Jesus is alive and lead the lost back to Me. You're doing a great job, and I'm proud of you!

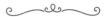

Proverbs 1:33; Isaiah 49:15; Hosea 13:5

Precious child,

Be encouraged today because the eternal hope I have given you is living and imperishable. The enemy works hard to combat this truth. He will put things in your path that will make you question My goodness. He will direct your eyes to see the world's evil and hope that you get distracted. The enemy wants you to wonder why I allow the hatred to continue. But I want you to wonder why I allowed My only Son, Jesus the Messiah, to be tortured and crucified for your precious heart.

This hope you have in Jesus is undefiled and will never fade. Through faith, My power protects you. So instead of giving in to the weight of various struggles, rejoice that the salvation of your soul has been made a reality. Death has been defeated. Feel My peace push away stress that has crept into your heart. I am for you. Today I want you to understand that My blessings are for you, and because your hope is in Me, you will learn that I am close to those who fear Me. I promise that when you put your hope in Me, you will not be disappointed.

There is hope in My words. Remain in the scriptures so you may be encouraged by the hope you find there. Hold on to the truth of My commands. The Bible isn't a collection of man-made stories, but a picture of a living hope that I have breathed out for you in redemption and grace. My words are a treasure. They were written to daily remind you to rely solely on Me. I have rescued you once from death through the sacrifice of Jesus. Keep your hope in Me because I am here to deliver you from the enemy's schemes. With all your strength, hope in My love.

Psalm 42:5; Isaiah 49:23; Romans 15:4;
2 Corinthians 1:10; 1 Peter 1:4–6

Precious child,

I have given you My Spirit so you will live each day in full confidence of My truth. He is with you to give you power to complete the tasks I am calling you to. He is there to fill you with My love and to teach you self-discipline. When you have to confront the enemy's lies, My Spirit will give you the right words to say. Don't be ashamed to tell everyone you meet about Jesus. Let His holy name resonate throughout your words and deeds. Today is a brand-new opportunity to reach the nations for My glory.

My Spirit is the Spirit of truth who is your advocate and helps you and will be with you forever. Dwell in Me. I formed the mountains and brought the earth into existence. From everlasting to everlasting, I am your God. I am with you, and I am also outside of time. When the enemy tries to send darkness, have patience and wait on Me. One day for you is like a thousand in My eyes. Let Me fill your heart with wisdom so you may discern truth from the enemy's deceit. I have given you all you need.

Let My love be brighter than the sun and feel its rays of hope warm your soul. Let Me be enough to fill your days with gladness. You will find nothing in the world as satisfying as My presence. Be content where I have you, and don't wish for things I haven't given. I am with you, and I am showing you favor by establishing the work of your hands. I do this so you can rest assured that My sovereignty will carry you through life's trials. I go before you to remove the obstacles, and I revive your heart and spirit. Don't be afraid. I am here to heal you and shower you with peace.

Psalm 90; Isaiah 57:15–19; John 14:16–17; 2 Timothy 1:7–8

Precious child,

Let today be a day for remembering the battle for your heart and what your Savior did for you. Let your thoughts go back to that day when Jesus picked up your sins and carried them with the cross. Try to comprehend how much Jesus loves you as you recall the sobering events of Calvary's hill. The enemy gathered his people and watched as the world tried to kill its Savior. A sign was made to mark the occasion: THIS IS JESUS, THE KING OF THE JEWS. What man wrote in sarcasm, I meant for good and truth. My Son, the one true king, was the living sign, nailed to the cross and lifted high for the world to see.

Bearing the weight of your sins, Jesus hung with open arms between two criminals. My Son's arms were stretched wide, not in submission to the soldiers' strength, but in submission to My will. My Son's arms were an invitation to receive grace. The enemy, blind to love, stirred the witnesses to hurl insults at Jesus. "He saved others. . .but he can't save himself!" Their words were an indictment. They were the ones who couldn't save themselves. They yelled out for Me to save Jesus, but they were blind to the fact that it was their own hearts I was trying to save.

For hours, day turned to night as darkness wrapped the world in a blanket of heavy despair. Jesus cried out to Me. With a shout, He asked Me why I had forsaken Him; then My precious Son gave up His spirit. The enemy rejoiced, thinking that his victory was secure. He had orchestrated a horrific assault, but My love was stronger. At that dark moment when Jesus died, love exploded through the darkness and tore the temple curtain in two. It shook the earth, split rocks, opened tombs, and brought the dead to life. And then truth was spoken: "Surely this man was the Son of God!"

Matthew 27:33–54; Mark 15:21–39

Precious child,

You are not alone in your struggle. I am with you always. Think about the hours of sadness that came in the wake of Jesus dying on the cross. The enemy had people believing that their Savior was finally gone for good. From a distance, the ones who loved Him stared in disbelief at the broken body of the one who had told them not to fear. They struggled in their hiding places to believe that hope had not died with Him too. But one man named Joseph was bold enough to leave the heartache and go to Jesus. He went to Pilate and asked for the body of his Savior.

You are not alone in your despair. I am at work in great and mighty ways for you. While you wait, do what Joseph did and in your grieving go to Jesus. On the outside, it may seem as though life is broken and filled with sorrow. What you hoped for didn't work out. Go to Jesus. Next to the hill where Jesus was slain was a garden where new life grew. This is where Joseph buried Jesus. He lovingly wrapped My Son's body in spices and linen. Even though the darkest hour weighed heavy on his heart, Joseph worshipped Jesus!

You are not alone in your weakness. The world works to keep your heart from finding hope in Me, but I am preparing wonderful things for you. Just like when Pilate ordered the soldiers to guard against the disciples from getting to Jesus in the tomb, the enemy still tries to keep you from seeking Jesus. Make today about faith in Jesus, your coming king, who wraps you in His infinite love. When the enemy works to make you believe that your hope in Jesus has died, trust Me that it hasn't. The Son is rising up above your struggles. He is shedding every drop of darkness that covers your weak heart. He is rolling away the stone of hurt and filling you with His mercy.

Matthew 27:65; Mark 15:42–46; John 19:41–42

April 5

Precious child,

Like falling rain heals dry land, the blood of the Lamb has fallen over sin, sent to heal dry hearts. The grip of death no longer has a hold on you. Nothing will ever stop you from reaching Jesus. The walls of guilt have been rolled away, and your enemy cowers at the sight of living water, who reigns over your soul. Rejoice, My child, rejoice! Your Savior is alive and well! He has risen! Today hear your Savior's sweet and holy voice greet you. Listen to Him say, "Do not be afraid."

Turn toward Jesus and worship Him. Believe Me. The enemy will try to convince you that you are all alone, but Jesus is right there in the middle of your heart, reaching out to you. He is there to comfort you and to turn your sorrow into joy. For you, Jesus allowed Himself to be handed over to sinners. For you, Jesus was nailed to a tree. And for you, He rose from the grave and has conquered your sin forever! He paid your debt and broke the chains that held you captive to darkness. Like the Lord's tomb, your life has been emptied of darkness.

Today, Jesus is filling you with strength to rise up from where you are and go tell the world the good news! Tell them that your Savior lives! Some may not believe you when your words point them to Jesus. They may say your testimony doesn't make sense. Tell them anyway. The enemy plants seeds of distrust in the hearts of many, just like the soldier guards were paid to lie and say that the disciples stole the body of Jesus. Some believe the lies. Some believe the love. Be bold and be My witness. Jesus is alive! He is here for you. Let Him hold you and wipe away every tear. Let My Son warm your soul with His radiant love.

Matthew 28:9–15; Mark 16:6; Luke 24:11; John 20:15–18

April 6

Precious child,

I am using your life to answer other people's prayers. My children are crying out from being held captive to fears and addictions. Their lives look good on the outside, like a kingdom of gold even, but on the inside their hearts are in mourning because they have lost all hope. By My plans for your life, you will help many. I know the current task I've called you to can be a burden some days, but deliverance comes from Me alone. I have so much more for you.

When it feels like I don't have a plan for your life, focus on Me. When the enemy persuades you to believe that you labor in vain, focus on Me. As you go through the wilderness of working hard without apparent results, stop and consider the mountain of My love. It rises over you and guards you against the enemy's lies. Meet Me there. Look for Me in the most unexpected places. For my servant Moses, it was a bush on fire. He wondered why it didn't burn up as it should, and that's when I called his name.

I am leading you in the same way. Hear Me call to you and know with all your heart that I am here. Spend quiet time listening to Me. Hear Me tell you about the suffering. Hear Me tell you about the tears. Listen to Me explain how the people I'm sending you to may appear okay but are really broken and waiting to be rescued. The world has enslaved them to lies. They are chained to the belief that they don't matter and are unnecessary. Go and rescue them from the enemy by sharing Jesus. Go and tell them He has risen and is alive! Bring them out of their suffering to a land of hope. Stand firm in every aspect of My will for you, because I am with you always.

Exodus 3:1–12; Psalm 3:8; Colossians 4:12

April 7

Precious child,

I know that you live to bring Me glory. An important way you can do this is to bear with the failings of the weak. Continue walking on the path of humility. Be a light to the dark world where the enemy seeks to tear down self-esteem. Build up the less fortunate. Be hope where there is none. Endure and encourage because that is what My Son did for you. I am here to give you the attitude toward others that Jesus had for humankind. He accepted people and forgave them, all to bring Me praise.

Encourage others. Jesus had been invited to dinner at the house of a certain Pharisee. A woman who lived in the same town heard that Jesus was near and grabbed an alabaster jar of perfume. She found the Pharisee's house and stood behind Jesus. Tears began to flow from her eyes as she thought about how her Savior's love was more powerful than her prideful mistakes. Drops of water fell over her Lord's feet. She washed them with her hair, kissed them, and then poured the perfume over them. With everything she had, she worshipped Jesus. She knew she was a sinner, but she didn't let shame keep her from Jesus.

Endure for others. When Jesus was in the city of Capernaum preaching at a house, the crowd outside grew, making it hard for the people to see Jesus. A group of men brought a sick friend to the gathering with the hope of meeting Jesus, but they couldn't get to Him. Knowing that He was the only answer, they endured the temporary setbacks and lifted their friend up to the roof. They pressed on toward Jesus by making a hole and lowering the man down into the house. Jesus saw the faith of the friends and healed the paralyzed man.

Love Jesus with everything you have and be the one who forgives. Show the world My love by putting down pride and picking up compassion. I am proud of you!

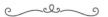

Mark 2:1–12; Luke 7:36–50; Romans 15:1–3

April 8

Precious child,

Don't try harder. Don't worry. Just have faith. Believe in Me. Trust that I am strong enough to carry you through the hard times. Walk with Me. Do all that I command because I am sovereign. I can see the other side of the storm. When the world doesn't understand, know that I am right there with you. Hear Me say that nothing can pull us away from each other. Consider Noah and his courage to believe in Me, even though the world mocked him and called him crazy. Noah had decided that walking faithfully with Me was more important than worrying about what other people thought.

Where Noah had the ark, you have Jesus! He is your salvation. Don't forget that just as Noah endured the floodwaters for forty days and forty nights, Jesus was in the desert on the floodwaters of temptation for the same amount of time. The tempest grew more powerful. The waters rose. But the ark remained safe by My powerful hand as it floated above it all. Can't you see that in Jesus, your life is in the same secure place? Today, feel My Son, your Savior, lift you above the storms that rage around you.

The enemy tries to turn your eyes to the swirling darkness. He labors all around you, hoping to capture your thoughts and focus them on the struggles. He longs to see you burdened by the weight of fear and the pressure of trying to make it on your own. But even when the world came against him with insults and pointing fingers, Noah had faith that I was bigger. Noah chose to see his Savior, not the storm. In faith, Noah obeyed me, even though he couldn't see the whole picture. He moved in holy fear with Me and condemned the ways of the world. Be courageous, child, because I am with you and I will never let you go!

Genesis 7:17–18; Ephesians 6:16; Hebrews 11:7

April 9

Precious child,

The enemy is real and doesn't want you to be close to Me. He is the reason you feel isolated. He is the reason that you feel like your life doesn't matter and that often the problems seem never ending. Today, I want to remind you that Jesus took up His cross and became a sacrifice so that you would be set free from the enemy's lies.

Jesus told a story about a farmer who went out to sow seeds for an amazing harvest. The seeds are the truth about My kingdom and how Jesus is My only Son. They represent the life-changing power of the blood of the Lamb who was slain for the forgiveness of all sin.

Some seeds fall onto the path and birds come and quickly consume them. For some, they hear the beautiful, wonderful, saving name of Jesus but don't understand how amazing He is. They shrug their shoulders in disbelief, and the enemy comes and snatches away the truth. Other seeds fall on rocky ground with little soil. Truth begins to take hold, but at the first sign of trouble, the heat of trials scorches, and these people fall away from Jesus.

Other seeds fall into thornbushes. These represent those who hear the name of Jesus but give in to the worries of life. They give in to the deception of prosperity and ironically live stagnant, unfruitful lives. The last seeds fall on good soil. This is when the sweet name of Jesus falls on tender hearts. They understand the gift of grace and deny the world with all the enemy's temptations and surrender everything to Jesus. This is the truth of your heart. Don't let the devil try to tell you differently. Your life in Jesus is meant to be spiritually prosperous. You have been set free to harvest a hundredfold what was sown in your heart. Your life does matter, and I love you!

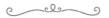

Matthew 13:3–8; Mark 4:14–20; Luke 8:5–15

Precious child,

My sovereignty means that I am actively involved in bringing things together for your good. I don't want you to just get by. My heart desires for your life to shine. I want you to be a force for love in a world that is starving for hope. I am with you, and I will rescue you from your troubles. I am here to give you wisdom and the ability to find favor among the people I'm sending you to. Stay in My Word and follow My commands. Live each hour in full reliance on My strength and guidance.

Someone close to you is seeking Me. Their heart longs for the truth of My Son and the treasure of knowledge found in Him alone. Be obedient and go to the places I am calling you to. Don't be afraid, because I am going with you. Remember My child Philip, whom I sent to be a witness to the Ethiopian. The traveler was reading the words of My prophet Isaiah, and Philip asked him if he understood what he was reading. The man replied that he needed someone to explain it to him. Philip used this divine appointment to tell the man about Jesus.

I want you to be bold and tell people who Jesus really is and what He really accomplished by His death and resurrection. Like Philip, let your life impact people in such a way that they leave you rejoicing because they have heard the good news of Jesus! Follow Me to the ones who are being lied to and deceived. Don't let the enemy tempt you into forgetting about the person who is hard to reach. He wants you to show favoritism by thinking they are unapproachable. He wants you to see people's behavior and not their broken hearts. Let your life be the sound of My voice, that they may hear truth and know who Jesus really is.

Isaiah 53:7–8; Acts 8:26–35; Colossians 2:2–4; James 2:1

April 11

Precious child,

See the hours I am giving you today differently. See them as a storehouse filled with gifts, all there for you to unwrap and learn more about My character. Don't get trapped in fear and worry. Don't let your own ideas about the way today should go prevent you from experiencing My gifts. Get closer to Jesus as you walk with Him. And through all these things, follow the Holy Spirit's leading and learn how to live out your calling.

I am all-knowing. I know all about the things you want and wish you had. I know about the things in your life that you want to get rid of. This is why I'm reminding you to put down your burdens and let Me take care of them. Because I am holy, no evil is found in Me. Read My words in scripture to see more of who I really am and not who the world wants Me to be. I am omnipotent and never tire. Let Me be God and you be My blessing.

Jesus, blessed Son and Savior, is your king. He has gone out into the biggest battle in the history of humankind and conquered sin for you. He died and rose again, conquering death. Your salvation is secure in Him! The devil is the grand deceiver. He tries to fill your mind with lies about who Jesus is. Because of Jesus, you are worthy. And if you make another mistake, it's going to be okay. Because of Jesus, you will still be worthy.

The Spirit is your counselor who walks with you and testifies about Me. He fills you with truth about who I am and My heart for the world. The Spirit is also your comforter who is with you forever. He speaks to Me on your behalf and helps you when you are weak. Put down your troubles and grab hold of My promises. I am never walking away!

John 15:26; Acts 9:31; Romans 11:33

April 12

Precious child,

Release your hands from the things of this world and stand firm in Jesus. Let His hands hold you close, and let His feet move you to places you could never reach on your own. Let go of your worries, because I have written your name in the Book of Life. Replace your fear with rejoicing. Be gentle so that the world will see something different when they see you. I am right by your side to erase any anxiety that arises when you put your faith in Me for everything. Come to Me always, not just in the hard times. Pray and ask for things with a thankful heart.

Practice My truth. Put all your hope in Me. Jesus has saved you from your sins, and I hear your cries for help, so let go of your fear. Let go of worrying what others think of you, and let your love for Me be the strength you rely on today. I'm showering you with My peace that is greater than you can ever imagine. It guards your heart and protects your mind in Jesus. As I do this for you, I want you to think about things that are true, noble, right, pure, lovely, admirable, excellent, and praiseworthy. I want you to think about Jesus!

The enemy speaks loud and clear the lies of hopelessness and shame, attempting to convince you that My power can't extend past the pages of scripture. Oh, just as I gave you life by My breath, so too are My words filled with holy power. Take Stephen, for example. You know about his courage as he gave his life for My glory, but he was also so full of My grace and energy that people who saw him knew that I was with him. I want you to be confident with the person I made you to be.

Psalm 39:7; Acts 6:8; Philippians 4:1–9

April 13

Precious child,

Seek My face with everything that's within you. Above all the things of the world that your eyes will see, I am the one who keeps promises by giving you grace. As you turn your eyes to Me, your feet will follow, causing you to walk away from your desires and begin walking according to My plans. Don't wait until this day ends. Come to Me now with an obedient heart and be confident that I will protect you when the wicked come and try to bind up your faith. They might try to make you forget Me, but by My power you will rise above the hurt and run after Me. My love fills your day so you have nothing to worry about.

I am here for you. I have good things for you just as I have promised. They will be found in both the highs and lows and everything in between. The enemy is waiting for the moment someone will disrespect you. He waits because he knows that you will want to respond in defense. When this happens, remember the cross. Remember how the world disrespected Jesus. Remember that even in the middle of that terrible suffering, My Son asked Me to forgive them. Keep trusting in My Word and learn to be a good judge of right and wrong.

Find delight in Me and don't fear. My hands are holding you. I made you, and I am so proud of you for putting all your hope in My Word. Your hope in Me will cause the people you meet today to rejoice in My name. Some who already know Me will be encouraged by your grace, while the lost will be encouraged to ask you where your humility comes from. In both situations, you will bring Me glory. And when the hours bring despair, remember that I am comforting you by My unfailing love. No matter what, let My grace be enough.

Psalm 119:58–77

Precious child,

I want to share more of My heart with you today. When it comes to My church, I don't want to see My children divided. That is the devil's desire. I made you different from everybody else, and I made everybody different from you. Don't let the enemy trick you with appearances. Don't let him deceive you into judging others because they talk differently or dress differently or even act differently than you do. My church, the body of Christ, is made up of more than just one person. There's you plus countless other believers. Be unified in love.

I know you have a desire to serve. For the moment, I want you to consider what it would look like for My church to serve each other. What if believers everywhere, who were all baptized by the same Spirit, would take care of each other in the same Spirit? I have placed everyone just where I want them to be. The enemy wants division. He whispers lies that some people are better than others. He tries to highlight weaknesses so your focus might stray from Me and onto judging. I am reminding you to submit to your neighbor out of reverence for Jesus. After all, Jesus submitted Himself to My will for you!

Show true concern for each other. Suffer and rejoice together. Pray together. Share the blessings I have given you with each other. Give without expecting anything in return. Meet each other's needs and be My love to a friend. The enemy desires isolation. He gains satisfaction when believers live two lives. He smiles when My children worship Me on Sunday morning and then worship themselves the rest of the week. I am all about unity. Let Sunday's fellowship spill over onto the rest of the days by lifting one another up. Remind others how special they are to Me and know that I am proud of you!

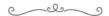

Matthew 7:1; Acts 2:42–47; 1 Corinthians 12:12–26; Ephesians 5:21

April 15

Precious child,

Shower the world with the affections of Jesus. Let your love abound. Let it grow as your knowledge of Me grows. You are a light in the dark world—I've called you to be different. Love others as Jesus loves you. He gave Himself up for your sins and rescued you from evil. Reflect on that powerful truth as you go out today. When you treat people the way Jesus would treat them, you're not worried about making them pleased with you.

The prophet Nathan had the courage to obey Me and confronted David. When the king had been mired in the deepest days of sin, Nathan was there to love him. When David was lost in his darkness, Nathan was there to speak truth. Both men were Mine, but David had followed his sins to a place where he couldn't hear truth. Nathan boldly faced David and asked him, "Why did you despise the word of the LORD?" Because of Nathan's obedience, David's ears opened. He took his broken heart and turned back to Me. David confessed, "I have sinned against the LORD."

One of My Son's disciples, Thomas, was trapped in a different kind of sadness. After Jesus rose from the grave, Thomas had heard the news but refused to believe. His faith wavered at the tragedy of the cross. Overcome by fear and isolation, Thomas was in his own dark place. He told his friends that his eyes had to see before the resurrection would become real to him. So Jesus met Thomas where he was. The locked doors were no problem for the Savior. Jesus walked through, into the house where Thomas was, and invited the man to experience His cross wounds. Thomas confessed, "My Lord and my God!"

My child, go and treat people with respect and be bold by speaking about the one true gospel. In this way, you will love them like Jesus loves!

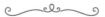

2 Samuel 12:8–13; John 20:24–28; Philippians 1:8–9

Precious child,

My prophet Elisha was in a certain town looking for ways to be used by Me. The people came to him and said that the city itself was a pleasing place to live because of the location, but the water was bad and the land didn't produce fruit. This is exactly how the enemy tries to tempt you away from thinking about Me. He strives to get you comfortable and hopes you won't realize that your soul is taking in the world's muddy water. When you're comfortable, you start to lose your desire to serve and bear fruit. Your faith walk begins to wither.

Elisha asked the men for a new jar and salt. They obeyed, and he went to the well and poured the salt into it. He told them that I made their water pure, and because I purified it, their water would never again cause death or loss of fruit. In a similar way, I am calling you to be the salt of the earth. Your life is so special to Me because you are the vessel to carry Jesus to the world. Your acts of love and sharing of the gospel are the salt you pour over a dying world. Speak to others with words filled with grace. Rejoice for the ones who hear you speak the name of Jesus and surrender by calling Him king and Savior. They will inherit eternal life and will bear life-changing kingdom fruit.

The enemy wants people to perish. He tries to separate people's hearts from the vine of Jesus by filling their minds with doubt. Call out to Me today. Let Me lead you to people who seem content, but underneath their masks of pride are tears because they're trying to live by their own rules. Pour My grace over their hearts and give them the living water of Jesus!

2 Kings 2:19–22; Matthew 5:13

Precious child,

The enemy is tempting you to build your own kingdom. Remember . . .he is the deceiver and is skilled at persuasion. Today, I want you to see through his lies and know that pride of life comes from the world.

There was a time when the world shared a common language. Some people decided to make themselves famous by building a special city with a tower that would reach heaven. They let pride blind them to the truth: that with Me there is nothing to fear. They were afraid that if they didn't create their monument made from the finest material, they would be scattered all throughout the land.

Their prideful arrogance caused the destruction of the endeavor. Their proud spirits brought about their fall. The pride in their hearts deceived them. I confused their speech and scattered them across the earth. Adam and Eve were tempted into the same trap of believing that they could become their own little gods. Even Cain had to be driven out from the land because of his pride. Everyone who is tempted by the enemy's lies quickly believes that they can be safe in their man-made kingdoms.

Let the thing you build up be the cross of Jesus Christ so that the world may see His glory. When people around you are looking inward, don't be pulled along and get swept away on the river of selfishness. Don't worry about how the world sees you, because I am here and see everything. Devote your entire life to building up the sweet name of Jesus. Instead of putting all your time into creating a tower of selfish pursuits, put all your energy into lifting up the strong tower of Jesus, so the faraway sinner who is lost may see Him and be found!

Genesis 11:4–8; Proverbs 16:18; Obadiah 3–4; 1 John 2:16

April 18

Precious child,

Stand firm in the middle of My will for your life. The enemy wants you to believe that you are stuck in a day that will never get better. He wants you discouraged and defeated so you'll believe nothing will ever change and that I am not mighty enough to solve your problems. But I am delivering you on the current of living water to new places. Jesus is your rock and on Him you will not be shaken. I want you to understand that the path of My will for your life winds through today for a reason! I haven't forgotten you.

Hold fast to every word that I give you in the Bible. My words will lead you and fill your life with righteousness. From the great storehouses of love that I have for you, I give you My truth so you may find freedom in life. Let My words take root in your heart so that you may love Me even more today than yesterday. Hold tightly to the words of Jesus, and listen to His voice. Hold His hands, for He is your life, and He will give you everything you need. He too has carried burdens and knows the pain and joy you experience. Don't let go!

Whether you are going or coming, I want you to remember that I am the one who will fight the battles. All you have to do is be obedient by taking up your position and remaining in the place I have called you. Until I call you to move, pray to Me. Tell Me what hurts and talk to Me about your dreams. Lift up praises for all the things I have done and for who I am. Stand firm and watch Me deliver you. Do not be afraid. Do not be discouraged. Go out to face the world and know that I will be with you. Always!

Deuteronomy 30:20; 2 Chronicles 20:17; Ephesians 6:14;
2 Thessalonians 2:15

Precious child,

I am the one who rescued you from the chains of darkness. I am the light that opened your eyes so you could see the way back to My everlasting heart. I am the stronghold where you find safety. There is absolutely nothing to fear. The enemy whispers to you that the wicked are advancing. In fact, he even lies that you will be devoured by the problems you are going through. But the truth is, Jesus conquered the enemy once and for all. The enemy has no hold on you any longer, so be strong.

You will experience stress and sadness, but those things will not overcome you. The hurting will last only a short time, but your heart will stay strong. Since the enemy knows full well where his final destination is, he will continue to torment My children. He will try to besiege your emotions and attack your will to worship Me. In all of this, remain confident that I am with you and will never let you go. Close your eyes and concentrate on My beauty. Hear My voice remind you that you are safe here. Be strong and wait on Me.

I am here to be your helper. I hear you and answer you with mercy. I am lifting your life higher than the wickedness that surrounds you. Let these truths encourage your heart to sing. Everywhere you go today, seek My face. In the beggar's dirty hands and the child's carefree smile, seek Me in strangers and in friends. Look for Me in the ones who live in poverty, and find Me in the hearts of the rich. The enemy desperately wants you to sort all these souls into groups. He wants you to rank them by appearance and status, but I want you to love them all! Remain confident that I am with you and you will taste My goodness. Be strong and wait on Me because I love you.

Psalm 27

Precious child,

One of My names is the rock of Israel. Remain in Me and know that you will not break when the wind blows. In Me, your life is secure. The enemy savors evil. He looks for ways to enjoy this wicked desire. Your hope is like a delicacy he wants to devour. He doesn't want you to believe that I am the mountain you live your life on. He wants you to think you can walk far enough away from Me where your feet will find sand. Be confident and know that I forgive you when you stray. I am here to nourish you and cultivate a compassionate heart in you for the world.

From heaven to earth, everything in creation declares My glory. All the works of My hands, day and night, speak of My love and reveal My wonderful grace. This is what the enemy fears most. He wants you to wander in doubt and confusion. He wants you to give Me a list of requests and then wait and worry about how I'll decide to answer them. Instead, I want you to be like the rest of creation that has no voice; glorify Me to the ends of the earth.

Don't wait. Worship. Let each moment of this new day I've given you bring Me glory. Not in words, but in the way you love your neighbor. Let your light for Me be like the sun and move across the hours. Let this command refresh your soul. Let it light your path. Let My words to you be purer than gold and sweeter than honey. These are the ways that the world will stop and consider Me. The enemy wants you to glorify yourself by putting your needs above My holy name. Ignore this scheme, My child. You have nothing to fear because I am your rock and Redeemer!

Genesis 49:24; Job 20:12; Psalm 19; Hosea 14:4

Precious child,

I am God over the whole earth.

As your Lord Almighty, I hold you close to My heart so you are able to walk before Me. I hold you with almighty hands that forgive you so that you can stand blameless in My presence. No one has any idea of my limitless power, and no one can keep you from Me.

My strength set you free. Today, My power, which is higher than the heavens, is in you to help you rise up for truth in a fallen world. Today, My power, which is deeper than the grave, is in you to help you speak out for the voiceless victims. Today, My power, which is longer than the earth and wider than the oceans, is in you to give you courage to be a leader.

I am God over your soul. I have redeemed you. I have brought you out of the murky night. The enemy is trying to keep you thinking that I only brought you part of the way out of the pit. But I have fully saved you. You have been completely redeemed. Don't let the evil one tempt you to believe you are still a part of that desolate place I snatched you out of. Your redemption is eternal. By the blood of My sweet Jesus you are forgiven.

I am mighty to get you through the trials. I am mighty to get you through the misunderstandings. I know, child. I know that your heart gets heavy from trying hard. I am proud of who I made you to be. Don't worry about tomorrow. I am over all. I have used My mighty power to rescue you from the enemy's dominion and have placed you down gently into the kingdom of Jesus. His love will always sustain you through life's battles. His heart beats for you every moment of every day of your life!

Job 11:7–9; Psalm 130:7; Ephesians 1:7

Precious child,

Don't make excuses. I just want you to make the name of Jesus known. Everywhere you go, people hurt for love. The enemy wants you to ignore them and come up with a million reasons why you can't stop and talk to them. When I called Moses to Egypt to confront the pharaoh, Moses focused on his weakness. I reminded him that I am the one who helps people speak and teaches them what to say. Even with My reassurance, Moses still asked Me to send someone else. Don't do this. The people I'm sending you to don't care about your weaknesses. They just need My love.

I called Jonah to bring My love and truth to a people in bondage. And like Moses, Jonah fully understood My abilities as God of everything, but he came up with so many excuses that he ran away. But when I call My people to do a certain job, I provide the strength and power to carry it out. For Moses, I had Aaron help him speak. For Jonah, I saved him from the deep, dark waters and the fish that swallowed him. The second time I called, Jonah obeyed and went to Nineveh. He understood that My power in him was enough for him to be faithful to the task.

Jonah's obedience in the hard things of life made the king of Nineveh renounce his wicked ways and command his city to call urgently on Me. When Jonah stopped making excuses and remembered that his life mattered so much to Me, hearts were changed forever. Eyes were turned from evil. Just like I showed Moses and Jonah, let Me show you how much I love you. Trust Me to do amazing things through you today. I will answer when you are in stressful situations, and My mighty name will protect you. Go and love people in the name of Jesus!

Exodus 4:10–16; Psalm 20:1–2; Jonah 3:1–10

April 23

Precious child,

Trust Me. I will reveal the plans I have for you, so be patient and wait on Me. Abraham is a great example of how I want to increase your faith in the waiting. He was seventy-five when I called him away from everything he held close to his heart: his country, his friends, and his father's household. He heard Me call him to a mysterious place, and Abraham obeyed. He didn't try to make My plans fit his schedule. He didn't give Me a list of reasons why he couldn't go. He simply trusted the promises I gave him and went.

Trust Me, even when you feel alone in the desert places of life. Remember that before Jesus started His ministry, He went into the desert for forty days and forty nights. My same Spirit that led Him into the barren wilderness is also with you. Let this truth lift your soul today, so you will know without doubting that I haven't left you alone. Jesus was hungry when the enemy came and tempted Him to turn stones into bread. My Son had faith that when I send, I save. Like Jesus, when the world leaves you hungry for more, want more of Me. Live on My words and plans for your heart.

Trust Me even when My plan for you seems confusing. When I called Paul, the light of Jesus penetrated his soul so deeply that he lost his sight for three days. He had to learn to rely on Me. My desire is for you to rely on Me, not the world. The enemy led Jesus up to the highest point of the temple and told Him to throw Himself down. He said the angels would be there to save Jesus. Instead of giving in and testing Me, Jesus relied on Me! And when, finally, the devil offered Jesus money and fame, Jesus refused. Come see the awesome plans I have for you. Trust Me. I won't let you down!

Genesis 12:1–4; Amos 3:7; Matthew 4:1–9; Acts 9:9

April 24

Precious child,

I understand how hard it is to wait on Me. The world is there beside you, whispering in your ear that there are more important things you could worship than Me. The enemy is trying to get you to see earthly gain as something worthy of your heart. The people I freed from captivity in Egypt fell into this trap. Moses had left them with Aaron while he climbed the mountain called Sinai. Moses was with Me for forty days and forty nights. The Israelites became so impatient they decided to make their own god.

They all thought that because their leader hadn't returned quickly, I must not be faithful. Aaron tried to fix the problem by having the people collect gold earrings. He took all the jewelry and made a golden calf for the people to worship. He then said that the idol was the very one who rescued them from the iron clutches of the pharaoh. A man-made statue! Then Aaron continued on this grace-replacement path by building an altar in front of the calf. And finally all the people threw a festival to celebrate their accomplishment.

I saw this corruption and told Moses what the people had done. But Moses sought My favor and prayed for his stiff-necked people. Moses worshipped Me by speaking truth about My power and might. Moses glorified Me and made his whole life about praising Me.

A similar thing happened to Jesus when his friend Lazarus had become very sick. When Jesus heard this, he proclaimed that the sickness wouldn't end in death. People in the crowd voiced their doubts that Jesus could give a blind man sight yet not prevent a good friend from dying. Jesus prayed to Me and called Lazarus back to life. He did it this way so people would know He is My Son. The pleasures of the world cannot see, hear, or walk, My child. Wait on Me and believe that I am for you!

Exodus 32:1–11; John 11:32–37; Revelation 9:20

April 25

Precious child,

The enemy wants you to question Me. He wants you to be satisfied with less than all of Me. He wants you to pick and choose which of My commands to obey and decide which people will be worthy of your love. I made you special and different from everyone else, but I didn't make you better. Allow this truth to set in, and feel Me rip away the chains of self that the devil tries to wrap around you. Read all of My words and let all of them take root in your soul. Let My instruction guide you today.

He doesn't want you to completely believe Me. His desire is to distract you so you might never fully stop and consider My wonders. I am calling you today to trust in My sovereign plans for your life. I am the one who cares completely for you. I never get distracted and take My eyes off you. And when I think of you, I consider you wonderful. Remember that the enemy doesn't believe Me. He wants to bring you down with him, but hear Me say you are so much more than what you feel. You are forever forgiven and free!

The devil wants you to keep your eyes closed. He'd rather you blindly follow the crowd than become My kingdom leader and take a stand. Jesus gave the early church in Sardis a set of commands that are still relevant for you today. He said, "Wake up! Strengthen what remains and is about to die, for I have found your deeds unfinished in the sight of my God. Remember, therefore, what you have received and heard; hold it fast, and repent." Hear Me remind you of these same principles. Open your eyes and strengthen your spirit by walking down the paths I am choosing for you. Remain humble and hold fast to Me. I won't let you down!

Genesis 3:1; Job 37:14; Revelation 3:2–3

April 26

Precious child,

The enemy wants you to forget all the things I have done for you. He wants you to focus on what's not going right to trap you into worrying about tomorrow. He speaks fear into you. He tries to surround you with people to whom I mean nothing. They might be powerful by worldly standards and will keep their eyes on themselves and what they can create. And even though I'm the Creator, they will believe that their ability to acquire resources insulates them from problems. Remember Me. Remember that I made you, not the other way around. The world is not your maker.

Do not put your trust in the things you see. Hide My commands in your heart and continue to fear Me. You don't have to do what the world says. My love and faithfulness for you will never disappear. There is peace with Me. Don't try to make peace happen by doing more. Find My peace in being who I made you to be. Lean on My knowledge and not your own understanding. Submit to Me and shun the evil one. I love you, so don't waste time looking for love. Slow down and be okay with the pace I set for your days.

I can't remind you enough that I am here to be your deliverer. Out of the hands of the enemy's dark plans, I deliver you every time. Talk to Me. I hear you, and out of My great compassion I will rescue you. Tell Me about the burdens of your heart. I never leave you alone. The world doesn't know Me. They think I'm just a word. An idea. But there are two words for Me: I Am. Look out the window and see. Look at the world I made. Out of all the things I've made, your heart is the most important thing to Me.

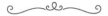

Exodus 1:17; Nehemiah 9:27; Proverbs 3:1–7; Jude 5

April 27

Precious child,

Oh, how wonderful you are to Me! I love you so much I gave you My Son, Jesus. Today, I want to describe the beauty of Jesus to you. I know you love Him, but I want My words to stir your heart to a greater awareness of His infinite love for you. King Solomon wrote that Jesus is the lily of the valley. Don't you see, your sweet Jesus is the most beautiful one. His hands hold you now as you read these words. The same ones that took the nails and carried your sins to the cross are still mighty enough to hold you close.

Oh, how special you are to Me! Stand firm in the freedom Jesus bought for you. Don't let the devil trick you into enslaving yourself by believing anything else. Jesus stepped down from His throne and walked among the sinners and broken people. He went to save the lost because part of His beauty is His unconditional love. Once, Jesus went into a synagogue to heal a man with a deformed hand. Even though people were waiting there to accuse Him, Jesus still went. The world didn't keep Him from healing. Let His feet lead you to people who need to hear about My love.

Oh, how dear you are to Me! The heart of Jesus that was pierced on Calvary is the same eternal heart that beats for you. His beautiful love fills your heart so it can beat again for the things His heart beats for. Jesus shines His love over you to remind you that the King of kings treasures your life. The enemy wants you to believe that all of this is nothing more than words on a page, not the Word on a cross. He doesn't want you to know how important you are. Go and remember your Savior's hands, feet, and heart are holding you, leading you, and loving you!

Song of Songs 2:1; Mark 3:1–5; Galatians 5:1

Precious child,

Grace is good. Grace is sweet and powerful. It's a mixture of love and mercy that the world cannot create no matter how hard it tries. It's something you can't earn, but it's everything you need. My grace is enough. Let it strengthen your heart today so you won't be enticed into the world's merit system. The enemy wants you to take care of yourself. Do what it takes to get on top. The enemy wants you to compare, rank, sort, segregate, manipulate. He wants you to think that as long as you're doing the right things you make Me happy. He doesn't want you to think about how life-changing My grace is for you.

My grace moves you to do courageous things. It paints new life over broken canvases and lets the world see a different love in the brushstrokes of forgiven hearts. I give an abundant provision of grace to you, so through Jesus you will reign in life. This is why I keep reminding you that you are not simply a shell of forgiveness but My chosen child. My grace meets you right where you are and lifts your head. My grace looks you in the eye and says that you are worth everything to Me.

Grace opens your eyes and shows you how the rest of the world lives. The enemy says the nations are someone else's problem, but he certainly isn't saving anyone. All the devil does is convince you that you were forgiven once but not forever. He wants you to believe that My grace isn't a gift but a burden. The enemy wants you to think that I only have a limited amount of grace for you and every time you mess up, less of it remains. My grace for you is limitless. Bring this truth to the world and start a revolution of thanksgiving all for My glory.

Acts 11:23; Romans 5:17; 2 Corinthians 4:15; Hebrews 13:9

April 29

Precious child,

Jesus, your glorious Savior, has done, is doing, and will do marvelous things for you. Long before you were born, Jesus tore down the walls of sin and destroyed death. In the wake of this epic battle for your soul, hope came flooding in. Jesus made it possible for you to step through the torn veil and draw near. Even though the enemy lurks, he is powerless to take you out of My hands. You have been set aside for a kingdom purpose. You have been set free from the worries of a life without Me.

The enemy seeks to drain your will to move forward. He wants you to stay where you are, not where I want you to be. But Jesus gives you authentic life. He made this a reality when you believed in His name. You became My child, not born of human decision but because I said you are worthy. Each day is a new gift for you to unwrap and discover more about who I am and the truth about all that you mean to Me. Now that your life is a new creation, each one of your breaths takes in more of My blessings. More grace. More love. More mercy. More compassion.

Jesus has given you the promise of eternal life. I want you to look forward to the moment when you will see Us face-to-face! Struggles and pain will not follow you here. Misery and misunderstanding cannot find you here. There will be no more sorrow and no more suffering. You will be covered in light and will never again see darkness approaching. Jesus said, "I am the Alpha and the Omega, the First and the Last, the Beginning and the End." Jesus has this day covered. From front to back, He knows what you need. He is more powerful than today's problems. Jesus loves you!

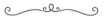

John 1:13; 1 Corinthians 15:27; 2 Timothy 1:10; Revelation 22:13

April 30

Precious child,

Listen to Me. Hear My voice speak to you through the scriptures. I want My love to recalibrate your heart. I've given you this day to remember who I am. I made the earth, the stars, and the galaxies. I formed them all and established them. I want you to see that I don't create and abandon. The enemy wants you to think I've abdicated My throne and that I've removed My presence from your life. These are cold lies. Call to Me. Call to Me in honesty. I have promised that I will answer you. Listen to Me tell you great and unsearchable things you do not know.

As you call to Me, I call to you. Hear Me say that I've made you unique. I have called to your heart and commanded it to be unchained. I didn't save you to be free to doubt. I am calling you to use your freedom to treat other people like you treat yourself. Humbly serve others in love. The enemy deceives you into thinking caring about others means simply a onetime act of compassion, but when things get hard the devil tempts your heart to withdraw. I made you special so that I can send you to the people who don't look, sound, or act like you. I have given you the power to take a stand for a lifetime.

Be like Jesus. He made each of His days point to Me. He didn't complain or argue. He walked in My will and loved people whom others despised. He gave the hopeless pure love so they would know that I valued them. Be like your loving Savior and shine like the stars. Where the enemy tries to sow confusion and apathy, I want you to sow clarity and concern. Hold on to My truth, and don't worry what people say about your willingness to help the oppressed. I love your heart.

Jeremiah 33:2–3; Galatians 5:13–14; Philippians 2:14–16

May 1

Precious child,

Don't carry yesterday's burdens into today. I don't look at you and see your sins. I look at you and see Jesus and everything He did for you on the cross. I don't see you as your next mistake or last disaster. I see you as beautiful because that's what Jesus has made you to be. A new creation wrapped in His mighty love, you are My child, and I am your holy Father. The world transmits a different message to your heart. It says that you are alone to fight your own problems and conquer your own fears. Tune out the lies. Turn to Me.

Put down yesterday's pain and keep your eyes on My heart and the things that it beats for. Walk with Me and know that no matter what feeling you might experience, the fact that I love you is your guide. Things won't work out if you try to solve life's problems without Me. You might think you're in control, but any plan carried out apart from Me will not succeed. But if you ask Me for guidance and wait for Me to answer, nothing will stop you. The enemy will not be able to stand in your way. He knows when you are in My will he is helpless to stop you.

Pick up today's grace. Hold My mercy close to your heart. Keep Jesus on the throne of your life and let Him be worth it all. I am teaching you My plans for your life through Jesus. He is the heir of everything. Through Him I made the universe. Let His majesty flow from your heart and cover each one of your steps. Let His righteousness be more than today's accomplishments. Live for Jesus. Let Him be your reason. Let Him be the answer to every prayer. It's going to be okay because you are covered in His hope.

Psalm 2:7; Acts 5:38–39; Hebrews 1:2

May 2

Precious child,

Read My words and learn from Me. Follow My directions so you will end up in places filled with My mercy. The Israelites had My ark of the covenant. Joshua commanded the people to move out from where they were camped and follow it. He also said, "Then you will know which way to go, since you have never been this way before." Your enemy searches for things to put in your path to distract you and keep you from following Me. He hopes you'll see My scriptures as one of many road maps for your life.

The world's knowledge can't take you to the places I have for you. Joshua instructed the people to keep a large distance between themselves and the ark. He also told them, "Consecrate yourselves, for tomorrow the LORD will do amazing things among you." There is freedom in My Son, Jesus Christ. And praise His holy name because, unlike the ark, He is in you with no distance in between! In Him you are made righteous, and the righteous cannot be uprooted. Don't accept the devil's lie that you aren't worthy of this grace.

Live today according to My directions. The enemy wants you to see your Bible as a collection of histories. He does not want you to see it as necessary food for your soul. He will try to persuade you Jesus was a good man who loved people instead of the sinless God-man who died for everyone. Follow Me by continuing to study My Word. Continue on the path I am leading you on. Don't be tempted to leave and go down roads that are wider and easier to navigate. I have made you complete in Jesus. Through Him I have set aside a special ministry for your life. I am doing amazing things, so be bold and complete the plans I have for you!

Joshua 3:3–5; Proverbs 12:3; Colossians 4:17

Precious child,

Today, remember that your life is hidden in Jesus. Find peace in Him. He has made you righteous. Please listen to Me. The fact that you are righteous in My eyes means that you are now blameless and justified. When the devil whispers lies that you are nothing more than a sinner, recall what Jesus went through. He took the mocking and nails because He knew you were worth it! I know it's hard for you to imagine, but it's true. Your Savior treasures your heart. Don't forget how important you are.

Jesus has made you holy. Even though this day may have a handful of tedious hours, you have been sanctified and blessed. Jesus cares about you. He's big enough to listen. I need you to be big enough to obey. Jesus cares about your heart too. I don't want you to spend your time regretting who I made you to be. The devil wants you to believe that you are nothing and that your life will never amount to anything. The kingdom work you do for Me isn't to earn My favor or to have a good feeling. Your work is worship. I want you to understand that I care about you and I protect you.

Jesus has redeemed you. Your Messiah has saved you when you couldn't save yourself. And He didn't just rescue you. Jesus said, "Everything is possible for one who believes." Everything. This isn't a challenge. It's a promise. Your life was never meant to be lived apart from My wisdom and love. Many in the world will tell you this is nothing more than inspirational talk from a holy king to his subjects. But this is not what Jesus was doing. He wanted to tell you that if you would just believe in who He says He is, your life will become a river of peace and grace.

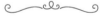

Mark 9:23; 1 Corinthians 1:30; Ephesians 2:14

May 4

Precious child,

I am your safe place. Take shelter from the enemy's wicked schemes in the shadow of My truth. I will never let you be put to shame. Know that I deliver you from the shackles of the world's description of your worth. I turn My ear to you, and I always save you. I am here to be your rock of refuge and the strong fortress you run to for safety. For My glory, I lead and guide you. I am looking ahead, and I know where the enemy is placing traps for you. I promise to keep you free from all of them!

As you breathe deep My new mercies today, commit your spirit to Me and know that because I am your faithful God, I will deliver you. All you have to do is trust Me. Be glad for the way I always see your affliction and always understand your soul's anguish. I know what tears you up inside, but I will not let the enemy take you into his hands. And while I constantly protect you, I have set your feet in a place of spacious grace. Today, this is where you will be free to find more mercy.

I know your eyes grow tired from sorrow and your body is burdened with grief. All you have to do is trust Me. Renounce the devil's advances by proclaiming My glory. I hold your life in My hands, and I cause My face to shine over you. Let My unfailing love save you. I will not let you be put to shame. I have an abundance of good things for you. Shout your words out for all to hear—praises that tell the world of My love. Let them know that I hear their calls for help. Let your life show them that I am just. Put all your hope in Me alone.

Psalm 31

May 5

Precious child,

Like the baby Moses drawn from the shadows of the Nile, so too was your life drawn from the shadows of sin. Because the pharaoh feared losing power, he had ordered every Hebrew baby boy be thrown into the mighty African river. The enemy will try to kill your spirit to serve and to relate with Me because your life is a threat to him. Your bold testimony of My Son's holy name causes the devil to flee. When Moses was three months old and too big to hide, his mother put him in a basket and hid him among the reeds. Of all people, it was the pharaoh's daughter who rescued him.

Once, Jesus had gone to Jerusalem for a festival when he entered the city through the Sheep Gate. Many people with disabilities were there by a pool. Society had given the order that they should be ignored. One man had been there for thirty-eight years. As with Moses, healing was about to take place in the least likely place, from the shadows of the ordinary. Right in the middle of nothing's-ever-going-to-change, Jesus said the word and the man was healed. Jesus offers this same healing over your life today. He is with you. He is in you. And He is for you. Hear His voice tell you to get up and walk!

My promise of what you will find in heaven is found wrapped in eternal hope. There is another body of water here, the river of the water of life. Clear and radiant like diamonds, it flows from My throne and from the Lamb's, giving nourishment to the tree of life. The enemy is powerless to take this away from you. I have given the order that he will be banished into water that burns, day and night, forever. But I am for you, My child. Breathe in My truth that you are important to Me. I love you.

Exodus 2:1–10; John 5:1–8; Revelation 22:1–2

May 6

Precious child,

Answer when I call. I am leading you to specific tasks that I created you for. I will affirm your steps through My Word so you'll know you are walking in My will. When you start to doubt and list reasons why you shouldn't answer My call, just believe. Abraham, whom I called from Ur to lead his family to the Promised Land of Canaan, questioned Me. He didn't doubt, but asked Me to clarify My plans. And just as I come to you in My Word, I came to Abraham and he believed. Ask Me questions. Tell Me you don't understand. I won't love you any less.

Listen when I speak. Hear Me say that you are justified by your faith in Jesus Christ. Listen to Me tell you more of who He is each day. Feel your heart being filled with His love. It is hard to hear Me sometimes when the world is shouting for your attention. Find time to rest in My promises. Go to the quiet places where you can listen to My voice. Remember that your will is not the same thing as My voice. The sound of righteousness and truth comes from Me. Let My commands be a symphony that moves and motivates you to be about My kingdom work.

With Me you will eat, drink, rejoice, and sing. For Me, you will proclaim the good news to the poor so their broken hearts will be made new. Don't do evil or choose the things that displease Me. Those are not the ways I've made you to take. Don't be like the world that forsakes Me to sit at the banquet of fortune and destiny. The enemy will tell you that your day is nothing but a random series of events. He'll push you to take chances instead of taking Me at My word. Nothing is ever meant to be unless I mean it to be. You matter!

Genesis 15:2–7; Isaiah 65:11–14; Galatians 2:16

May 7

Precious child,

I can't remind you enough how special you are to Me. I created the universe and everything in it to display My glory, and I have made your heart to do the same. I have called you by name and set you apart to be My humble servant. Just as I have commanded you to listen when I call, so too do I hear your voice every time you call to Me. Continue in My Word so that you maintain your holy fear of Me and keep from sinning. And when it is time for rest, I want you to be silent and search your heart to make sure you are trusting Me in all things.

The world prospers without Me. They make their own lights to shine in the dark places. But eventually their lights dim and fade. Not so for you! I am your prosperity. The light of My face—a light that never fails—shines upon you. You are in a wonderful place where I alone am the one who fills your heart with joy. You understand that all blessings come from Me and are grateful. I give you peace, so even when you lie down you are safe because I have made it so.

The enemy tries to alter your perception of Me. He tries to have you believe that the earth is your throne and heaven is your footstool. I am not bound by the world. Human hands have made nothing new. Even though it is My hands that make everything, your heart is on the front lines of a battlefield of deception. Remember, child, Jesus is on your side. He is for you. And He is the one who cares. When you are wrongly accused, remember that Jesus holds the scepter of justice. He loves righteousness, and I have set Him above everything and have anointed Him with the oil of joy. Praise Him forever!

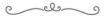

Psalm 4:3–8; Isaiah 66:1–2; Hebrews 1:8–9

May 8

Precious child,

Seek My favor by turning from your sins and paying attention to My truth. I am righteous in everything I do, and for My sake I will answer you because of My great mercy. I forgive you, and I am here to act on your behalf. I will not delay in helping you. Your life bears My name and shows a small piece of Me to people who see you. When it's hard to rejoice because the enemy surrounds your hope in Me, don't despair. Feel the breath of My Spirit stir your heart to beat in time with Me. Run to Me and find freedom that restores your soul.

And not only do you bear My name, but you are My living letter to the world. They don't have patience because they race from one distraction to another. Your life is a letter written by My Spirit for the world to read, not with their eyes but with their hearts. I have strategically put you where you are so they can see your heart and read about Me. As you go, serve Me by following the leading of the Spirit. Don't stay rooted in fear. The enemy wants nothing more than for you to disregard My call. He is hoping that you will crumble up your letter so the lost won't be able to read it.

Boast in Jesus. Take a stand against the evil one. Put all your confidence in Me, not the flesh. Remember, My mercy is great and new every day. Trust Me in the little things. I know that a great deal of your time is spent going through the motions of daily routines. I am right there with you. I don't walk away only to show up in the big deals of your life. Let's make the daily grind something big. Turn each breath I give you into worship!

Daniel 9:13–19; 2 Corinthians 3:2–3; Philippians 3:3

Precious child,

Open your entire heart to Me. Don't give Me almost all of you. Always keep My Word because I do. I am going to make sure you experience My majesty and feel the might of My hands. When the enemy pursues you, I will overwhelm him and drown his plans to distract you. I am right there with you, sweet one, and will ruin plots made against you. My outstretched arm is a wall of protection around you. Whether in the wilderness or gardens, let your eyes see the great things I am doing. Continue to place your trust in Me because I am faithful.

The world battles for your heart. The enemy doesn't ask for all of you. He is content with enticing you to worship just one thing other than Me. The devil tries to see you bow down to the idol of time, knowing you'll run yourself ragged filling your days with things instead of filling them with My grace. Take the time I give you and read My words. Keep my directions in your heart and mind. Meditate on scripture when you're at home and when you are out in the world, before you sleep at night and when you get up each morning.

Let your heart absorb My truth until I am everything you seek. When the enemy tries to put your shame on trial for all to see, I will be your witness. Jesus sent out His disciples to bring the gospel message to the world. He specifically told them not to take anything with them on the journey—no staff, no bag, no bread, no money, no extra shirt. He knew that they would be distracted by material possessions. Put down your burdens and let Me protect you. Be filled on My words and believe that I will provide for your needs.

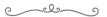

Deuteronomy 11:1–20; Luke 9:2–3; 1 Thessalonians 2:5

May 10

Precious child,

Jesus is your Lord of all. Of every cell in you and every second of your day, He is your glorious Savior. Jesus is the true champion of your soul. He isn't trying to find you in a crowd of billions. He is eternal, outside the constraints of time. He doesn't spend a little time with you and then leave to be with someone else. He is with you no matter what negative feeling or emotion the enemy tempts you to experience. If you are drawn to sadness, let Jesus be your Lord of joy. If anger, let Him be your Lord of peace.

In Jesus, you are victorious. When your strength fails and the world calls you a failure, you have My promise that I see your heart. I see it filled with the love of My Son, and nothing the world tries to cover you with can make Me see you differently. Give everything you have to the work I am calling you to. Don't let anything move you away from the path I have you on. Your work for Me is never in vain. Be encouraged by this. What you're going through matters. Every misunderstanding. Every tear. Every laugh and every cry. They all matter because I care about all of you!

And because of Jesus, you have the power to turn away from sin. The blood of Jesus shed on Calvary's hill has washed your soul. Death no longer holds its shadow over you. You have passed from darkness to light. The light of the world is in you! Let Jesus shine on your day. Let His light expose the enemy's dark schemes. Your debt has been paid! Spend your hours rejoicing and praising the one who set you free. When the devil paints sin as a masterpiece, you see it with forgiven eyes and call it forgery. Turn away and see Jesus leading you to pleasant places. Follow Him alone.

Romans 10:12; 1 Corinthians 15:57–58; 2 Timothy 2:19

May 11

Precious child,

I hear you and consider your words. I think about you all the time. I listen when you praise Me, and I hear your cries for help. When you pray, you are letting the enemy know that I alone am your king and your God. Lift your voice to Me in the morning. Tell Me the most intimate things on your heart. Lay them before Me and wait. I want you to get in the habit of expecting My answer. Lift your voice to Me in times of struggle and times of blessing. Let Me lift your tired head and hold it gently in My hands. Feel Me look into your eyes and hear Me say that everything is okay.

I am alive, and I am your ever-present shield. The world conspires to make you feel that you should live between church, work, and home and not venture into the places where people don't worship Me as king. Jonah went to Nineveh. Moses went to Egypt. And Jesus went to you!

I need you out in the world to show them the way back to Me. Persevere, My child. Breathe and persevere because I am for you! Even when the air seems thick with unanswered prayers and unwanted burdens, breathe in Me. I will breathe into you and you will find peace. Like Job, I want you to know without a doubt that you will see Me.

I haven't redeemed you to feel alone. Jesus, your Savior, didn't take the nails so you would feel lost and abandoned. My Son did that so you would feel empowered by His love! I am full of compassion and mercy. All of Me is for you. Let the trials be used for good. Let what the enemy sets up for evil bring you closer to Me. Let the unbelievers see your Jesus-filled heart. Even when your circumstances are hard to handle, remember that I am God.

Job 19:25–26; Psalm 5:1–3; James 5:11

Precious child,

The enemy roams around trying to defeat your spirit. He dumps many distractions along your path in hopes you will pursue them. Jesus died on the cross to set you free so you could pursue Me. If you give all your time to the distractions, you have no time for Me. If I become an afterthought, I lose majesty in your eyes. I become an option. My mercy becomes an item to grab off the shelf of quick fixes. Pray hard. I won't let you go. When you let go of the world's distractions, you will see Me correctly. Your heart will sing, "The Mighty One, God, the Lord! The Mighty One, God, the Lord! He knows!"

I do know everything you need. When you open your heart to My will, you begin to see your life from My eternal perspective. True wisdom begins with Me. As you fill your heart with My Word, your understanding of Me widens, and you are able to see clearly that I am the Holy One who made you and loves you more than anything. I made you to prosper in My love for you. I made you to grow in learning who I am. Remain rooted in the scriptures. Let them nourish your soul.

This isn't an easy task because your adversary is a cunning opponent. I want you to see sin as something that needs to die in you. Anything that belongs to your earthly nature (greed, evil desires, immorality, selfishness) is an idol and should be destroyed. Because I am just, My wrath is coming to erase these attacks on My character. These words describe who you once were. Anger and rage were attributes of your old self. You no longer have to fight for control and self-promotion, because I am your defender!

Joshua 22:22; Proverbs 9:10; Colossians 3:5–9

May 13

Precious child,

You are safe because I am your God, and My mighty hand protects you. I have set you free, and I drive away the enemy when he tries to tempt you into darkness. You will see My power covering you today in ways you never could have imagined. I push back the forces of evil that try to thwart My plans for you. I am the Lord God Almighty. Keep learning more about Me and know that I am making Myself fully known to you.

Just as I established My covenant with the Israelites to give them the Promised Land, I have given you Jesus. He is your Savior, the living covenant between us. He has made a way for us to be reconciled. I hear the groaning of your heart as you tell Me all the things that burden you. I see how the enemy tries to enslave you with feelings of regret. The world might ignore you, but I am your God who seeks you out to shower you in mercy. The world might say hurtful things to you, but I am your Lord who speaks love into your heart.

Jesus fights for justice too. Just as He scattered the coins of the money changers and overturned their tables in the temple, so too does He scatter the enemy's soldiers and overturn their plans to bring you harm. And I don't stop fighting for you either. I always stand up for what's right. My justice will be served forever. In the end, I will even send fire down from heaven and devour every ounce of evil. All of the enemy's angels will be destroyed. And finally, the devil who deceived the world will be thrown into burning water. He will not perish but will be persecuted day and night for ever and ever. Don't fear because you will be with Me for just as long!

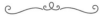

Exodus 6:1–8; John 2:13–17; Revelation 20:9–10

May 14

Precious child,

I remember you. I know where you are and what you're going through. I know the floodwaters are rising and the winds are increasing. I haven't forgotten My promise to save you from these things. I need you to gain strength and wisdom by following My commands through the trials of life. Your struggles do not determine your future. Noah remained faithful to Me, and even though he didn't know when the storms would end, he believed. When the ark came to rest and the floodwaters receded, Noah worshipped Me. I smelled the pleasing scent of his sacrifice and decided to never again curse the ground or destroy all living creatures.

Whether in the middle of a struggle or the center of blessing, spend your time telling the world of My kindness. In the barren places, remember My good deeds for which I am to be praised. Remember everything I have done for you. Remember that I am compassionate and kind. You are mine. Be true to Me and know that I feel what you are feeling. By My love and mercy I have saved you. Don't rebel because your enemy convinces you there is life apart from Me. I have given you the Holy Spirit so you will not be left without knowledge.

I have sent you My glorious arm of power to help you divide the seas of misunderstanding. Feel My strength help you run through fields of forgiveness and never stumble. And I always give you rest. In the waking hours, let Me teach you how to see people with the eyes of your heart. This will encourage you to know the hope that I have called you to. My power is incomparable, and it is for you. This is the exact same power that raised Jesus from the dead! You don't have anything to fear. Ever!

Genesis 8:20–22; Isaiah 63:7–12; Ephesians 1:18–20

May 15

Precious child,

I love you. Feel My mercy wash over you. Let it strengthen your weary heart. Let it heal your aching soul. I hear you ask Me how long will the trials last. I hear you and want you to know that I am with you. I keep My face shining on you. I am delivering you from the current storm and setting you down on still waters all because of My unfailing love. I am drying the tears that have made your eyes weak with sorrow. My strength keeps you safe from those who do evil. I accept all your prayers. Your enemies will be overwhelmed with anguish.

I have hidden your life in Jesus so the enemy can't reach you. This doesn't mean the adversary will stop trying, but he is powerless to snatch you out of the mighty arms of your Savior. Make your life a sermon that will preach to the people that Jesus is the one I've appointed judge over the living and the dead. Just like the prophets who sacrificed their comfort to make My name known, I'm calling you to sacrifice your fears and concerns to testify about Jesus. Tell the world the truth that everyone who believes in His holy name receives forgiveness of sins.

The enemy has sold the world a lie that they have to fight for themselves. He speaks anger into their minds so they will react and be defensive. Where there is injustice, be My ambassador of truth. Where there is hatred, be My giver of love. Make this new day I've given you all about Jesus. Make everything about today be a continual sacrifice of praise to Me. Let your heart beat for Him, and let the fruit of your lips openly profess His sweet name. Push the enemy back by doing good and sharing with others. I am pleased with these kinds of sacrifices.

Psalm 6:2–10; Acts 10:42–43; Hebrews 13:15–16

May 16

Precious child,

All of your days are laid out before Me. I am with you through every one of them. Let go of all your hardships and find your strength in Me. Do this by making Me the source of every ounce of your joy. Keep the royal law that I have given you in scripture. Love everyone as deeply as you love yourself. I want to remind you again that I do not approve of showing favoritism. Don't let your enemy trick you into following the crowd in doing wrong. Let your life represent justice. Don't grieve, because I am holding you. Dwell in the shelter of My love.

Continue to see people through My eyes. I have chosen the meek, the ones who are poor in the eyes of the world, to be rich in faith. You are a loved member of this body of believers chosen to inherit My kingdom that I have promised to those who love Me. So let your desires be for honoring the poor. I'm proud that you try to share the gospel with strangers, but also remember that many souls whom you will never meet are watching. They see you putting all your trust and hope in Me. Your only expectation is Me.

I have poured out My divine power over your life, which is everything you need to live in a way that reflects My integrity. I have called you by My glory and goodness. Consider that My promises to you are great and precious, and by them you are able to fully participate in the divine nature. My love for you is powerful enough to help you escape the world's corruption. Evil desires that are sown over your path will not take root and grow.

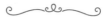

Exodus 23:2; Nehemiah 8:10; James 2:5–9; 2 Peter 1:3–4

May 17

Precious child,

I want to be your encouragement. I want to lift your spirits so you won't have to carry yesterday's sadness into today. I want to be the only one you wonder about and the only one you seek. Rejoice in the strength I give you. The enemy wants you to feel like nothing you do will ever succeed. But the victories I give you are great, because the truth is that I work through you and everything I do is successful. I made you, I love you, and I protect you from the enemy's lies. Cry out to Me and know that I do not withhold My rich blessings from you.

I want to be your life. I gave you life, and I breathed into your lungs to start your real living. Spend your gift of days with Me. The enemy wants you to share your time between Me and the world. This is not the way I made you to be. Please believe My words in scripture. I am here for you, and I want to make you glad with the joy of My presence. When you pray, I am here to listen and strengthen your trust in Me. My great and unfailing love for you means you will not be shaken.

I want to be your story. When you talk to people, let it be Me they think about when your conversations are done. When you lead people, let it be Me they follow. Jesus told the people, "Whoever acknowledges me before others, I will also acknowledge before my Father in heaven." This is the sweetest story your life can tell the hurting world. The enemy tries hard to hinder the gospel from being shared because of the salvation and freedom it brings. When you help people, let it be Me they thank. I am proud of you!

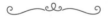

Psalm 21:1–7; Matthew 10:32; 1 Corinthians 9:12

Precious child,

I am your sure foundation. Build every thought, every choice, every step on Me. My blessings for you are endless and include a rich bounty of salvation, wisdom, and knowledge. The devil tries to trick you into thinking you are blessed if you have things the world can measure with their eyes. But My blessings are those things that you can only measure with your heart! As you submit your will to Mine, a holy and reverent fear of Me swells within your soul. This is the key that opens My treasure of saving grace, wisdom that unlocks My mercy found on every page of scripture, and knowledge that opens your heart to desire more of Me.

Do the work I have called you to do. I know you feel discouraged as you wonder just what exactly My plan is for you. Stay strong in faith and let My courage course through you, for My promises do not fail. I will not forsake you. Don't be afraid of the enemy's threats. Be committed to My will and let your words and actions exalt Me. I have built up justice and righteousness as walls of protection to guide you down the path I have for you. When you need reassurance, I will give you more love. When you need to know you matter, I will give you more hope.

There is only one Me. The enemy labors to divide your heart among many desires. I made your precious life to yearn after Me. There's no room for division in our relationship. I give you all of Me, and in return I want all of you. I am the only God. I am the only one who made you. I'm the one who lifts you up and carries you across the days. I am the only one who will never let you go or leave you. I love you.

1 Chronicles 28:20; Isaiah 33:5–6; Romans 3:30

May 19

Precious child,

I give breath to all living things. When you were born, I filled your lungs with the breath of life. When you were reborn, I filled your soul with the bread of life. Jesus, My sweet Son of infinite love and mercy, made a way for you to put down your burdens and run free. Free of the enemy's grip that pulls you into the depths of sin. Free of the lies the world speaks to you about your lack of purpose. Free of the whispers that say you don't matter. This new day is for you to breathe in My breath and exhale praise that will rise up to Me.

I give you exactly what you need, when you need it. When My children were in the wilderness, I gave them manna from heaven to eat. I do the same thing for you today. The world tries to sell you on temporary satisfaction, but My provision satisfies forever. The Israelites were a month and a half out of Egypt when they came to the Desert of Sin. They forgot the power of My mighty hand that had only weeks before rescued them from the pharaoh's cruel oppression. They actually said it would have been better if they had died in Egypt, because they thought I had led them out to the desert to starve.

I want you to know that I am God. I love you so much that even on your bad days when you find yourself full of complaints, I provide you with everything you need. I provided for the Israelites in the evening and in the morning, giving them as much bread and meat as they wanted. I want you to know that Jesus is your true daily provision. My Son gives you real life. He said, "Whoever comes to me will never go hungry." Find satisfaction at the good feast of His eternal love and grace.

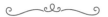

Exodus 16:1–8; Numbers 27:16; Nehemiah 9:15; John 6:31–35

May 20

Precious child,

Your own strength cannot save you. When Gideon had amassed an army of many men, I told him to greatly reduce its number. I did this so when he went to battle and found victory, the people wouldn't say that it was by their own strength they won. There is real power in keeping My commands and walking in the way I have laid out for you. Being with Me and letting Me hold your heart through all of the hours is the key. Trying to problem solve without Me creates more tension and dishonors My name.

Let all of My words mean more than anything. The enemy wants you to see your Bible as a box of words. He wants you indifferent to the treasure you have on its pages. My words guide your feet. They remind you that I watch over you while you sleep. They speak truth into your soul while you are awake. So listen! The enemy loves closed Bibles. My scripture that I have given you is your lifeline that keeps you tethered to My truth. It is a lamp that lights up the darkest day.

Let Jesus have His way in your life. Let Him be the rightful king and ruler over you. His energy is limitless, and He works powerfully in you. Don't let the evil one tell you faith is wishful thinking. Don't let him tell you that I am just a product of your imagination. Don't let him convince you that I must not be real because you feel alone sometimes. Don't believe the lie that Jesus took His last breath on the cross. Through My power you tell the devil the truth. You tell him that I am thinking of you and making your wishes real. You tell him I alone give you real life. You tell him that Jesus conquered death and is your breath of life!

Judges 7:2; Proverbs 6:21–23; Colossians 1:29

May 21

Precious child,

Remember that you don't have to earn My favor. It was My will that Jesus died for your sins. You have been forgiven. The enemy wants you to believe you've been condemned. Jesus took your condemnation onto the cross. His heart for you is more than you could ever imagine. Remember your forgiveness comes from Me, and there is nothing you can do to help or add to this truth. I love you. Not who you might become with hard work and sacrifice. I love who you are, who I made you to be.

There was a king named Manasseh who did evil. He desecrated My temple and undid everything that his father, Hezekiah, had done before him. Where Hezekiah strove to keep My name holy in Jerusalem, Manasseh worked to make his own name famous. His actions angered Me. I spoke to him, but he wouldn't listen. So I brought an army against him, and they took Manasseh prisoner. In this state, he sought My favor and humbled himself greatly before Me. When he prayed, it was a rich heart song of contrition that moved Me, and I listened to his plea. At that point Manasseh knew that I am the only true God.

This is the life I am calling you to live. Your life is a gift for you to unwrap and find more of who I am each day. Consider Jesus who, unlike Manasseh, made My name known every minute of every day. Jesus habitually prayed in solitary places. He called out to Me in all situations. Jesus knew that staying in My will was all that mattered. Be like Jesus and pray. Know that your prayers matter and that I hear every word of every one, and know that I alone am your God!

2 Chronicles 33:12–13; Mark 1:35; Galatians 1:3–4; Revelation 8:3–4

May 22

Precious child,

Remember that everything you have comes from Me. From the heart you've been given to love others to the mind to read My Word and follow My commands, all of you comes from Me. Abraham lived this out when he said to the king of Sodom, "With raised hand I have sworn an oath to the LORD, God Most High, Creator of heaven and earth, that I will accept nothing belonging to you, not even a thread or the strap of a sandal, so that you will never be able to say, 'I made Abram rich.'" This is a wonderful example of how to keep things in perspective. I make your life rich.

I also cause you to flourish. Continue to trust in Me because My love for you never fails. Live an intentional life for Me. Look for Me in all the people you meet. Go to them in grace. Always praise Me with your words. Not only the ones you lift to Me in prayer, but the ones you speak to others. The enemy wants you to hope in things of the world, but I want you to hope in My name because My name is good. The enemy has tried to pull My children away with lies that their real worth is in praise from other people.

I want you to be glad in Me. Be thankful and rejoice forever in what I will create, expecting great things. I am for you, which means I don't want you to wait for happiness. Let Me be your joy. Let Me be your reason for everything. You don't have to go looking for approval. I approve of you. You don't have to worry about the next hour or tomorrow. Let Me be enough. I look over you and see the good plans I have for you. Your life is so important to Me. I didn't create you to worry. I love you.

Genesis 14:22–23; Psalm 52:8–9; Isaiah 65:18

May 23

Precious child,

Be at rest where I have you. My angels are with you. They protect you and keep you safe from the enemy's forces. My apostle Peter experienced this when Herod arrested him. The king's intent was to persecute him for believing in Me. He put him in prison, handing him over to be guarded by sixteen soldiers. While Peter was imprisoned, the believers earnestly prayed for him. Your prayers matter. I don't want you to simply exist. I want you to talk to Me. Tell Me what matters to you and be confident that I hear when you call.

Peter was bound with chains, sleeping between two guards, when an angel appeared. He struck Peter on the side and told him to wake up. At that same moment the chains fell off his wrists. Put yourself in Peter's shoes. I know many days you feel trapped in a position of hopelessness. It seems as if the enemy has your mind locked in a prison of fear. But then angels who will break you out of the enemy's grip surround you. You are never left to defend yourself. You are a treasure in My kingdom, and your heart is protected here.

Know without a doubt that I will rescue you from the enemy's clutches. My angel armies are ministering spirits sent to serve you. Even though you cannot see them, they are there for you. My Son also sends out the angels to go into every part of His kingdom and weed out everything evil that causes sin. When the enemy's intent is to bring persecution over your life, My angels will hold back the forces of evil. They will not be successful. My armies will open a way for you to run to the safety of My arms.

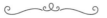

Matthew 13:41; Acts 12:1–11; 1 Timothy 3:16; Hebrews 1:14

Precious child,

My child Joshua was approaching the city of Jericho when he met the commander of My army. Joshua fell facedown in reverence and asked, "What message does my Lord have for his servant?" This is the attitude I want you to have today. In all situations and in all places I want you to expect a message from Me. This new day isn't for you to be disconnected from Me. The devil wants you to see your life as a Sodom and Gomorrah. He wants you to feel like I am not there. He wants you to see your Monday through Saturday as a Nineveh where strangers don't know about Me and the goal is self-worship.

I have new lessons I want to teach you today. Jesus reminded the leaders of His day of an important truth when they began to persecute Him for doing kingdom work on the Sabbath. Jesus said to them, "My Father is always at his work to this very day, and I too am working." I want you to listen for My message, and I want you to be about the work I call you to. You can't do any of this by your own strength. Set down your will and your dreams. Turn your eyes toward Me and watch the work that I am doing in the world. Let Me show you what I am accomplishing.

Love. Be humble. As you set about the work I have for you, don't give evil back to the people who give it to you. As you let Jesus transform your soul, repay the dark world with blessing. Sympathize with the people I will have you meet today. Show them compassion, because the world is certainly not giving it to them. As they begin to see that you are not like the world, they will ask where your choices originate. Be bold and tell them the sweet and holy name that is above all names. Give them Jesus!

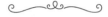

Joshua 5:14; John 5:16–19; 1 Peter 3:8–9

May 25

Precious child,

What are the things in your life that take your mind away from Me? Who do you listen to? Do you follow what certain people say because you think they might be wise? Do you spend a great deal of your time working and never really have time to sit and listen to Me? Do not make idols either of the people in your life or of the activities you do. Don't set up someone or something above Me. I am the Lord your God. Don't bow down to anyone but Me. I am glorious, and the things the world worships are worthless. Don't exchange Me for those things. Like the time Jesus flipped the temple tables to rid My house of money worship, so I want you to overturn the idols that have set up tables in your heart.

The world worships what it makes. Abundance. Extravagance. Silver. Gold. The idols of nations cannot speak even though advertisements call out to get your attention. The things of the world that attract you can never tell you how important your life is. Idols cannot see, they cannot hear, and most of all they do not breathe. When you make something your idol and put your trust in it, then you become like the idol yourself. Your eyes go from Me to the idol and you become blind to My presence in your life. At that point, you can no longer hear My voice, and My breath becomes nothing more than the wind blowing across your path.

Think about Me. Pray. Listen to My voice teach you. Tear down the thoughts that keep you from thinking about Me. Tear down the words that keep you from praying to Me. Tear down the noise that keeps you from hearing My voice. Let Me be the sole object of your worship. Let Me be all that you run after. Raise your hands and glorify Me. I love you.

Leviticus 26:1; Psalm 135:15–18; Jeremiah 2:11

May 26

Precious child,

I want your life to be so much more than it is. Life will not make sense unless you follow Me with highest reverence for My holy name. When you obey My words and continue keeping My commands, your life will begin to reflect My power. You will serve Me in humility and hold fast to Me. The apostle Paul is a good example of this. He went from Christian hunter to Jesus lover. Paul sold his life for the sole purpose of telling the world about his Savior. He walked miles and miles to make sure as many people as possible would be able to hear the name above all others!

My child, don't see this new day as an obstacle course filled with traps and temptations. See today as an opportunity to be My witness. Remember that I am with you, so you have nothing to fear. You are that important to Me. I am just and want you to continue to sow justice where injustice abounds. Defeat the enemy by proclaiming to the world that My salvation is near. I am righteous and want what's best for you. The world has hidden motives, but for Me your heart is My only motive. Hold on to My promises and don't let go. Worship hard every day of the week.

Your inheritance is secure. Your salvation is guaranteed. You have received mercy upon mercy. Grace upon grace. An endless supply of forgiveness and love. All of it from Me so you don't have to spend your days worrying that you're not worthy. Jesus, the perfect and holy one, died in your place and redeemed your life from the clutches of sin. Remember this, and the enemy's lies won't reach you. Do not be shaken by his attacks aimed at your heart. Do not listen to his cunning whispers. Let each of your steps today be taken in worship and awe of who I am.

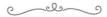

Deuteronomy 13:4; Isaiah 56:1–2; Hebrews 12:28

May 27

Precious child,

Let Me move your heart to desire My will. This is the way I designed our relationship to be. I am the potter. You are the clay. I created you and formed you into a very special person. Be strong today and rise up over the waves of hurt that the enemy casts at you. My love is your shield that the rising waters will crash against. The raging force that was sent to destroy will itself be destroyed. Breathe. Look for Me in every small thing. Every smile, hug, sunrise, flower, encouraging word. Let these fill your heart.

Pray constantly. As we talk, your heart will be filled with the understanding that I am here to bless you. Your soul will awaken and know that I am making you worthy of My calling on your life. I plant My power in your soul so I may make a reality every good thing you desire and every good deed that is prompted by faith. All this is so that the great name of Jesus Christ, your Lord and Savior, will be glorified in you and that your life becomes glorified in Him. All this is according to My grace and His for your precious life.

Be strong because I have called you by name. I love you so much, and I have saved your life for Jesus! The enemy desires your sadness. He thrives when you forget that you are Mine. He waits for you to feel abandoned and attacks your mind with lies. He tells you that nothing is ever going to change. He whispers that you don't matter. He says that I'm not listening to you. He wants you to be lonely. Close your eyes and think about how My mercy, peace, and love are all yours. And I shower you with these in eternal abundance.

Ezra 1:5; Romans 9:20–21; 2 Thessalonians 1:11–12; Jude 1–2

May 28

Precious child,

Today I want you to be more aware of your enemy's never-ending attacks. He wants you to doubt Me. So be on your guard by resisting his lies. When he says you are weak, hear Me say I made you strong. When he says you are alone, hear Me say I am with you forever. And when the enemy says that you are fighting a losing battle, hear Me say that Jesus has already won the war! When the enemy whispers "Quit," I want you to shout "Conquered!" When he whispers "Sinner," you shout out "Saved!"

Your heart is My treasure. In your quiet time with Me, continue to find this truth throughout the pages of My Word. Find My promises there and use them to stand firm in faith. From Genesis to Revelation, read truth and let it fill your soul. Connect with Me and become courageous. Be strong and resist the devil. When the world tries to bench you because the enemy says you're in the way, I want you to stand up. Let the dying world see how I love them as they see you love. Do everything in My love so you can thwart the devil's attacks.

Keep your heart protected from the world's selfish desires. Don't let the enemy's wicked words penetrate your defenses. Don't let his hatred stain your thoughts. I am calling you to be your heart's watchman. Through every waking hour, be alert and ready. Walk slowly across the walls of truth that surround your heart. Look for apathy and loathing that will try to sneak past your defenses. Don't let them in! Above everything, keep your heart sheltered from the devil's storms. Jesus rescued you from darkness, so His peace rules in your heart because everything you do flows from it.

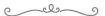

Proverbs 4:23; 1 Corinthians 16:13–14; Colossians 3:15

Precious child,

Jesus taught His friends a lesson that I want to remind you of. He used a story about a man who planted a vineyard to teach them that He would be like a rejected stone. But I would not reject My Son. Instead, I would make Him the cornerstone upon which all of creation is built.

Jesus went on to say that the man put a wall around the vineyard and also constructed a watchtower on the property. When all of the preparations were complete, the owner rented the vineyard to some farmers and then moved away. When it came time for the harvest, the owner sent a servant to collect some of the fruit from the vineyard. But the farmers captured the owner's servant and beat him, sending him away with nothing.

Then the owner of the vineyard sent a second servant to the renters. They assaulted this man and treated him shamefully. Jesus knew that He would be treated the same way by His accusers. The owner sent a third servant who received death in exchange for his attempt to help his master.

The man sent many others to try to retrieve some of the harvest. Some of them were beaten, while others were killed. The owner's final option was to send his own son, whom he loved. He thought that they would surely respect his son. But they killed him too and threw his body out of the vineyard. I want you to see that this is what happened to Jesus. The enemy watched Him get beaten and crucified, thinking that he'd won. He watched as the people buried Jesus with nothing.

What did the owner do? Jesus finished the story by saying the owner would go and take the tenants' lives and give the vineyard to others. Those who reject My only Son will meet a similar fate. The gift of salvation is here for those who call on Jesus. Go and tell the world that He alone saves!

Mark 12:1–11

May 30

Precious child,

I know it's hard to wait. It's difficult to feel My presence in the desert, but know that I am at work! I never stop fighting for your heart. My timing for all the events and appointments in your life is the only thing that matters. While the enemy leads the world away from My heart at a frenzied pace, I am calling you to resist him and wait on Me. When your heart is burdened with worry and fear, I want you to wait with Me. My patience is the comfort you've been searching for. When the enemy tries to make you believe the desert never ends, remember I have not forsaken you.

I hear your soul's cry for love. Please know that I care. I know you want answers, and I am still on My throne. Trust Me. Just as I delivered you from the heavy chains of sin and gave you never-ending grace in Jesus, so I am delivering you now. My promise to you today is that I will not disappoint you. The daily struggles you face are not bigger than Me or My love for you. When the world despises you and they shake their heads at you, remember that they did the same thing to Jesus. I carried you from the womb, and I have carried you through all the days of your life. I have given you the strength to trust, so trust Me now.

I have plans for you. Wait, and through the heart of Jesus, continually offer up praise to Me. Long before you were born, I ordained your life and the beautiful story that I would tell the world through it. I planned every one of your days, and now I am bringing them to pass. Continue to walk with Jesus and wait on Me. I won't let you down!

2 Kings 19:25; Psalm 22:1–9

May 31

Precious child,

I am calling you today to stand firm in My love for you. Remain connected to My promise that there is absolutely nothing on earth that you need to fear. Nothing. Your eyes will see My glory and power. Jesus suffered so your heart could be saved. This new day is for rejoicing. And just as My beautiful Son delivered your heart from the power of death, so today I am delivering you from every evil that the enemy puts in your path. Your feet will not stumble over stones of hate or roots of indifference. Raise your eyes and see that the people around you need to hear from Me today.

Where the world sows sorrow, I am planting peace. In your heart, Jesus is giving more of His love so you will see more of Me. Let My Spirit fill your heart with mercy so you can rest in the hope of your Savior. Where the enemy sows anger, I am planting forgiveness. Where darkness sows confusion, I am shining My glorious light. Harvest these blessings and carry them to the lost and hurting. Give them to the ones who need Me. Don't wait for someone else to move. I have equipped you to undertake this life-changing task, and I know that you are going to do an awesome work in the world.

So, My child, don't be afraid to keep speaking truth. Don't let the world silence you. Your words about Me are a sweet song that cannot be unsung by the enemy's lies. Your forgiven heart beats a symphony for Me that the enemy cannot unplay. Your life is a story of redemption to glorify Me that the enemy cannot erase. Keep serving the ones in need and don't let the world stop you. Your hands that lift a stranger's eyes toward heaven are like the eagle's wings that help broken hearts soar above the pain. I love you.

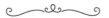

Exodus 14:13; Judges 6:23; John 12:15; Acts 18:9

June 1

Precious child,

I fight for you. I am here to protect you. I know that sometimes all the hours I give you seem to blend together and make you wonder about the reason I created you. I have so much more for you today. There is so much more of Me for your heart to experience. My servant Joshua wanted the people to exalt My name over every other. After a certain victory, Joshua wanted to give Me all the credit and glory. He wanted to teach his people a lesson, and where they all could hear, Joshua called out for the sun to stand still. And when I held the sun in place for a full day, the people were reminded that I am the Almighty.

Armed with only your forgiven heart and prayer, fight for others. Moses found himself in a place where the people he cared about were turning their backs on Me. Instead of walking away, Moses lifted his voice and prayed that My name would be magnified. He knew that I am just and loving. Moses opened his heart and prayed that I would remember My promises I had made to Abraham about numerous descendants and the Promised Land. He prayed that the world would see My glory.

Jesus lifted you up way before you took your very first breath. He called out to Me and said, "I pray also for those who will believe in me through their message, that all of them may be one, Father, just as you are in me and I am in you. May they also be in us so that the world may believe that you have sent me." Your Savior prayed that you would remain in Us so that the world would believe in Him. Just as these three men called out to Me, today I want you to do the same. Pray for My power to fight injustice. Be the one who cares!

Exodus 32:12–14; Joshua 10:12–14; John 17:20–21

June 2

Precious child,

I didn't make you just for today, but I created your heart to be with Me for all eternity. The narrow path of life I have you on has been secured for you by the blood of your Savior! Remember, the road that leads to destruction is wide. There is no joy on it despite what the world will tell you. I am here to fill you with My presence, which will bring you abundant peace and joy. Spend time today thinking about the day when you will see Me face-to-face and enjoy eternal pleasures at My right hand.

I am proud of you because you have left everything comfortable and safe for Me. For My kingdom, you have decided to put Jesus above family members and even above the work of your hands. For the sake of Jesus, I know your heart beats for the things of My people. You will receive a hundred times more blessings sacrificing for Me than trying to find happiness and security in people or things. You are inheriting eternal life, and this is My gift given to you in grace.

Jesus is for you. He is the mediator of our new covenant because I have called you by name. If a moment comes when you feel down and defeated, please remember that I have chosen you. Jesus knew you by name when He went to the cross! He will make sure that you receive the eternal inheritance I have prepared for you. Jesus has set you free from every last tangle of sin. Don't let the enemy ensnare your mind with lies. Don't let him make you believe that you are unwanted. Go and be the one who makes a difference in someone's heart. To the ones who act like everything's fine, be My love, so when they are alone they will know that I am here to give them what the enemy can't.

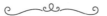

Psalm 16:11; Matthew 19:29; Hebrews 9:15

June 3

Precious child,

My peace isn't a sweet-sounding word or a mere idea. It isn't a goal that I want you to race after and hope you have enough strength to reach. My peace I pour over you is like a summer rain, sent to refresh your weary heart. But unlike the rains that eventually end and do not return for a while, My peace never ends. It is a sweet treasure that is yours forever. Let this gift open your eyes to the green, wide-open pastures I have placed you in. The chaos and disorder that the enemy throws in your daily path will no longer rule over your feelings. These things of the world bow down to My peace.

So what I want you to do today is to seek My peace by extolling Me at all times. Let praise for Me be on your lips always. Feel My peace as you glorify Me so that the afflicted both in body and in spirit will be able to hear truth and rejoice. Exalt Me with other believers, and together let your voice lift up a symphony of praise. Today, I want you to pursue peace. Run after it. Seek Me and know that I am answering you. And I promise that I am delivering you from all fears. Keep your eyes on Me always and your face will become radiant, never to be covered in shame.

Let My peace guide you in your relationships with others. When you call out to Me, I listen. I am here to save you from all your troubles. I want you to act this way toward others so they too will see more of Me. Remember that you can have peace because My angels surround you and are ready to deliver you. Take refuge in Me and know that I am good. Go and face the day I have for you knowing I love you.

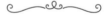

1 Kings 2:33; Psalm 34:1–14; 1 Thessalonians 5:13

Precious child,

I want to speak grace into your heart today. I have taught you before that My grace is enough to make your life complete. But with Jesus, I am giving you even more grace! Jesus, your sweet and mighty king, the holy and righteous one who surpasses everyone and everything, lives in you, and His grace satisfies. The enemy wants you to keep your eyes on the pain. He hopes you won't look away from the fear. But I want you to look at Jesus. He is your minute-by-minute grace giver and your day-to-day truth teller.

Take these promises and live boldly for My name's sake. Because of the grace I am giving you, go and proclaim the gospel message to the ends of the earth. This means the same thing as going to the ends of your neighborhood and being Jesus to the people who live around you. Pour into them as I am pouring into you. Don't just tell them about Jesus. Show them by the work of your hands and the love of your heart. Continually invest in them. Let them know they matter. Their hearts are part of the big plans I have for your life. Lives changed by My mercy and grace are what I want you to give your own life to.

I am grace, and through My promises to you, I will cover your days so you will never feel alone. And if a moment comes when you feel isolated and misunderstood, please remember Me! Remember Jesus! Remember My Spirit! We are with you. We are guiding you and loving you. We are teaching you the ways you should go. The enemy tries to stand between us so you will feel abandoned. The enemy doesn't understand grace. From the beginning, he has wanted to exalt his own name over all creation. This is the way of the world you are stepping into today. Remain in Me, and go show the world grace.

John 1:15–17; Romans 15:15; Galatians 3:18

June 5

Precious child,

My servant David lifted up a prayer to Me that will remind you of just a handful of ways I am blessing you today. David began, "Who am I, Lord God, and what is my family, that you have brought me this far?" When the enemy tries to attack you with lies and make you wonder if you are really Mine, remember this promise: you are My chosen child, saved by My Son's blood, and I am never going to see you differently! And even though David knew he would continue to make mistakes, he understood that My will is always best.

David continued: "For the sake of your servant and according to your will, you have done this great thing and made known all these great promises. There is no one like you, Lord, and there is no God but you." Please don't get discouraged when you mess up. You're not perfect, and I forgive you. The enemy lurks around encouraging you not to forgive yourself. He wants you to think that every time you make a mistake, I turn My back on you. These are his lies. I love you, and I will never take my eyes off you. Nothing in the world is better than Me.

Expect Me to keep My word. I know people have let you down, but I'm your heavenly Father. I will never disappoint you. David said, "Do as you promised, so that it will be established and that your name will be great forever. . . . Your servant has found courage to pray to you. You, Lord, are God! You have promised these good things to your servant. Now you have been pleased to bless the house of your servant, that it may continue forever in your sight; for you, Lord, have blessed it, and it will be blessed forever." I give you the courage you need for every situation, and I love you with a love that never ends.

1 Chronicles 17:16–27

June 6

Precious child,

Today is another gift I have for you. Remember, your enemy whispers lies that this day is nothing special. He will try to tell you that nothing good will come from it. The devil will try to turn your eyes to all the evil in the world. His goal is to try to get you to feel defeated before the day even begins. But remember that one of the biggest ways I'm working in you today is changing your heart. My prophet Joel reminded My people, "Rend your heart and not your garments." He was reminding them that I am not concerned with outward appearances.

Return to Me. My Word is close at hand. Open it and read of My mercy and grace from the pages of scripture. Read throughout the chapters and verses how I am compassionate. See in the stories how I am slow to anger. I'm not here to judge you. Jesus is judge over all creation, and since He is your Savior, He has deemed you forgiven! When I think of you, I smile. My endless heart abounds in love for you. When your plans don't work out exactly as you wanted, please don't worry. I am there working everything out for your benefit. When it seems as though I'm far away, I will let you know that I am actually closer to you than ever.

Before you surrendered your life to Jesus, you disobeyed My commands. You allowed the enemy to enslave you to the world's treasures. You detested the things of My heart by caring only for your own. In selfish pride, you carried your own dreams around, but now you carry My light. Jesus set you free because of His love and kindness. And through it all, hear Me say that from the very beginning, I have loved you with a love that never ends, and that is why I will continue to be faithful to you.

Jeremiah 31:3; Joel 2:13; Titus 3:3–4

June 7

Precious child,

I know you hear how other people live for Me and love Me and sometimes you don't feel like you will ever be good enough. Sin still lingers. You try to be good, but after a while your heart feels like nothing special. Don't listen to the enemy's lies. Jesus has gone to the cross for you. He conquered death and the power of hell for you. Jesus is the only one good enough, and He thought of you when He rose from the dead. What He has done for you makes you more than good enough in My eyes.

Look back through the pages of My Word and see how I protect My people. With My mighty hand I drove out the enemy and planted My children in places where their hearts could take root in the promises I made from the beginning. I made them flourish so they would know it wasn't by the power of weapons or their own hands that all of this happened. By the power of My love, it was My right hand and strong arm and the light of My face that won the victories for them. It's the same for you today. I am here to walk ahead of you and push back the enemy's forces. By My name you will trample your fears.

Spend every minute of today boasting about My holy name and lifting up praise. I am with you when you walk through the rough waters of life, and I keep them from washing over you. When the path you're on seems to head into fiery situations, I promise to keep you from getting burned. I need you to focus on My love for you. Understand how great My heart is for you. I want you to rely on My love. You are so valuable to Me. Live today in My love for you, and know that I am with you always.

Psalm 44:1–8; Isaiah 43:2; Matthew 6:26; 1 John 4:16

Precious child,

I am your maker. I want to paint a word picture today for you to ponder how amazing I made you. I want to describe some features of the ocean that you can't see. There are so many amazing things that lie beneath the surface. Likewise, your heart is a very intimate place because that's where Jesus pours His love for you. His love for you is deeper than anything you have ever experienced. This love fills you with more of Me so you can continue to be sanctified. Jesus dwells in your heart so your entire life may be rooted in love. His love is your life's foundation.

There's a place in the ocean called Challenger Deep that is seven miles down. The great Mount Everest could fit in that abyss and still be covered by a mile of water. The love that Jesus has for you is deeper!

The oceans are so wide that they cover more than 70 percent of the earth's surface. The love Jesus has for you is wider still!

The longest mountain range in the world is the Andes Mountains located in South America. This chain is close to 4,500 miles long.

Out of sight far beneath the water is a rock formation called the mid-ocean ridge that is ten times longer than the Andes. The love that Jesus has for you is longer still!

Mauna Kea is an island in Hawaii, but if you were to travel underneath the Pacific, you would find that this island is really a mountain. Even more amazing is how I created this as the tallest mountain in the world, but most of it is out of sight, hidden in the ocean's watery depths. The love of Jesus for your heart is higher!

My powerful hands that made the oceans also made your heart. I created you special to reflect My majesty, and your tender heart is a mighty ocean of My Son's love.

Job 35:10; Ephesians 3:17–19

June 9

Precious child,

Take each breath I give you today and sing a new song to Me. Let each one of your heartbeats be a sound of praise for the life I have given you. Sing to Me by the words of kindness you speak to everyone you meet today. Join the earth's chorus by making My name glorified throughout the world. Sing to Me and keep on proclaiming My goodness all your days. Tell everyone of My glory. Tell the world about all the wonderful things I have done for you. My grace is great, and I have proven Myself worthy of praise.

Let the people see that you live in awe of Me, so that more and more souls will hear the glorious name of Jesus. The world is filled with idols. The nations worship technology and inventions created by their own hands. They worship themselves at the expense of finding real grace in Jesus. The idols are not Me. I alone am worthy to be worshipped with all your heart. Splendor and majesty surround Me. Strength and glory fill my dwelling place. Show the world that your life is a daily offering to Me.

Show others that your heart trembles in love before Me. Be the example of My peace to everyone you deal with today. Show them My love and guide them to the place of mercy at the foot of the cross of Jesus. Let the lyrics of your life teach the world of My holiness. Let them know that I reign over all creation. I promise you that I will provide for every one of your needs. I want you, in faith, to rejoice and be glad that I gave you life. I am righteous and faithful. I have established My love in your heart so you can let My freedom loosen the chains of fear and tell the world that Jesus is their Savior!

Psalm 96

June 10

Precious child,

Please wait on Me. Don't run ahead. I know your need to work is great, and when you get things done you want to celebrate. Remember that your accomplishments glorify Me as you tell people that I am your provider. Your patience also brings Me glory. The world watches how you react to things. As you tell them your patient heart is the fruit of My harvest, you are reminding them to look around and see My grace. Encourage your friends to remain true to Me. Pray that they would give Me everything. Show them all the things My grace has done in your life.

Jesus, your Lord, is the one who gives you the strength to wait. Be thankful and learn from Him who is patient with you. He has given you the task of proclaiming the gospel because He has judged you faithful. Building relationships with the ones you share the good news with is key. Be patient with them and watch their trust in you grow. And just like Jesus showed you mercy during your days of unbelief, show the world mercy. Let His grace overflow from your heart as you patiently wait on My timing. Whether the enemy tries to bring you down or you feel as if your labor is in vain, I want you to know how much your life means to Me.

Continue to live and breathe in Me. In faith and love Jesus obeyed Me by stepping down into your world. He did this to save sinners. As you go about your day, magnify your Savior by sharing His mercy. Show the world that patience is better than selfish pride. The enemy hopes you will harvest anger and block people from hearing truth. As My faithful servant, commend every part of your life to Me. Endure hard times by feeling My strong hands and heart surround you. You are Mine!

Ecclesiastes 7:8–9; Acts 11:23;
2 Corinthians 6:3–7; 1 Timothy 1:12–14

Precious child,

I have plans for you, not only for today, but for all of your tomorrows. My heart beats for you, and I will accomplish everything I have for you. When you feel alone, don't let the enemy tempt you to find things in the world to replace Me. I am holding you, and I am never letting go. When you feel like no one cares, I pour compassion over all of you. When you feel like no one thinks about you, I am! How great is My desire for you. You cannot imagine how much you mean to Me.

I was faithful to you when I formed your life, and I remain faithful today. My love for you lasts forever, and My dreams for you will work out. I will never abandon you. Your heart is in My hands, and I will never put it down. I made you for Me, but the enemy wants you to believe I made you for the world. He wants you to have an intimate relationship with idols. He wants you to think about time, money, technology, and people, when all I want you to think about is My love for you. Think about Jesus and how much He sacrificed because He wanted to give you new life.

You know the truth because I have shown it to you. I have given you Jesus! He is the beginning and the end and everything you need in between. My purpose is to make your heart know the amazing love of My Son. The evil one cannot stand in the way of this plan. I do all that I please, and it pleases Me to see you sanctified. It pleased Me to call you Mine, and it satisfies My heart to protect you. Every attractive idol the enemy tries to put in your way does not love you. They might look nice, but they don't have hearts to care about you. Hear Me call you My beloved.

Psalm 138:8; Isaiah 46:10; Jeremiah 30:24

June 12

Precious child,

The battles that loom on the horizon are Mine to fight. Today, I am the one who will protect you against the giants your heart will face. Do not be afraid or get discouraged by the mighty armies of life. I am here to lift your heart above the fray and make you feel secure. You are, and always will be, safe because I am with you. I promise to keep you shielded from the enemy's schemes. Don't waste time figuring out how to combat the enemy. That's My job. I have your life nestled in the palm of My hand, so as you go about your day, no evil will be able to overwhelm you.

Jesus told His disciples, "Don't be afraid; from now on you will fish for people." The enemy wants you to worry about your life, but I want you to wonder about others. Wonder about their struggles and fears. Wonder about how their hearts are burdened by the enemy's lies. Leave everything that you have been running after and follow Jesus. Let Him lead you to these souls who are stumbling around in darkness and need a Savior. Let Him show you what sharing the gospel really looks like, and be the one in your world who stands up for Me.

Jesus is the start of this new day, and He will be with you at the end of it. Fall at His feet and feel His hands holding you. Hear Him speak to your heart: "Do not be afraid. I am the First and the Last." Jesus goes before you to face your fears, and He is after you to guard your back. Every minute of this day belongs to Him, so spend your time worshipping your Savior. Don't worry about what to say or how to act. Arm yourself with My Word and fill your mind with My truth. I want you to know without a doubt that Jesus loves and protects you all day long!

2 Chronicles 20:15; Luke 5:10–11; Revelation 1:17

Precious child,

When Jesus was baptized, the crowd of witnesses looked up and saw the sky open. They saw My Spirit descend like a beautiful dove over Him. I have given you this same good Spirit to offer you wisdom and instruction for all aspects of your life. The enemy roams around day and night constantly trying to make you forget everything that I've done for you. He dumps one distraction after another in front of you in hopes that you'll forget the plans I have for you. The devil toils for your soul. Even though your life is Mine, and your salvation secure, the enemy still wants you to doubt.

My Holy Spirit brings you joy as He reminds you who you really are to Me. Spend your day thinking about Jesus and how He brought grace to the graceless. Think about how He brought mercy to the merciless. Spend today imitating Jesus. You have the same Spirit that led Jesus through each of His days. My Spirit is My gift to you for guidance and understanding. He will teach you the right things to say when the enemy tries to leave you speechless.

The enemy sends out false prophets into the world. You will have wisdom and discernment to determine these forces of darkness because they do not confess that Jesus is My Son. The false teachers proclaim that Jesus was a good person but not the King of kings. You are Mine, and you have overcome them. Rejoice! You have Jesus in your heart, and He is greater than the enemy who roams the fallen world. Keep your eyes open. The world listens to the enemy's prophets. They hear the lies loud and clear and hold on to them as truth. But you have My Spirit—the Spirit of truth—and He will guide you down My narrow path to avoid the evil one's traps.

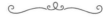

Nehemiah 9:20; Matthew 3:16; 1 Thessalonians 1:6; 1 John 4:2–6

June 14

Precious child,

Jesus is My anointed one. My only Son. Your king. He is set apart from all others. Think about how He set you apart from the world when He saved you. Think about the new life He has given you. Make choices today that keep Jesus set apart. I want the people who see you and hear you today to see Jesus held up high. I want them to hear you talk to them with the sounds of forgiveness. Keep the name of Jesus sacred.

You matter to Me. Even though long hours of despair prowl around your heart, you are a mighty force in the world. Even though sometimes you feel weak and strength seems far away, remember that Jesus was born in a stable. His entrance into the world was seemingly not fit for a king. But from that humble start, your Savior grew, and His name became known throughout the lands. And today, Jesus is transforming your heart so you will have confidence and power to carry His name throughout your world too.

Remember that your enemy hopes you will look at this new day I'm giving you as an opportunity to advance your own agenda. He wants you to fill up your heart with worldly experiences that will make you jealous for more. He will show you what others have and plant seeds of desire in your mind. The evil one toils night and day to find ways to make you think more about your life than My intense love for you. I'm giving you this new day to cultivate a thankful heart. Be intentional with your desire to serve Me. Let your heart cry out to Me with words that shout love and mercy and grace to the world. Let your hands move mountains of injustice for My glory so the world can see justice and hope and forgiveness.

Psalm 2:2; Daniel 9:25–26; Micah 5:2; Colossians 3:17

June 15

Precious child,

I am here to bless you today. The world toils to reap blessings by the fruit of its labor. But My blessings are eternal. The riches of the world fade and break down, but My treasures for you are forever. My gift of grace is not earned by your hard work but bestowed by My giving heart. By grace, I have given you Jesus, and through Him you are eternally blessed. Through Him you are being blessed in life and also in heaven. The enemy wants you to get lost in the day's confusion and strife. He wants you to feel unloved and outside of My grace. But you know the truth. I have adopted and forgiven you. I am here to love and protect you as My child and shower you with new mercy every day.

Take this truth and go into the world as a bearer of My holy name. Feel My favor pour over you and be renewed by My constant provision for all your needs. Reach out to the people around you. Whether they are a family member, a friend, a neighbor, or even the stranger standing next to you in line, I want you to have a humble heart and treat them all with the same kindness Jesus shows you. Wherever you go today, carry the sweet fragrance of My love and heart-saving sound of My name.

The enemy is satisfied when My Word is closed, collecting dust on your shelf. Keep your Bible open. Read My commands. Read about My Son who gave it all for you. Read about the people who have gone before you in faith. Read about My heart for you. You will be blessed as you plant My Word in your heart. Pray and ask Jesus, the living water, to rain over you and cultivate a rich harvest of truth in your heart. I am proud of you.

Proverbs 10:22; John 12:13; Ephesians 1:3; Revelation 1:3

June 16

Precious child,

Be encouraged today as you remember that you are inheriting eternal life. You will be with Me forever. Build My kingdom with the hours you've been given. Forever we will be together in heaven. No more sadness and guilt. No more worry and fear. No more of the enemy's games and temptations. Let this reality pull you forward today as you help build towers of hope for the world to see. Be about the business of giving the world Jesus. My will is that everyone, regardless of background, culture, or traditions, who looks on Jesus and believes in Him should receive eternal life.

I am your eternal God, and your new dwelling place isn't in the world but in My everlasting arms. Your life is covered all the way from this moment to forever. There won't be a second today or an hour tomorrow when you will be out from under My wings. The enemy says that you're alone. He wants you to doubt that I'm here protecting you. He wants you to invite hopelessness and fear inside your heart and keep them company. But Jesus is the only one in your heart, and His sweet love for you fills every inch of it.

Feel My grace pour over you and give your tired bones strength. Let it wrap you in the warmth of My glory and move you into this new day. Let My love for you bring you to people who will rejoice and glorify Me as you plant the seeds of My Word into their lives. You are loved and you are free because of Jesus. I am taking care of every one of your needs today. Go out and be Jesus to the hopeless world. Show them His truth. Use your hands to hold theirs and your feet to lead them to the cross of Christ. I love you forever.

Deuteronomy 33:27; John 6:40; Acts 13:48

June 17

Precious child,

You are not alone. The enemy wants you to believe you're heading out today all by yourself. He would be satisfied if you think that I'm at a distance just watching over you, but not with you each step of the way. But not only am I with you; I send My angels ahead of you to guard and protect you along the way. And not only are you watched over as you go, but I am bringing you to the places I have prepared for you. Today isn't a random mix of hours but rather intentional meetings with people who need to know I am God and I love them.

Before the city of Sodom was destroyed, My angels found Lot sitting in the gateway. He greeted them and invited them to his house. He told them to get rest, but at first they refused his offer. Lot continued to insist that the angels follow him home. Lot prepared a meal for the angels. Soon after, many men from the city surrounded the house with wicked intentions. The angels protected Lot and blinded the intruders so they couldn't get in. The angels warned Lot to take his family and leave the city because I was about to destroy it. Because of My mercy, I commanded the angels to lead Lot and his family safely out of the city.

I send angels to you too. They go through this day alongside you to lift you up in their hands. I have commanded them to look out for you. You are My treasure. I think so much of you. When the enemy throws a stumbling block in your path, My angels will keep your feet from hitting it. You are not stranded on a sea of mistakes and bad decisions. Don't let the enemy trick you into carrying yesterday's burdens. Carry My love to the lonely world instead.

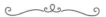

Genesis 19:1–17; Exodus 23:20; Mark 1:13; Revelation 5:11

June 18

Precious child,

Today I want you to focus on trusting Me for everything. Trust Me that My love for you is limitless and never-ending. Trust Me that you are right in the middle of My will for your life. The enemy is a liar, and he desires wickedness. He doesn't want you to live by faith. The enemy wants you to be like him and chase hard after the things that will inflate your ego. Think about all the ways I have taken care of you in the past. Think about the ways I have blessed you. You are beautiful to Me, and today won't be the day I stop feeling this way about you. Trust Me when I say I will never stop loving and blessing you.

Today I want you to focus on My plans for you. I will hold you in perfect peace, and I need you to keep your mind on Me. Talk to Me all day long. Ask Me the best way to handle things. I want you to come to Me with all of your burdens, big or small, but I also want you to praise Me with every ounce of your life. My child, the enemy wants you to believe that because you make mistakes, I won't accept your worship. He wants you to believe that because you still sin, I won't love you as much. These are lies.

As you continue to trust Me, devote yourself to doing good. People will see you lifting up My holy name and wonder about your faith. Remain steadfast in your love for Me. Let the world see that you trust Me for everything. Whether in pain or praise, let them see that your heart remains tethered to My righteousness in all situations. Build others up so their eyes are high enough to look over the top of pride and see the beautiful grace of Jesus.

Isaiah 26:3; Habakkuk 2:4; Titus 3:8

June 19

Precious child,

Live today to show the world that Jesus is your king. Live so the entire earth will hear the song your heart sings of your love for Him. Live for your king in such a way that the farthest lands will know My Son's mighty name and be glad. At times your heart is attacked with hurt and you're stuck trying to decide how to respond. The devil uses these attacks to get you to doubt your own worth and question My mercy. He would love for you to think that your problems are the only ones I cannot solve. Let go of those lies and hold on to Me.

My fires of justice spread out before Me, burning up the enemy's plans so your heart will remain protected as you walk through the hours. I am righteous. My light will shine over every part of your day, so you won't have to worry about getting lost in the darkness. It will warm your heart and grow the joy I have planted there. Remember My strength will melt the mountain of problems that looms over your path. Glorify Me by the way you love others. Share the love of Jesus so hearts will see and tremble. Join the heavens in proclaiming My holiness, and help the nations see My glory.

Many souls walk around hurting. They have been worshipping idols and are burdened with disgrace. They have been boasting of the worthless gods who cannot save them. They don't realize that everything in creation must bow to Me. Let your heart rejoice in Me. Be glad that I am just. Let your words and deeds show the world that I really am worthy to be exalted. Hold on to the fact that I am supreme. In your love for Me, take a stand against the evil schemes of the enemy. Don't forget that I am here protecting you, and I will always rescue you from the wicked ones.

Psalm 97

June 20

Precious child,

I want to remind you that true love is Jesus. He is your everything because He did what no one else could or would do. Jesus laid down His life for you. Jesus allowed Himself to be mocked and humiliated and even pierced by the soldier's spear for your sins. Jesus was broken by the weight of your sins to redeem your life. He chose to do this for you so that the punishment of death would be on Him and you might receive peace in its place. This new day is for you to praise your holy and loving Savior with everything in you, because you have been healed by the blood of the precious and perfect Lamb.

Make today about running to the feet of your king. Spend time learning more about Him and the way He sees people. Understand from our time together that you were like a sheep that had gone astray. You were once walking down an uncharted path of pride and self-worship. You felt that going your own way mattered until you met Jesus. He showed you the end of the path you were on, with all its pain and suffering. My Son showed you that He carried all of your sins to the cross so you will find comfort within the boundary lines I've set for you.

Make today about showing My mercy and grace to the world. In Jesus, there is no difference because of skin color or birthplace. Everyone is one in Jesus. The enemy wants you to remain ignorant of what other people go through. He wants you to stay trapped in your misconceptions. Jesus associated with you when you were still lost in your sins. Live in a way that shows sin is no longer your master. Let everyone know that Jesus is your advocate who pleads your case before Me. Let them know Jesus is truth and righteousness!

Isaiah 53:5–6; Galatians 3:28; 1 John 2:1

Precious child,

You will go through today unafraid of the struggles. I am giving you the strength to rejoice with all your heart as you seek Me in everything. No matter what you have to do, look for Me in all your interactions. In every person you meet and every place you go, I am there to show you joy. If a stressful situation arises, remember that I fight your battles. Talk to Me through it all, and watch how I take care of your heart. You will see My light shine in the darkness. You are a part of this light, and your life shines brightest when you are an example of humility.

Pray. Let your heart rejoice as you see My face today in all the people you meet and in all the places you go. Let My love for you restore your weary soul. Remember, I find favor with you. Don't be afraid of anything, because I am with you always. Show the world that it's okay to say you're sorry. Don't be afraid to admit your mistakes so you can be a witness to My grace. Let them know when it comes to your destiny, you did not get what you deserved. Show them My love, because this is your act of praise. Tell them how I delivered you out of the pit.

This day is for your heart to be filled with inexpressible joy. Despite the heavy burden of sorrow in the world, I am still your glorious God. I am working in all things to bring about good. Move out in faith to show the world how My love changes hearts. Proclaim with your actions that I am worthy of all praise. Tell the world of your passion for Jesus. Teach them how the cross rises higher than their sins and that the love of Christ raises their eyes from evil to eternity. Show them what true love is!

Job 33:25–26; Zephaniah 3:13–15; 1 Peter 1:8

June 22

Precious child,

Grace pulled you out of the darkness and brought you from death to life. My grace made you alive in Jesus. When you were dead in your sins, My grace found you and embraced you. When you were running after the temptations of the world and were lost, My grace held your hand. When you were satisfied with selfish pride, My grace came down and opened your eyes. My grace showed you My heart, and you were amazed.

I am giving you the gift of today so you can continue walking in this grace. Let it lead you to a greater understanding of My love for the nations. The story of My servant Joseph reveals this truth. It expresses the great depths of My compassion for people. When his brothers were starving because of the great famine, they went to Egypt to find relief. After they were reunited, Joseph told them not to be distressed that they sold him into slavery because I had used it for good. I made Joseph a blessing for many as a ruler who shared My grace.

It is through My Son, Jesus, that you receive My grace. Daily, He directs your heart to beat in grace for the dying souls who don't know Me. He teaches you in grace to go and do life with people who are different from you. Instead of a wave and a smile, My grace gently moves you across the street and gives you the chance to talk to your neighbor. Grace gets into your words and lets your friends hear something new. It shows them more of Me and that I am here for them too. Through Jesus, My grace takes you to places that are filled with people who need forgiveness. Go and be a grace-giver.

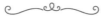

Genesis 45:5–8; Acts 13:43; Romans 1:5; Ephesians 2:5

June 23

Precious child,

I know you're tired. Exhausted. You feel like no one truly understands what you're going through. First, I want to remind you how proud I am of you. Today, I want to take you back to the hours just before Jesus shouldered the cross. To the hours when He was beaten and mocked. Back to the minute when the guards blindfolded Him and hurled insults. Trust Me when I tell you that Jesus does know what you're going through, and He knows exactly what you're feeling. After that initial torture came the cross. Think about how Jesus bore it and the weight of all your sins to Calvary.

Trees that I created beautiful were chopped down and shaped into an instrument of wicked desire. Today, through your words, I want you to keep the gospel message beautiful. Keep the work of Jesus sacred. The only thing I want you to boast about is the cross of Christ. You should do this by denying yourself. Live in such a way that you serve others instead of serving yourself. When you hear Jesus tell you to carry your cross, hear Him say that He is your strength. Hear Him say that you are completely forgiven. This day will indeed have its burdens, but hear My voice speak grace into your heart. Bear the temporary burdens as you carry the gospel to the nations. As you go, let Jesus develop in you a rich, deep faith.

Lose your life for Jesus. Don't let the enemy tempt you into trying to gain the world's riches. Spend your days preaching the gospel, not with fancy language, but with the power of the cross. Jesus is power. Your life has been forever changed. You are no longer a slave to the world's authority. You have been set free from the chains of guilt and fear. Continue to courageously follow the narrow path of truth that I have set you on.

Matthew 16:24–26; Luke 22:63–65;
1 Corinthians 1:17–18; Galatians 6:14

June 24

Precious child,

I want the best for you, and I know what's best for you. Submit this day to the plans I have for you. Be humble and study My Word. Hold on to your teachable spirit and let My commands be a sweet relief, not a checklist of burdens. My discipline is for your benefit, not punishment. My ways are a blessing for your soul because I made you and I breathe life into you. The enemy is also trying to teach you lessons. He uses the world to train you in the ways of selfishness and greed. He gives speeches through the words of lost strangers who don't know Me. The enemy loves it when you listen to them.

But I wait for you. I wait in order to show you grace. You mean so much to Me, and since I am the God of justice, I will always protect you. I am here to show you mercy and compassion. So in light of these truths, I want you to be patient and wait for Me. You are Mine and a light for Me in the darkening world. As you wait for Me to move, shine in the place I have you today. Be a blessing to everyone and stand up for what's right, even when no one else will.

My words, My ways, and My will are perfect. When you spend your time in these, you find a freedom you can never find in the world. When you give up your dreams for My sake, you discover pure joy because My dreams for you are greater. When you ponder My words with your entire being, you stop being a casual observer who forgets what is heard and become one who acts. You can accomplish great things for Me because that is how I made you. Find all the courage and confidence you need in My Word and My love. You will always be blessed.

Psalm 94:12; Isaiah 30:18; James 1:25

June 25

Precious child,

I want you to think about running to Me in the waiting. When the day calls for you to be patient, I am calling you to be faithful and wise. You draw closer to Me the more you wait. You learn more about Me the more you wait. The enemy shouts at you that waiting means nothing is happening. He works hard to make you believe that I have abandoned you when the waiting seems unbearable. He whispers that I must not care. He hints that you should question My sovereignty. The enemy attacks you in these quiet ways because he knows that there is great blessing for you in the waiting.

Let your faith in Me strengthen your heart and mind. Drink in the refreshing waters of My love and promises so you can move and be useful for My purposes. The enemy would rather you be lazy—someone who takes in My words but doesn't do anything with the grace and mercy I've given you. The devil wants you to be like a worthless desert of thorns. Don't let him trick you. Your life is special, and I am calling you to be about the business of sharing the good news of Jesus. Be about the things of salvation.

I am just. I will not forget you and the work that you do for Me and My children. I am proud of the love you show others, and I love the way you constantly give. This is what Jesus did for you, so keep being diligent. Carry on in hope, never doubting that I keep My word. Don't worry about anything. The world's business is self-worship and hate, but Mine is salvation. Be faithful to complete the work I am calling you to. So many people need to see your faithful heart today. Lead them to Jesus!

Proverbs 19:11; Hebrews 6:7–12; 2 Peter 3:15

June 26

Precious child,

Jesus is more than a word. He is much more than a name. He is the name above all names. My only Son, Jesus, stepped down from heaven to rescue you. Live each minute of today giving Him praise. Let Him teach you your great worth because of what He accomplished on the cross. Every blow of the soldier's hammer pounded the heavy nails farther into your Savior's hands and feet. Every ping from metal hitting metal rang out across the Jerusalem sky, sounding the warning that evil had come for a fight. But you know that's not where the story ends.

Some in the world hate the idea of Me because they don't know Me. The devil has blinded them to the truth. I am in the middle of loving you and the rest of My children. Continue in your love for Me and keep My commandments as you spend your day telling the world what happened after darkness fell over Calvary's hill. I have said in My Word that I am the Lord your God and I am jealous. I love you, and My jealousy is for justice. Today, I will make sure your heart is protected. I want you to go out and take a stand for My truth so that the nations will know Me.

I am making Myself complete in you. Until we see each other face-to-face, you will never fully grasp how deep My love is for you. Find all the hope you need for today in the fact that I have given you eternal life and will keep you from perishing. When the enemy suffocates your hope, think about the truth that I do not condemn you. I have given you eternal life through Jesus. Tell the people you meet that Jesus is alive and ready to rescue them! Give them the same hope you have. Give them Jesus!

Exodus 20:6; John 3:16–18; 1 John 2:5

June 27

Precious child,

Remember that I am not a God of disorder. Confusion in your life doesn't come from Me. Let go of those thoughts and submit your plans to Me. I want you to be filled with My peace. The enemy looks for ways to twist your thoughts so you will become tired and weak. In pure vanity, he smiles when his lies overwhelm you. The devil enjoys piling lies upon lies on your heart so you don't have enough strength left to run after Me. But hold My hand and let My peace erase the enemy's lies and free your heart. This is what it means for you to prosper.

My peace is here to renew your soul. My kingdom isn't about accumulating an abundance of worldly riches. Don't spend your time worrying about eating and drinking. I provide those needs for you, so don't chase after them. My kingdom is about righteousness and peace and joy in My Holy Spirit. So be content with My sovereignty. My peace goes before you to make your way peaceful and secure. Your struggles don't mean I have removed My presence from your life. There is peace in the journey, even if some days are hard to endure and even harder to understand. Though you wrestle with daily stress, My peace still remains to cover your heart.

Rest in the goodness of My promise to keep you close. Love My words. Feel the peace that comes from knowing you have My desires safe in your soul. Nothing can stand between our hearts. Nothing can pull you from My hands. Read My words. Plant them in your tender heart and let them help you grow into the beautiful person I made you to be. Go and bring My peace to a world that is burdened by pride and selfish hearts. I am proud of you.

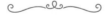

Job 22:21; Psalm 119:165; Romans 14:17

June 28

Precious child,

My servant Daniel loved Me and found himself in charge of an entire kingdom. But some were jealous of Daniel and his new position. Because of his love for Me, Daniel was trustworthy and had a great attitude. Once the men knew they wouldn't find fault with Daniel, they tried to attack his relationship with Me. They convinced the king to issue a decree that made praying to Me illegal, with the penalty being thrown to the lions.

Daniel's heart was consumed with a desire to thank Me for who I am and all I had done for him. The wicked men who had tricked the king found Daniel asking Me for help. The king had compassion for Daniel, but since he had signed the law, he had no recourse except to arrest Daniel and put him in the lions' den. However, the king knew who I was because he said to Daniel, "May your God, whom you serve continually, rescue you!" Soldiers moved a stone over the mouth of the den. Daniel was trapped.

That night, I sent My angel to shut the lions' mouths so they could not hurt Daniel.

The following morning, when he was lifted out of the den, no wounds were found on him because he trusted Me and I protected him. After witnessing My saving grace, the king issued this proclamation about Me: "For he is the living God and he endures forever; his kingdom will not be destroyed, his dominion will never end. He rescues and he saves."

Be encouraged by Daniel's story. Your heart for Me is just like his, and the enemy tries to interfere with our relationship. He doesn't like that you rely on Me for everything. He'd love for you to feel isolated in a den of despair. Remain faithful to Me no matter how overwhelming your situation. Be like Daniel and the king. Trust Me and proclaim My goodness to the people you'll meet today.

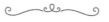

Daniel 6:1–27

June 29

Precious child,

This new day is for you, through the power of the Holy Spirit, to get closer to Me and also for you to grow in your love for Jesus. Once, when Jesus was walking with His disciples, they came upon a crowd. One of the men in the gathering came up to Jesus and knelt before Him. He had a son who was demon possessed. The father's faith was enough that he knew Jesus could heal the boy.

This is how I want you to live each day! Kneel before your Savior and cry out to Him. Ask Jesus for mercy. Tell Him about your sufferings and downfalls. Confess that you've tried to solve all of your problems on your own and that while you were going through the darkest times it was hard to believe that Jesus was still your king.

The enemy has drafted an army of unbelievers. And even though you are not one of them, they surround you. They get in your way and mock your love for Me. That's okay, child, because when you give this day to Jesus, you are rebuking the evil one and all his perverse tactics. You are not a part of his wickedness. Do not live like you believe his lies.

Jesus believes in you, My child. Have faith that He is there to protect and guide you through this day. When His friends asked why they couldn't drive out the demon, Jesus said, "Because you have so little faith. Truly I tell you, if you have faith as small as a mustard seed, you can say to this mountain, 'Move from here to there,' and it will move. Nothing will be impossible for you." When you have beautiful faith, no matter how big or small, no amount of difficulty will stand between us. No mountain of guilt or fear can rise high enough or wide enough that your faith will not be able to move it out of the way!

Matthew 17:14–20

June 30

Precious child,

Spend time with Me today thinking about where you were when I first called out to you. Think about the time you cried out for Jesus and He saved you from the dark well filled with sin. I took you out of the desert of pain and carefully laid you down in My endless green pastures. Jesus, your good shepherd, guards your heart, and nothing can enter in and harm you. You have been washed clean by your Savior's blood. The living water, Jesus, has cleansed you from all of your sins and all of your desires to worship idols.

I have given you a new heart to love others and a new spirit to care and give compassion to the world. The enemy speaks lies into your soul. He says that you are weighed down in grief because of all the bad decisions you've made. He wants you to believe that everything I say to you isn't true. He wants you hurt and defeated. But I have taken your old heart of hardened stone and traded it out for a heart made of flesh. I have given you My Spirit who moves you to follow My commands and helps you keep My laws. I have done all this so you will feel alive and blessed.

I can't remind you enough that one day you will be with Me in heaven. The burdens that hinder you in this life will one day be gone forever. You are My child, and I am your God. I am here to save you from desiring things that will lead you away from Me. I will always provide for you. You will not go hungry, and I will make sure you have more than enough. From that first day I made you until this moment, I am so grateful for your life. It makes Me happy to take care of you. You are worth it all to Me.

Ezekiel 36:24–30

July 1

Precious child,

Trusting Me in both easy and difficult times strengthens your faith. The enemy sneaks around trying to convince you that you are a failure, but I am making you victorious. I have anointed you. Listen and you will hear Me give you answers to all your problems. There is no problem you will face that I can't solve. My right hand holds victorious power. Run to Me and see that I am hope, and I am here filling you with joy and peace as you trust Me. You are ready to face this new day and overflow with hope by the Holy Spirit's power to be a blessing to many.

Don't trust the things of the world. Many trust what their money can buy and the possessions they have worked hard for. Don't worry about that. Just put all your trust in Me. The world will be brought low and eventually fail, but you and the rest of My believers will rise up and stand on solid ground. The ones who trust in their own accomplishments are easily disappointed because grace comes from Me alone. Jesus died on the cross, alone. Come to Me empty-handed and trust that I will fill your hands with everything you need.

You are a leader for Me; and, like Moses, you will do great things for My people. People trust you because they know you love Me. They know we are Father and child, and they trust that. Stay connected to Me in your quiet times and in the crazy times when life seems to spiral out of control. Remain in Me, because you know the enemy is out there trying to get the world to distrust you by uttering little lies here, insinuations there. Soon, the evil one has many who don't know you but will be quick to judge your character and attitude. But their thoughts of you don't define your worth. I do!

Exodus 19:9; Psalm 20:6–8; Romans 15:13

July 2

Precious child,

I am here to bless you. I am here to love you. I am here to listen to you pray and lift up your voice to Me in song. You are constantly with Me, so be confident today. You are constantly in My power, so rejoice. Because I have blessed you and will continue to, live this day like one freed. From the life of hopeless toil to the one of merciful kingdom work, your life has been transformed.

Spend time today proclaiming My name to the world. The enemy wants you to be distracted by all the little things that bother you. He wants you to linger in stress so you will get to the place where you expect it. But that is not what I made you for. I made you to bring Me glory and rejoice that I am your God. I saved you to trust Me for everything. Rejoice and be glad in My salvation. The world can't rejoice in truth. They do find ways to celebrate, but those celebrations end. Rejoicing in My provision and My gift of salvation is forever. Be intentional and ask Me to realign your priorities so your life is a song of thanks to Me.

And if this day should find you in a hard place, I want you to focus on letting your spirit rejoice. I say this so you will remember the suffering Jesus endured for your sake. When you go through today remembering what Jesus went through, your heart will rejoice and be grateful. Remember how He left His throne all for you. Remember how Jesus gave His time to teach life-changing truths by His actions and words so you would know how to be set free. Remember how He died a criminal's death under that dark Jerusalem sky to save you.

Deuteronomy 12:7; Isaiah 25:9; 1 Peter 4:13

July 3

Precious child,

Rely on My Spirit to find the right words to speak. May everyone you meet hear the sounds of My love and grace in every word you say. May mercy come from your tongue and righteousness from your lips. This is the day I have made for you to go and be a voice for My sake. You can't do life on your own. I created you to need Me and depend on Me. Rely on the Holy Spirit to guide you and give you the words to say and the ways to say them. People will listen.

My Spirit helps you avoid the devil's traps. The world tries to dominate your thinking by ushering in sinful things to distract you. The enemy finds you there and tempts you to go further away from Me and My truth. Let the Holy Spirit control what you consider. Let your thoughts be pleasing to Me. You have been remade, a new creation, and that means everything about you has been changed. Sin doesn't define you anymore. My words define you. Study them and learn more of who you really are in Me. Don't let the world tell you what you're worth.

Remember that this new day is for you and Me to be together and for you to grow in My love for you. But today is also for you to practice yielding to the Holy Spirit. There are always opportunities for you to share the powerful name of Jesus. There are always people in your life who will act like they are not interested in what you have to say. Don't worry, because Jesus has called you to be fishers of men. Your kingdom work is to take the good news to the ends of the earth. My job is grace. Salvation is Mine!

2 Samuel 23:2; Romans 8:5; 2 Peter 1:21

July 4

Precious child,

I have all of this day—everything you'll experience and everyone you'll interact with—in My hands. Don't forget this once the hours go by and the temptations rise. When the enemy intervenes and convinces you that your actions determine how close you are to Me, resist this scheme. Only the actions of Jesus have determined that you are Mine. Devote your heart to Me and raise your hands in response to all that I have done for you. I help you throw away the sin that you hold on to and bar evil from your home.

Look up and rejoice because Jesus has deemed you free. Stand firm and don't fear because I am with you always. I want you to know that troubles will pass you by and life will soon become brighter than the sun. I give you hope all day long so you will be secure. You will find rest because you are safe with Me. You will be able to lie down and fear nothing because you are protected. Dedicate your life to Me. I will give you mercy all day long, so worship Me today by sacrificing all of your thoughts and actions to Me.

Pray that you will dedicate this day to Me. Consecrate yourself to Me. Give Me everything you have. The enemy wants you to hang on to your pride. He's okay with you giving Me everything else. But when you are intentional about worshipping Me through your holy living, you show the world how much I mean to you. You show them that you refuse to conform. The enemy entangles the world in a pattern of self-worship. Once that habit is formed, it's easy for the world to ignore Me. Avoid this scheme by renewing your thoughts with scripture. Fill your mind with My Word and devote yourself to My perfect will.

Exodus 32:29; Job 11:13–19; Romans 12:1–2

Precious child,

I created you to experience an array of emotions. I know that some days you feel powerful and ready to do great things for My kingdom. Other days you feel weak and powerless to do the work I've called you to do for My glory. But whatever you feel, I need you to remember that I don't change. Spend all of your day with Me, and you will hear Me tell you over and over that no matter what you might feel, the facts are unchangeable. I have chosen you to do great things for Me, and because of Jesus you are powerful, even on the days you don't think so.

I am here to show you My greatness and strong hand. Nothing in the world is mighty like Me. I Am. Don't worry about not being strong enough. I Am your shield. I Am your support. I Am your everlasting source of mercy, grace, and hope. With these truths I want you to go out into the world and be brave for My people and My kingdom. In what you say and how you treat people, be strong and courageous. Don't listen to the world when it claims to have more resources to solve your problems than I do.

You are Mine. I created you. I knew you in your mother's womb. I have watched over you every day since. By My grace, keep My words alive in your heart. By the strength of Jesus, you resist and overcome the devil. Don't stop now. Today will have obstacles, but they aren't big enough that I can't carry you over them. The cross you carry shouldn't be a cross of guilt or shame. The cross I want you to take with you today is a burden of love. Carry a burden for people. Look at them and imagine how I see them. Be brave enough to tell them about Jesus.

Deuteronomy 3:24; 1 Chronicles 19:13; 1 John 2:14

July 6

Precious child,

Let Me test your heart today. Don't hold on to anything but My strong hands. Let Me fully sanctify you. I am leading you to be a bearer of integrity to all the earth. This pleases Me, and I will show more of My dreams for you. I am filling your heart with My desires so you will be able to know truth and freedom. I am here, and I will keep your heart loyal to Me. I have many things planned for you, but for today I want you to devote your heart to Me. Follow My commands so you can build up the name of Jesus in the broken world.

I have made your heart as mighty as I have made the mountains. I have made your spirit move like the wind. I have made you strong to face the opportunities this day holds. I am revealing My plans to you so you can follow My path for you. All creation knows My name. I created the dawn, and I can ascend to the highest heights. I am the Lord God Almighty. Spend your time sharing the good news that Jesus saves. Spend your time telling people that Jesus is the only answer.

The enemy is trying to amass armies of wickedness. But Jesus came so that the wicked would forsake their evil ways and surrender their sin-stained hearts to Him. Go tell everyone that it's time to turn to Jesus. Tell them that through faith, He will have mercy on them and I will pardon them.

The devil tries to build a mental wall around your thoughts so you might be held prisoner to his lies. This isn't what I made you for. I made you to shine. I made you to be in fellowship with Me. As I reveal My plans for your life, you will be able to tear down the lies and see yourself as I see you!

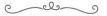

1 Chronicles 29:17–19; Isaiah 55:7; Amos 4:13

July 7

Precious child,

Whatever thoughts might come today, please remember that I am the one who rescues. Just like I rescued the Israelites from the hands of the pharaoh, I delivered you from the clutches of sin. I sent Jesus for you. He reached down and drove out the darkness that had been growing in your soul. I am the one who saves you each day from the enemy's oppression so you can be free to focus on My heart. I rescue you from apathy and fill your heart with compassion for people who are not like you. People who are poor by the world's standard are rich in My eyes. I rescue the fatherless and give them hope.

Learn from Me by keeping My Word in your heart. Let My goodness overwhelm your whole way of looking at the gift of days I have given you. Pray to know My purposes and be a humble servant who lives each moment by faith. Have patience to wait on Me and My timing for your life. Don't forget to love people by speaking words of kindness and concern. Endure the hardships of life, knowing that I will rescue you from them all. The world runs after evil, and once the enemy knows you are Mine, he will try to attack your self-esteem. He will try to deceive you into thinking that you don't matter.

But I will rescue you from all the persecution and deception. Your job is to continue living what you are learning from Me. Continue planting My words in your heart. I breathed out the words of holy scripture so they wouldn't just be words on a page. They rescue your mind from the enemy's accusations and lies. They make you wise by teaching you more about Me. They help you teach others that salvation comes only through faith in Jesus. I am here, and I love you!

Judges 6:9; Job 29:12; 2 Timothy 3:10–17

July 8

Precious child,

Make time with Me a priority. Guard your time with Me. I need you to pray and let Me help you develop a habit of listening to Me rather than doing things for Me. The service to Me and My kingdom will come, but for now I want you to practice listening to My words. Protect your days with Me. Step out every day with an attitude of worship. Let the world see your joy as you go about your hours working to bring Me glory. Be with Me, and focus on listening to Me and My plans for you. They enemy likes to tempt you with busyness, but you can avoid this trap by remaining in My Word and listening to Me.

I have called you to be patient in your actions, but I am also calling you to be slow to speak. I know your heart is passionate to do kingdom work and take up a cause, but I need even your heart to be patient before Me. I am the God of heaven and earth, and I formed you and gave you breath. I am the potter. You are the clay. Remain humble and let Me mold this day for you. Let Me build you up into the person I want you to be. Then, in faith, you will have the power to pray and know without a doubt that I hear you and that I am here to vindicate you.

The world runs after its own passions. The enemy has tricked them into believing that I don't exist and that they need to make their own future. The wickedness that you see in the world around you today is the same wickedness that plagued the earth when Jesus was there sharing truth and preaching repentance. His disciples said there would be scoffers who run after ungodly desires. The problem is these people don't listen to Me because they don't have the Spirit. I am with you to help you tell them the truth. You are worthy, and I am proud of you.

Genesis 30:6; Ecclesiastes 5:1–2; Jude 17–20

July 9

Precious child,

Think more about Jesus today. He was the only one who could redeem your life because He was the perfect sacrifice. He lives to conquer fear that creeps into your thoughts. No one else and nothing the world may offer can compare to the sweet name of Jesus. He was your ransom, and I'm sending you to tell the world, no matter what title a person has, that everyone is equal at the foot of the cross. Everyone! Treat everyone you meet today with dignity and respect. Let your words and actions help them understand what Jesus looks and sounds like.

The enemy has tricked the world into trusting their wealth and encouraged them to boast of their riches. Money isn't bad, but it can't buy salvation. A perfect person had to pay the price, and His name is Christ Jesus! Now that Jesus is your Savior, you have been given eternal life. The enemy has also tricked people into trusting themselves even though he knows they can't save themselves. I am sending you out today as My gospel witness. Let the people you meet today hear you boast in Me. Let them know that you boast through Jesus because He made a way for you to receive the forgiveness of sins.

Jesus has made you upright. He has redeemed your soul from the darkness, and one day He will bring you home to heaven. I remind you of these things so you don't spend time worrying about what you have or don't have. You have Jesus! He is in your heart, and He is all you need. Be awed by His majesty and goodness. Spend time thinking about the splendor of His holy name. The world wastes its time praising people who are prosperous, but Jesus is Lord and Messiah over all the earth. Take boldness from Him and go tell the world that He is the only one they need.

Psalm 49; Acts 2:36; Romans 5:11

Precious child,

Walk with Me today. Noah did, and I found him blameless. He decided to run after Me with everything he had. No matter how dark the world was around him, Noah walked faithfully with Me. The people didn't care about Me and did whatever they pleased. They weren't interested in having anything to do with Me. They worshipped evil and even mocked Noah as he faithfully followed My commands to build the ark. Noah found salvation in Me by My grace. I want you to be the one who stands up for righteousness when no one else will. I want you to be the one who stands up for Me when the world around you won't.

Serve Me faithfully. Our relationship isn't meant to be one of force. I chose to save you by sending My only Son to rescue you. Jesus took the nails and the weight of all your sin to the cross for you. Let your actions be worship. Love Me faithfully by getting rid of the idols in your life that take your time and heart away from Me. I created you to be Mine. I gently made your heart to beat for Me alone. When you let yourself be pulled in the direction of idols, your passion for Me withers and your holy, reverent fear of Me fades.

When you give Me your whole heart, you will experience the life I have for you. You will remember all the great and wonderful things I have done for you. Jesus gave all of Himself to save you from the wicked clutches of sin. Giving Me all of your heart means you will live an undivided life. You will choose Me and My plans because all I want for you is Jesus. He will be enough because He is your holy and mighty King. Faithfully keep running after Me. I made you. I love you. And I'm never letting go!

Genesis 6:9; Joshua 24:14; 1 Samuel 12:24

July 11

Precious child,

Let your whole life be about My grace. Make each choice by grace. Let each word you speak be spoken in My grace. I have given you the gift of grace through Jesus. Take this gift and be a blessing to many as you share the gospel among the nations. The enemy is trying to lead you to live a life of selfishness and shame. Don't be tempted to walk away from grace. Let My grace lead you. Let it transform you so today can be more about us than about you. Remember that Jesus died so that you could be set free, not shackled to pride. You are no longer tethered to your old ways!

My grace is a gift, given for you to also give away. Jesus knew your name and decided you were worth it all. You didn't do a thing to earn My grace. Not one thing. But today I want you to do everything with it. Take grace with you and minister to hurting people in need of Jesus. Let grace open your eyes to people you wouldn't normally think about and let it move you to serve their hearts. You have been given grace to be a blessing to others. You have been given grace to shine. I have made you to grow in love for Me.

I showed you My kindness when I gave you Jesus. Grace flows from Him, and it fills your heart so that you can continue being sanctified. The enemy knows about grace, but he doesn't understand. His pursuit of evil blinds him to the truth. He would love for you to ignore grace and chase after the world's empty treasures. He knows that the worth of worldly gain quickly fades. What looks attractive today quickly breaks down and shows its real value. But not so for grace. Marvelous grace is priceless, and it's a gift that I don't want you to ignore.

Romans 5:15; 2 Corinthians 6:1; Ephesians 2:7

July 12

Precious child,

Jesus is the light that shines over you today. He is like the sun, giving you rays of hope to warm your soul. He is your wonderful Savior and glorious dawn of this new day. Jesus is in your heart because of My tender mercy. You have salvation because of Jesus. Eternal life in heaven is your destination because of Jesus. These truths are brighter than the sun. Feel His love for you uncover hidden fears. Let His light push them away and drench this new day in courage. Jesus reveals more of His heart to you when you sit at His feet and learn from Him.

You once walked in deep darkness, but then you saw a great light. Jesus broke through the blanket of heavy clouds like the dawn, lighting up your heart so your eyes could finally see Him. Today, I am calling you to be a light-bearer to the world. The enemy has tried to convince the masses that salvation is a lie and that Jesus was nothing more than a good man. He has tricked them into believing that being good is good enough. The devil is blinding their eyes to My Son's beautiful light.

Just like the morning is a new beginning, today is the wonderful day that many souls who have been traveling through life in darkness will finally see the light of Jesus. Today they will run to the light and find saving grace in the arms of Jesus! My child, these people were living in the shadow of death, but they will be saved from its sinful grip. You will walk with some of these same people today. Think about this as you go about your work. Bring Jesus everywhere you go. Let His light shine from your words, and let it radiate out of the acts of grace you perform. You are so important to Me!

Job 38:12; Isaiah 9:2; Matthew 4:16; Luke 1:78

July 13

Precious child,

I know your heart. I know you struggle with feelings that leave you wondering if My compassion is real. I know the loneliness and confusion you experience when you work hard to do something for Me, but all your planning comes undone. Everything you wanted to build falls apart and the pieces get blown away by the winds of the world. You set out to accomplish something beautiful for Me, but you wind up with a handful of hurt. Your heart is left heavy and your words to Me are full of questions. But please don't feel defeated.

The world will not be victorious in its battle for your heart. It will not oppress your faith in Me. I am in control, and I am your almighty God who loves you more than you will ever know. The moment that Jesus became your Savior, the ropes of the wicked that had you entangled in sin were severed. You were cut free, but the enemy still wants to overwhelm you with worry and grief. He wants you to go through this new day thinking about yourself instead of your life in Me. Remember, the devil is a wicked deceiver. He wants you to live by your feelings instead of living by Jesus.

Jesus has set you free from failure. Live this day released from the weight of sadness that comes from listening to the lies that you'll never amount to anything. Even the feelings of great strength you get from accomplishing great things are not what I want you to focus on. I don't want the highs and lows to define you. I am the potter. I have made you beautiful, but the enemy tries to reshape your thoughts into a bundle of anxiety. You have been set free, and My grace keeps you that way. Forever!

Psalm 129:1–4; John 8:36; 1 Peter 2:16

July 14

Precious child,

I hear your prayers, and they mean so much to Me. Even the ones you've been lifting up for a long time are just as important to Me as the ones I answer quickly. I am answering you. Trust Me in the waiting. The world is bound by time, but I am timeless. Believe Me when I say every second is used for your sanctification. I use every minute to send blessings over your life. I love you, and I will not let anything come between us. Use the days of waiting to release everything you're clinging to.

Jesus chose to be born in a manger. He took up the hours and grew through the slow movement of days and years. He sacrificed His position in heaven to take on flesh and become your Savior. Jesus let Himself be bound by time, going about My kingdom work as He spent three years delivering My message of forgiveness and salvation. Then He spent hours on the cross for you. In each moment, Jesus used the waiting to show the enemy that My glory cannot be tarnished and that My mighty name can never be weakened.

I want you to live today like Jesus. I want you to wait on Me by growing closer to Me. Wait on Me by reading My Word and soaking in truth. My instructions will satisfy your soul. Live for Jesus. He is with you always. Learn from Him while you wait. Listen to Him speak. Practice bearing grace to the broken world just like Jesus did. I never take My eyes off you. The enemy wants you to believe I go help other people and leave you alone. He wants you to feel abandoned. He doesn't understand that your love for Me grows deeper over time. So don't stop praying, but while you wait for answers, continue walking with Jesus!

Zephaniah 3:8; Luke 8:40; 2 Peter 3:12

July 15

Precious child,

I am the God of commitment. I want you to commit all the hours of this day to Me. I am the God of covenants. When I give you My Word, I keep My promises. No one knows you more than I do. No one can or will love you like Me. No one. I've made a special covenant between us. It's a covenant of love unlike any love you could ever hope to find in the world. It's a commitment bound by My Word. I promise to love you, and I do not go back on My promises. Continue giving Me your entire heart.

I also give you peace. Just like I have made a covenant of love with you, so too have I created a covenant of peace over you. Like My love for you is everlasting, so is My peace. You are My wonderful creation, and I want you to be a fruit-bearer of love and peace. I have placed them in your heart. Today, I am calling you to do a beautiful kingdom work, to be a minister of a new covenant. Not one written on paper by human hands, but the one written on hearts by My Spirit. Be strong, child. Go and tell the world about Jesus. Speak love and peace into the darkness.

Remember that I am committed to you forever. I give you My word. Stay with Me. Read My scriptures and be blessed. Don't let the enemy tempt you into thinking you aren't important to Me. Don't let him lure you into a dim place where you don't think I love you. I am pouring into you, so don't run away. Stay in the warm glow of My glory. Let go of everything that keeps your heart from being fully committed to Me. And most of all, hold on to Jesus.

1 Kings 8:23; Ezekiel 37:26; 2 Corinthians 3:6; Hebrews 8:6

July 16

Precious child,

Don't hold anything inside. Draw your courage and encouragement from Me. Speak the feelings in your heart and the words on your tongue. The thoughts on your mind, the dreams that rest on the wings of your spirit—give them all to Me. Think of these as seeds. Give them all to Me and let Me plant them in My everlasting love for you. Let Me water them with My never-ending compassion. I promise to tend to all of them with careful hands and watchful eyes. Don't keep anything back. I want to bless you.

After you hand over your heart, hold My hand and follow Me to a place where we will look at the brand-new day from My perspective. I will show you marvelous things. First, I will show you how this day sits in the shadow of the cross. The sacrifice of My Son reaches out to cover you as you go. Look and see that His love that was poured out for you still flows like a river right through the middle of today. Look closer and see that the river flows to your heart and fills it with merciful hope. And out past it all, look and see the people wandering far and wide on the horizon. They are the seekers. Run and tell them Jesus is who they're looking for.

Look ahead to the day's end. I never let go of you. See the blessing that comes from giving Me everything. You had the awareness to reach more people for Jesus because you weren't weighed down with time spent wondering. You were completely free to run to the lost and tell them how much Jesus means. You had all the energy you needed to bear the light of Jesus to every dark place.

Now go and remain in Me. Untethered. Free. Be the child I made you to be!

Exodus 24:12; Jeremiah 29:12; 1 John 3:21–22

July 17

Precious child,

My arms are wrapped around you to keep the forces of evil at bay. The enemy cannot penetrate My love that is built up around you. Don't worry about what happens today. Just concentrate on Jesus. Let Him give you new thoughts to ponder. Dwell on all His teachings. Life's strong winds are no match for your blessed Savior. Rough waters of daily living rage below His feet. Jesus walks over the problems and despair. Hear Him call for you to hold His hand and let Him help you do the same! Walk in faith with Him through every hour of this new day.

I have told you that I am your refuge because I am the one who provides safety and security. I will not take My arms from around your life for a single moment today. Be still and know that this is truth. Don't let the enemy plant fear in your heart. I am always there to protect you. Always! Even when the world trembles from chaos and mountains of your hard work collapse into dust, I am your everlasting, almighty Father. I will keep your heart protected through all of it. When waters rise into pounding waves of uncertainty, I am there to stand in front of you and keep you safe.

Moses was leading My people when a powerful king's army intercepted him. I told Moses not to worry because I had everything under control. In faith, My child obeyed and found victory in My promises. I fought the battle for him, and today I will do the same thing for you. Kings that rise against you in the form of fear do not hold authority over you. Armies of worry are not big enough to overpower you, because nothing in the world is big enough to overpower Me. Go and strike down the enemy's injustice for My glory.

Numbers 21:33–35; Psalm 46:1–3; John 6:18–20

July 18

Precious child,

I love you. Let this be the truth that leads you through today. My heart desires that you experience all the blessings I have for you. Tell Me what occupies your thoughts. I want to hear everything that's important to you. I love to listen to your prayers. I love to hear your worship. Your praise is a symphony because I made you wonderful. But the enemy wants you to be quiet. He tells you that since there are so many people in the world, you will only get a small portion of Me. He tries to persuade you that I stop loving you the minute you mess up. These are lies. I give you all of Me because I love all of you.

I want you to know My love for you is extravagant. It leads and rescues. When you find yourself trapped in a mire of doubt or the quicksand of insecurity, I love you so much that those things have no grip on you. They might hold you for a moment, but My love pulls you free. I'll never let you sink into the waters of shame because My love declares you forgiven. My love is also powerful enough to deliver you from the ones who hurt your feelings. Floodwaters of hate will not engulf you because My heart is a wall that rises in love, higher than the raging seas of anger and accusation.

Because I love you, I will answer you. While you go through this day, I am calling you to love others. As you do, My love for you will become more apparent. When the enemy tries to make you feel alone, remember that I love you. Before anything you ever felt, cared for, wanted, or loved, I loved you. It is because I loved you first that you are able to love. Like summer rains that bring relief, My love pours over you. My child, you are My treasure, and I adore you.

Exodus 15:13; Psalm 69:13–16; 1 John 4:19

July 19

Precious child,

I use the delays to strengthen you. Your faith in Me is a powerful tool. I craft each of your days and your experiences to increase your trust in My plans for your life. Be still. Let Me teach you how to react to conflict so you don't get trapped with constant worry. The enemy bears anxiety and can't wait to give it all to you. Don't accept his offerings. He wants to pile burden after burden on your shoulders so you will feel weighed down and tired. But remember that Jesus suffered all the pain of the cross to release you from the enemy's clutches.

I use the long stretches of time to teach you to rely on Me. I want you to long for Me with everything that's in your heart. When you bring a need to Me, I know exactly how I will provide for you. At just the right time, I will deliver blessings to fill the voids the world has caused in your life. Remember that your wisdom grows from being patient. As you live by faith in My holy name, you learn more about Me. You lose interest in trying to have all the answers and rely on My knowledge to navigate the daily paths I have you on.

In the waiting, I also want you to practice being more patient with others. Everyone you meet needs to feel your patience so they'll remember you were different. Your life is part of the harvest, and when you treat strangers with respect and give them your time, they will start to consider Me. The world is obsessed with first place. There is no room or time for waiting. Seeds of truth, however, have been sown across their paths. Proclaim the gospel. Your patience will help you be right where I want you. There you will be able to speak the sweet name of Jesus and witness broken hearts become saved!

Psalm 37:7; Proverbs 14:29; 1 Thessalonians 5:14

July 20

Precious child,

Rejoice. Let your heart seek Me all day long. Lift up your voice and worship Me. Let your songs of praise rise and be carried on the winds so many people will hear My holy name. Keep a grateful heart as you take My grace to the broken down and disregarded. I have created this day for you to tell sinners they can still find hope and forgiveness in Jesus. Pray for them and rejoice with them as you see My Son take away their sins. Be thankful that I am calling you to be a part of this glorious journey from darkness to light.

Celebrate because you also have a great reward in heaven. You have been given eternal life—death no longer holds any power over you. Live out this day unchained to your past. Let Me fill you with heaven's joy so you will have the strength and mindset to remain thankful for all I have done for you. Enjoy My everlasting provision of mercy and grace. See today as a new chance to sing songs of thanksgiving because heaven is your new home. Live free. Live for Me and rejoice for each breath I give you!

Rejoice with a glad spirit that Jesus is your Savior! Let your joy be evident in the world and they'll see you give Him glory. Jesus has brought you ultimate relief from the enemy by conquering your sin on the cross. Jesus reigns victorious over death, and since He also is king of your life, you have been released from the enemy's bonds. You are no longer the world's servant. Jesus has turned your sadness into celebration. His ultimate sacrifice on the cross has transformed all your sorrow into joy. All your debts have been paid!

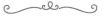

1 Chronicles 16:10; Esther 9:22; Matthew 5:12; Revelation 19:7

July 21

Precious child,

The blessings I have for you go past your heart and touch many of the things you rely on. My blessings for your life increase your sphere of influence as I enlarge the areas where you will take the gospel and the number of people you will be able to share Jesus with. I bless you with provisions and quiet times to find rest. In the stillness of life, I give you peace. I provide so you can go and tell the world about Jesus.

Jesus said it was more of a blessing to give to others than to worry about receiving things from them. A part of My blessing for you is found in helping the weak. Pray for wisdom so you can reorder your priorities. Pray that you will have the courage to help others and make that your new spiritual lifestyle. Giving really means taking the blessings I've given you and sharing them with as many people as you can. In this way, you are making My name known in many hearts and many places. Give. Turn your eyes toward more of the people who need a Savior.

My blessings will pour over you in the midst of persecution and hardship. Your witness during these dark moments is a powerful weapon in defeating the enemy's advances. Trials give you the chance to deepen your faith in Me and show others what real hope looks like. In all this, you are eternally blessed by having Jesus, the Messiah, the Lord of lords, and the way, by your side. He is blessing you through each step today, and I am renewing your spirit even in the struggles. The enemy wants you to believe that I leave you to fight for yourself during trials. Don't listen to that lie. I love you too much to ever let that happen!

Deuteronomy 7:13; Acts 20:35; James 1:12

July 22

Precious child,

Prince of Peace. Glorious Savior. Jesus is in you, and He is for you! Trust Him for everything you need today because He cares about you. Just as He went out to minister to the hurting hearts and feed the hungry, Jesus cares for your heart and feeds your hungry soul. With Him, you have all you need to face this new day. He is your righteous king who reigns in victory. Rejoice that this is your eternal reality. The world is not your master, so let go of worrying about the things that are out of your control.

My Son. Your Messiah. Live today for Him alone. Experience His love that surpasses all others. His love for you is like a wave of peace that crashes over you, leaving pure contentment in its wake. Jesus is the anointed one over all others. He is your high priest who gave His life as the sacrifice for your life. Jesus is your king who reigns in heaven and in your heart. His royal splendor is more beautiful than anything the world can fashion. I have made you a valuable treasure in His kingdom. Listen to Him teach you how to treat others and how to live a life that worships Me and brings Me glory.

Jesus found you when you were completely powerless. By grace, He reached down into the dark world and found your lifeless heart. In sweet mercy, Jesus saved you from the powerful clutches of death. Please let this beautiful, ultimate sacrifice be the masterpiece your soul ponders. As you go, think about the brushstrokes of compassion Jesus painted for you. He opened the door of salvation and called your name. He reached out His hand and led you into His wonderful light. This is what I want you to think about today. Consider where Jesus has brought you and from where He rescued you. You are free to go and help others meet Jesus.

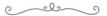

Zechariah 9:9; John 20:31; Romans 5:6

July 23

Precious child,

I want to remind you of My servant Gideon who walked through paths of hardship just like you. The Israelites had done so much evil that I gave them over to Midianite oppressors. For seven years the enemy ravaged their lands and impoverished My people's desire to go on. I sent My angel to meet Gideon and tell him that I would be with him and he would be a mighty warrior. I reminded him to take a stand against injustice and save My people from the Midianites. At first, Gideon tried to ignore My calling by claiming weakness as an excuse for not stepping out in faith. I reminded Him I am the one who fights the battles.

Today, I am calling you like I called Gideon. Be about My work in the world and don't waste time making excuses. The enemy cannot thwart the plans I have for you. Also be encouraged that Jesus is coming soon. He will send angels to sound the trumpet and gather My children. That day is coming when all the weights and burdens and struggles you carry will be wiped away. Forever. Live today anticipating that moment when you will see Jesus and look into His eyes! Live today expecting that moment when you will join heaven's chorus of angels and believers eternally loving your King!

My Son is with you. My angels submit to Him. I want these truths to build your confidence today as you go into the world and sow seeds of the gospel. Jesus is your loving Savior who takes you to places you could never find on your own. He leads you to people who are yearning to be released from their chains. The enemy is out in the world commanding his evil forces to destroy goodness. He is trying to conceal truth and extinguish light. But you too are a mighty warrior for My kingdom. You matter!

Judges 6:12; Matthew 24:31; 1 Peter 3:22

July 24

Precious child,

After Jesus rose from the grave, He brought His friends peace and comfort as He showed them His hands and side. Jesus saw their joy and added to it when He reminded them of their real calling. A very beautiful thing happened. Jesus breathed on them, and in that breath was the Holy Spirit. I have poured out My same Spirit over you. You are covered with truth and the power to discern right from wrong. You need this today as you step out into the world that idolizes selfishness. The enemy teaches people to take their desires and make them truth. My Spirit teaches you how to make My truth your desire.

My Spirit bears fruit for your life. He helps you love others in such a way that their hearts turn toward Me. My Spirit also fills you with a joy that can never be made by human hands. It's a joy that doesn't fade. My Spirit will bring you peace today and teach you how to give kindness even in the middle of hard times. He will give you the strength to carry goodness into dark places that harbor hatred and greed. My Spirit will teach you all about faithfulness so you will be able to follow Me wherever I lead. My Spirit will show you how to be gentle in stressful times and how to practice self-control when everything in you wants to lose it. My Holy Spirit will give you patience so you can wait on Me.

Live by the Spirit. Let Him lead you through each moment, experience, and conversation. Walk with the Spirit, and you will avoid the enemy's worldly traps. My Spirit teaches you truth by explaining the rich meaning of scripture. He will fill your mind with understanding and show you the Bible for the treasure it is. Ask the Spirit to be your guide. He will give you counsel in both quiet times and in storms!

Joel 2:28–32; John 20:22; Acts 2:17; Galatians 5:25

Precious child,

Jesus calls you friend. He is with you today as your trustworthy Savior who gave up His life for you. He is your best friend who cares about all of you. Through each of today's hours, Jesus will remind you how special you are to Him. Your heart is His desire. The enemy will try to surround you with selfish people to make you forget your bond with Jesus. But your Savior gave up His life so you could be forgiven and find new life. He is the one to confide in. Let your friendship with Jesus be what satisfies your heart. Let it be the unbreakable bond I created it to be.

Jesus is your friend who forgives you and strengthens your faith. He builds you up and constantly speaks encouraging words over you. Jesus will never let go of your hand. Ever. Feel Him comfort you in the middle of the pain. He is the light of the world, so let Him shine over every moment of today. Your enemy loves to hide in the shadows, but the light from Jesus in you helps take away the devil's hiding places. Your mind basks in your Savior's radiant glow of righteousness. Don't change a thing. Let your soul take comfort from His lovingkindness.

Jesus is loyal and will never break your heart. During His earthly ministry, My Son sought out sinners. Even though many mocked Him, Jesus never stopped looking for the lonely and outcast. He does the same for you today. He holds you and seeks out your cares and fears. He never laughs at you or your dreams. Jesus loves your hopes and wishes. He wants you to be full of peace. Talk to Him. Tell Him how much He means to you. Tell Him how grateful you are for His friendship. Listen to Jesus all day long and hear Him call you friend.

Matthew 11:19; Luke 5:20; John 21:5

July 26

Precious child,

When the world quits on you, I am here. When the enemy convinces you your strength has run dry, I am here to replenish your heart's desire for righteousness. I am everlasting. Think about the choices you make today. Think about making them with Me. Let your decisions help make a stand for My glory. Let your entire life rise up above the fallen world so people will look and see what real worship looks like. Don't allow the enemy to trick you into thinking I'm far away. I can't tell you enough that I will never give up on you. I am from everlasting to everlasting.

When the days are long and the struggles seem endless, please hear Me tell you they will all end. I am not bound by the time I created, so I see where everything begins and ends. I never get tired, so I will help you carry your burdens. I never grow weary, so I will bear life's heavy loads alongside you. My understanding of everything you are going through is so deep that it is impossible for you to comprehend. I just want you to surrender to Me. Let Me be the potter who shapes this day into a fantastic design of love and compassion.

When the hours seem to be laden with grief and confusion, remember that Jesus is your holy, powerful king. I've given Him all authority and sovereign power. He is for you! Just worship Him today and give Him glory. Even in the little things, find new ways to glorify your precious Savior. His dominion in the world and in your heart is an everlasting reign. Nothing will ever destroy it. And as far as your heart goes, no act of wicked darkness or amount of hurtful slander can take Jesus out of it. You are loved forever!

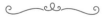

Nehemiah 9:5; Isaiah 40:28; Daniel 7:14

July 27

Precious child,

This new day means another opportunity for you to grow closer to Me. I know the hours can wear down your spirit, but I pour My compassion over you. I am here to restore your weathered heart. I am here to reenergize your will and to give you new determination to work on the kingdom plans I have for your life. Cry out to Me. Don't let the enemy tell you I get tired of hearing you or that I'm ignoring you because I have bigger things to care about. I gave you life so that you and I can be together.

I hear you because I'm compassionate. I am here for you, and I will be gracious. Take the concern I show you and bring it into the world where people are adrift on their oceans of pride. Just like I have made a covenant of love with you, sealed by the blood of Jesus that He shed on the cross, I am sending you to bring compassion to others. Be My grace for each other. Don't let the world sell you a lie that people don't have time for the gospel. Don't listen to the enemy's whispers that people are content with life and don't want to be bothered with what you have to say about Me.

My compassion for you leads Me to show you mercy. I don't get angry when you make mistakes. When Jesus said, "It is finished," that's what He meant! Your mess-ups can't undo the work Jesus completed on the cross. He gave everything to cover each failure. The world turns on an axis of selfish pride. People try to outdo each other and run ahead of everyone else. Everything they accomplish is at someone else's expense. But not with you. Be the one who shows compassion. Be the one who rises above the trials and shows mercy. I love you.

Exodus 22:27; Deuteronomy 13:17; 2 Kings 13:23; John 19:30

July 28

Precious child,

I want to encourage you. I want to remind you of some important truths that will help you today. I remain firm in My purposes for you. The plans I have for your life will come to pass, and they will be for your good. My love for you stands firm. I don't take My eyes off you for a moment. You mean everything to Me, and nothing in the world can undo our relationship and the awesome things I have prepared for you. I am mighty, and My love for you is great. I cannot be moved by the world's forces. The enemy is powerless against Me. You are with Me, safe in My arms.

Live your life grounded in these truths. Then, by My power, you will be able to make firm your decisions to run after Me and My righteousness. Be firm in your desire to serve Me and tell the world about Jesus. Bring Me glory by believing that I am not against you. That's the enemy's grand deception. He paints pictures filled with lies so the world might see bleak days filled with despair instead of beautiful days of grace found in Jesus. Be with Me. Give Me your heart and soul. Don't define your view of Me in the moment. I am so much bigger!

Let your life be a song of praise to Me. Let it join with the heavens in praise for My wonders and faithfulness. Nothing compares to Me. So stay here and I'll continue leading you. I won't waver in My desire to see you sanctified. Above every dream you have, I've already given you the ultimate blessing. I have made you able to stand firm in Jesus! I have anointed you and set My seal of ownership on you! And to make you a new, complete creation, I have put My Spirit in your heart because you are special to Me!

Job 36:5–7; Psalm 89:2; 2 Corinthians 1:21–22

Precious child,

It doesn't matter what your job title is. Now that you have been saved, I have given you the title of spiritual leader. I am calling you to bring people to the cross of Jesus. Whether your worldly title defines you as one who serves or one who makes decisions for others to obey, what matters most is that you remember your spiritual calling. Your real job is to get the whole world to see that I am kind and faithful. I don't forsake My promise to take care of you. I have made a way for your redemption, and I have called you friend.

My love is in you, and it goes before you. I will not take it away from you. So trust Me completely, without wavering, to be the God I say I am. Unclench your hands from the world's fading treasures. Let go of the desire to store up praises from men. My opinion of you is the only one that matters. Be confident, and don't abandon your work of loving others. Take an unwavering stand against deceit. As you conduct yourself, avoid hypocrisy. Keep walking in My truth. Fall deeper in love with Me. Make bringing Me glory your highest concern.

Lead people back to Jesus. I am with you all day long, and I will always keep your feet on solid ground. I will always be here to show you mercy. My grace ensures that you are forever forgiven. I love you! Please don't forget that nothing can ever cancel My faithfulness. If you have a bad day and don't feel like praying to Me, I am faithful to you. If the enemy tempts you into thinking I have left My throne, I am faithfully loving you away from temptations and holding your heart. I will be with you today like I was with you yesterday and like I will be with you tomorrow.

Ruth 4:14; Psalm 26:2; Romans 3:3

July 30

Precious child,

I want you to put all of your confidence in Me because I am not a man but your unchanging God. I will never lie to you or change My mind. The enemy is a liar and disguises his wickedness as truth. He changes like the sands pulled back and forth by the tides. He will lie about Me and hope you begin to question My integrity. He wants you to believe in yourself instead of My spotless name. He wants you to trust in others more than you trust Me. He wants you to think that if you look for peace in the world you will find it. I am your peace. I don't adapt. I don't change. I Am.

The world is constantly changing. People constantly change their minds. When Jesus came to save the lost, the enemy used change to tempt Him. "Turn stones into food." Jesus said everyone needs to live on My unchanging words. "Defy God." Jesus said that people should never test Me. "Be your own god." Jesus said that everyone should worship Me because I am your God who never changes. Temptations change. Evil changes its face. Darkness changes its hiding places. But I, your almighty God, am on My throne. Keep your thoughts on this truth. I am the same sovereign God who created you. You have changed since I gave you your first breath, but I have not.

I have called you by name. I have chosen you and have given you an eternal inheritance with all the saints. Don't be ashamed when you are tired and forget just how important you are to Me. I am timeless, and every time I will remind you that each heartbeat I give you is sweet to Me. I will never change My mind about you. Jesus, My sweet, holy Son, never changes His mind about you either. He is your perfect Lord who loves you!

1 Samuel 15:29; Malachi 3:6; Matthew 4:1–10; Hebrews 13:8

Precious child,

Pray. For your family. For your friends. Pray that My desires will open doors for you to share the good news. The world blares the sounds of false doctrines and self. So many people don't know Jesus. They fill their days with worthless desires. They are going through the motions of religion and don't make time to talk to Me. I love you and want you to know the truth. Prayer keeps your mind on the things of My kingdom. The enemy doesn't want you talking to Me. He wants you to solve your own problems.

There is power in prayer. It is effective. Use your quiet time to lift up the needs of others. I want the truth that I gave you life and have saved you to radically change your perspective on sharing your heart. Pour out your soul to Me. I love you and want you to hear Me say over and over that I want the best for you. Your prayers wield power in My holy name. They are forces of goodness for the building up of My people. And pray for the ones who are lost, blindly running after false teachers and material idols.

Talk to Me about all the things on your heart. When you make prayer a habit and not a have-to, you will find humility to help you grow in My grace. When you pray, pause to hear My reply. Have an open mind when you talk to Me. I know what you need, and I will provide. Listen to Me and let your prayers be a response to all the things I'm saying to you. Hear My voice in quiet times. Prayer leads you into My presence. Follow My calling to pastures of peace. Be the one who shows others what living life with Me sounds like. Let them know you value our time together.

Ezra 8:23; Romans 1:10; 1 Corinthians 7:5; James 5:16

August 1

Precious child,

Being with Me throughout the day will keep your heart connected to Mine. This is how you gain strength to do all the work I have for you. The world drains your energy. The enemy doesn't want you to remember how strong you are in Me. My mighty power is in you and goes with you wherever you go. If you find yourself in a situation that makes you feel weak or unqualified, remember that I am your strength. Call to Me. The enemy says you are not strong enough to fight the battles, but he forgets that in Me you are a brave soldier.

Because I am with you, you can sing the same lyrics My prophet Deborah sang: "March on, my soul; be strong!" I live this new day with you and give you the strength to fortify your soul. I go before you so that you can live intentionally to be about My kingdom purposes. The same power that made the world is here for you. Use it today to reach the unreached and make My name known. The same power that parted the Red Sea is here for you. Use it to separate the shadows to find lost souls and tell them about Jesus. The same power that conquers death is here for you. Use it to boldly proclaim the saving grace of Jesus!

You are strong because of Jesus. By His grace, all is possible. Think about His love and how it wrapped around you and pulled you out of the abyss. His grace was powerful enough to endure the cross for you. These acts of mercy came from your Savior's heart, but today they are still here for you to hold on to and use. Give your battles to Jesus. Let Him be every ounce of strength you need to be victorious. Let Jesus help you avoid distractions and remain focused on My love.

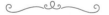

Judges 5:21; Ephesians 6:10; 2 Timothy 2:1

August 2

Precious child,

Live your life confident in Me. I will never go back on My promises to you. What I tell you today will be true tomorrow; you can build a strong tower of faith on the rock of Jesus Christ! I am giving you this new day to learn more about Me. The enemy wants you to doubt Me by encouraging you to believe in yourself. He doesn't care about your soul. His lies are "Do your best," "Keep trying," and "Work hard." When he says these things to you, he wants you to stop relying on Me.

Live your life dependent on Me alone. Don't depend on your own strength. Don't depend on family or friends. Want Me more than the world's treasures. Those things might bring temporary comfort, but they do not give you unfailing confidence like I give. Find biblical examples of My children who had confidence to complete all the tasks I planned. In the same way, I fill you with heavenly courage, not like anything found in the world, that you will use to finish the jobs I've prepared for you. You will also use it to stand up for My truth. Let your confidence come from the hope I've given you—the hope of eternal life.

Be confident in Me because I am the one who loves you with a love so deep you cannot comprehend it. I promise you all these things are true because I do not lie. As the morning sun brings light for the new day, so too does My heart deliver love to yours. Feel it rise in your soul and shine over your spirit all day long. Don't let the enemy tell you that you're not good enough. Don't let him take away the gift of grace I have given you. I am so proud of you!

Philippians 1:6

August 3

Precious child,

Don't forget that I made you and I always want what's best for you. The enemy wants you to doubt My plans. He wants you to question Me. You are My creation, and I am your Creator. Like clay, I have formed you. Like a potter, I have shaped you into a beautiful person. The enemy wants you to concentrate on the world. He wants you to find meaning in the words of others instead of in My Son, the Word. The enemy wants you to find love from the actions of others instead of the actions Jesus took for you. Because Jesus died on the cross, My love was able to reach you and save your life from the oncoming darkness.

I formed you in your mother's womb, and I continue to shape each day of your life. I can form great things for you—more than you can imagine. Today is in My hands. Don't work against Me. Let Me shape this day to be more than you could ever plan or achieve on your own. Don't get caught up in the enemy's game of building your own day. He wants you to get wrapped in a tangle of problems and re-grets. When you rest in Me and let Me mold these hours for your good, nothing will distract you from bringing Me glory.

I have created you beautiful and have put My light in your heart so you can shine in the darkness. Live like a servant for Jesus. Make everything you do preach His righteous name. As I spoke light into the dark void, today I speak the light of knowledge for you to under-stand My glory. As I make this new day, consider how I made a path for your salvation. Look for My fingerprint on all the blessings that come to you. Pay attention to the details. See that I have formed today to be a blessing of faith for you to grow closer to Me.

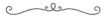

Isaiah 45:9; Jeremiah 18:6; 2 Corinthians 4:5–7

August 4

Precious child,

Stay in My Word and believe Me when I say I care about you. I see everything, from your days of rest to your days of sadness. I see every beat of your heart, and I want to remind you that I made you special. Don't fall into the habit of putting your trust in the things of the world. Believing in things of the world will bring disappointment because man makes those. Eventually, if you keep all of your heart and mind in the world, you will begin to believe in anger and pride as justifiable reactions to your problems. By keeping all your hope in Me, and believing that I love you, your heart will react in grace.

When Jesus raised His friend Lazarus from the grave, He told Martha that if she believed, she would see My glory. My Son went on to raise Lazarus, and He is with you to raise the sad times to a living peace, all for My glory. I believe in you, and I always will. Believe in My promises and I'll open your eyes to unlimited examples of My glory. Don't forget that I am proud of you. I know it's easy for the enemy to slip in and distract you from the path I have you on. It's that simple moment when you are tempted to take your eyes off Me. But remember that you have been saved by My Son's blood that was shed on the cross for all your sins. Claim this truth over and over again.

Listen as the gentle whisper of My voice reminds you that no matter how long you may doubt My ability to change your circumstances, I still love you. I never want to see you drowning in doubt, but I understand. Let go of the enemy's lie that Jesus died for only some of your mistakes. Be My mighty believer who lives each moment in My truth. I love you.

Exodus 4:31; John 11:40; 1 Corinthians 15:2

Precious child,

My words are perfect. Today, I want you to spend time reflecting on the gift I have given you in My Bible. Keep it with you and see it like the treasure I intended. My child David said My words are like gold that has been refined seven times. They come to you and teach you about all the things I have for you. Find yourself in the stories. Sing the psalms. Imagine yourself in the crowd, inching your way closer and finally finding a seat at the feet of Jesus. Listen to His perfect teachings. You won't hear any judgmental tones. Hear His love for you in every lesson.

My words are not just for you to read. I give them for you to consume. Let them bring you a happiness the world can never bring. Read My words and delight your heart in their goodness. They will sanctify you from the inside out and change you so much that complete strangers will look at you and know you are a bearer of My mighty name.

Go into each hour with Jesus because He speaks words of eternal life. My Son chose to be broken for you. He covered you with love yesterday and is doing the same today. And when the dawn opens wide and another day's sun rises over the horizon, Jesus will shine the same rays of love over you. Follow His example and be free from the chains of sin. The enemy wants you to believe that Jesus only forgives your little mistakes. If you say something that isn't quite true, Jesus has that covered. If you hurt someone's feelings with a harsh word or an ungrateful heart, Satan would have you believe the power of the cross can't mend that sin. No! Don't listen to him. Let his lies fall on deaf ears. Repent and know you are completely forgiven. You will be with Me forever!

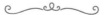

Psalm 12:6; Jeremiah 15:16; John 6:68

August 6

Precious child,

Live all of today with a thankful heart. Be thankful for all of the wonderful things Jesus has done for you. Be intentional in your conversations with people. Let them know that Jesus is your king and in Him alone you put your trust. Don't put yourself above anyone. Call on Jesus to help you understand that living is so much more than breathing. Being thankful for each breath and abiding in Me is what today is all about. Tell the world that Jesus saved you from your sins and gave you eternal life.

Your life is in Jesus, and there you will always find victory. Each day may not look like a triumph, but I am sovereign and I see things that you cannot see. Your day may have some pain, but I am your healer. The enemy tries to cover your eyes so you can't see My blessings in the middle of storms. He loves to watch you doubt. He wants you to quietly slip away from My promises when things seem out of control. I have put your life in Christ so that as you go about your daily routine, you may spread His name to everyone and know that you are protected from the devil's schemes.

To see someone know who Jesus really is means everything to Me. A sweet fragrance fills the air from knowing your Savior. Focus on Him today. Take His name to work and share Him with your team. This is your real occupation. Your primary job description is to bring glory to Jesus by bearing His name to everyone, not just your friends. Your goal is to honor Him in all situations by giving grace to everyone. Show thanks to your loving king by living all of today for Him. Make each moment reflect your thankful heart for His saving grace!

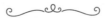

1 Chronicles 16:8; 2 Corinthians 2:14; Revelation 4:9

August 7

Precious child,

Take refuge in Me. Don't walk away to find safe places in other people or things. No one can protect you like I can. I made you, and I will fight for you. I didn't have to send Jesus to the cross for you, but I wanted you to know how much you mean to Me. I didn't have to give you My words, but I wanted you to have the Bible as a daily reminder that you are dearly loved. I am your sanctuary. Run to Me and find peace within My heart. I didn't have to give you life, but I wanted to have a wonderful relationship with you. Your heart beats by My creativity. I will protect it.

Fear Me and know that I am your secure fortress. Nothing in life can break through Me. No matter what the enemy tries to do, he is not powerful enough to reach through Me and hurt you. In Me, you have nothing to worry about. Darkness will crash around the walls of your life, but it cannot crash over Me. In Me, you have eternal security from the demons who try to whisper words that question your worth. You are safe from the lost and broken people who think your identity should come from them instead of Jesus.

I am a refuge for you whether you are in need or have plenty. I am a refuge for you whether you are stressed or at peace. I am a refuge for you whether you feel that I'm far away or nearby. When the enemy creates storms around you, I am your shelter. When the enemy turns up the heat, I am your shade. I am greater and more powerful than anything. Think about Me and how I always want what's best for you. See that I am here to build you up and give you rest. To have Me as your safe place is worth everything. I love you.

Psalm 2:12; Proverbs 14:26; Isaiah 25:4

Precious child,

My presence surrounds you. It is many things, but in particular My presence keeps you from falling. The enemy lures you away from Me. He wants you to run away and choose the path you believe will be the easiest to navigate. The enemy wants you to be in charge. He wants you to live your life apart from Me. He works to separate us because if he does, you will fall. And when you've stumbled, he knows it's hard to get back up. But not only do I keep you safe from falling, I also lead you in My glorious presence.

Because I keep you in My presence, you nurture a holy fear of Me. You worship Me, and I receive the beautiful sounds. You remain in Me, and I listen to every prayer. Let your life continue to honor Me as you remember what I've done for you. Jesus became your sacrifice so you can stand before Me, faultless and joyful. Continue to reflect on just how far away I have removed you from that dark jungle of selfishness and sin. Remember that lonely place where Jesus found you.

Preach the saving name of Jesus, because a day is coming when everything I created, both on land and in the seas, will tremble in My presence. Every fish I made to swim in the deep and every bird I created in the sky will stop and shake because of My holy presence. Both the animals that walk the earth and every person who inhabits the face of the earth will tremble before Me. I will lift and overturn the mighty mountains. I will tear away the cliffs and watch them crumble. And I will cause every wall to fall to the ground. But My presence washes away worry and fills your heart with peace as you tell the nations about the blessed name of Jesus.

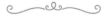

Ezekiel 38:20; Malachi 3:16; Jude 24

August 9

Precious child,

I have given you My word so you will know where to go. I have given you My promises so you will stay on the path I have forged for you. The enemy will be waiting to tempt you away from My will for your life, but I am here to love you. My plans for you don't change. I won't hear your dreams one day and then leave you alone to figure out your own way. I am your just God. All creation declares Me righteous. I am judge, and I show you what is good and true. I won't leave you alone to navigate the hardships on your own. I will always lead you.

Stand up for kindness. Love it. Live it. Give kindness away to everyone you meet. Don't hold on to any of it, because I am your kindness and I will continue to keep your heart full. I am always with you, bringing you justice. I always listen. I hear your cries, and I will never forget to answer you. The enemy wants you to focus on sin. He compares the sin in other people's lives to My righteousness. When someone acts unjustly, the enemy wants you to internalize the hurt and think that My justice is full of holes. Don't fall for this deception.

I want you to focus on Jesus. He took your sin far away. According to My justice, even though you were drowning in pride, Jesus rescued you! All I want from you today is justice. Be fair to others. Consider how I have treated you and do the same. Give compassion. This is the difference between you and the world. Doing justice creates rivers of mercy that flow through your day and carry you to people who are searching for Me. As you reach them, walk humbly and show them how beautiful My love is. I am always proud of you.

Psalm 50:6; Micah 6:8; Luke 18:7

August 10

Precious child,

Pray to Me about everything. Give Me all the feelings of your heart and all the concerns in your mind. Your words remain with Me day and night. The enemy says that your prayers are blown away on the wind and you're better off not talking to Me. But I am the one who listens. I am the one who knows what you need each day, and I am the one who lifts you up over the temptations and pitfalls. I want you to make a habit of trusting Me for providing what you need and answering your prayers at just the right time.

Don't let your mistakes hinder our relationship. The enemy wants you to feel like you let Me down over and over. He persuades you that you'd rather not talk to Me in fear of messing up and having to come to Me seeking forgiveness. Nothing takes Me off My throne. He whispers that you are letting Me down. In fact, the opposite is true. When you sin and come to Me with a repentant heart, you are lifting Me up and giving Me glory. You show the enemy who your king really is. Satan wants you to stop asking Me for forgiveness because he wants you to live in isolation.

Bring every decision to Me. No matter what you want to accomplish or what particular challenge today might bring, lift all of it up to Me. Let Me direct your wants. The world is full of dreams and fleeting treasures, and your enemy is quick to lead your eyes and heart to rest on them. Let the holy name of Jesus be all that you need today. Hear Him call you with two simple words: "Follow Me." The enemy says today is a complicated series of problems to solve. But I am your problem solver, and I love you.

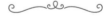

1 Kings 8:59; Ezra 9:6; Nehemiah 2:4

August 11

Precious child,

I am here for you. My love for you comes from My eternal heart. It doesn't run dry or lessen over time. Today, and every day after, My passion to protect you and see you do great things remains. I won't let you down today, and I won't fail you tomorrow. The only thing I ask is that you don't judge My promises against the world's standard of love. The world always wants something in return. It gives temporary love but expects worship back. This bears the devil's fingerprint. He only gives to get something back, but I love you because I adore you. You make Me proud.

Show the world who I am by acting like Me. Just like day after day I am here for you, spend each day telling the world that Jesus is their risen king. Tell them that He is waiting for them. Don't assume that people will hear His name from someone else. People at your work and in your neighborhood are waiting to hear about Jesus from you. Don't be like the enemy. Go and tell them about Jesus even though the world gives you a hundred excuses not to.

I am writing you these letters so you don't lose heart. I always want you to understand that nothing in the world can come between us. The enemy likes to destroy. He corrupts your thoughts so they will break down and crumble into tiny pieces of doubt. He trains your eyes on the rampant evil in the world in hopes that you'll focus on the waste and decay. The enemy does this to make you forget who you really are in Jesus. You really are saved. You really are eternally forgiven. And your heart is really being renewed. This is your everyday reality. I am here with you. Forever.

Zephaniah 3:5; Acts 5:42; 2 Corinthians 4:16

Precious child,

Part of My character is kindness. Today, find all the ways I will be kind to you. I am here to help you and guide you in kindness. Through each hour I will act kindly because that is My nature. The enemy covers over this truth with lies that I am only here to judge. The devil wants the world to forget My miracles and all the ways I pour out My kind heart and to rebel against Me. I remind you of these things so you will know how important your life is to Me.

I formed your life, and I am shaping this new day for you to see more of Me. I mold you with My compassion so you can be brave and help people today. Let the Spirit guide you to serve others so you won't get trapped in selfish excuses. Give kindness even when the world doesn't understand. Meditate on My will for your life. Right now, even though your mind is on many things, let Me be God. Let Me make everything okay again. I will guide you through green pastures and refresh you by clear waters.

I give you My everlasting kindness because I want you to be satisfied with all of Me. I didn't create you to love Me and the world. The enemy wants that, but Jesus died for all of your sins so when you worship Me it can be with all your heart. Don't divide your passions between Jesus and earthly pursuits. Just pursue Jesus with every ounce of strength I have given you. Run after Him alone and be satisfied with His heart. This will bring about a revolution in your soul. You will begin to understand that My kindness is for you and that Jesus has made you worthy to receive all of it.

Psalm 106:7; Isaiah 54:8; Romans 11:22

Precious child,

My mercy is for you. It pulls you on even when the world tries to tell you that your life doesn't matter. When the enemy works to make you feel unloved, My mercy becomes your heart's loving refuge. It grows inside you so you don't ever have to worry that I am somewhere far away. I am with you. I am the one who gave you life, and I am the one who sustains you. My mercy takes your hand and leads you away from your mistakes and gives forgiveness in place of sin. My mercy treats you with kindness and shows you all the ways I made you wonderful.

No disaster or act of malice can overtake you. My mercy covers you from the storms, and I want it to be your anchor on the world's oceans of judgment and ridicule. No matter how dark the day may be, Jesus is the light of your world. He shines over you so darkness cannot remain. My mercy protects you from being overwhelmed by the day's unrelenting pace. I know you have times when you don't feel loved. The world has a way of draining your heart with its burdens and expectations. Don't let the enemy trap you into thinking that an empty heart is what I want you to bear.

Instead, share all the ways I've had mercy on you. Tell people how I answer prayers and bless you in ways that far exceed how you hoped I would answer. Mercy originates in Me. Come to Me when you feel alone and misunderstood. Mercy replaces those feelings with My compassion to help you feel valued and wanted. I can accomplish so much through you. The enemy wants you paralyzed with worry— frozen right where you are, not where I want you to be. I will keep your heart filled with My love and creativity. I want you to know that you are important to Me, and today is better because you're in it.

Psalm 57:1; Mark 5:19; 1 Timothy 1:2

Precious child,

Give everything to Me. I know all the things you want, but above all those you need to trust Me. I watch you, and I know your heart. The world sells the idea that wealth is the perfect protector of problems. Keep working. Keep striving. Keep going. The enemy sells these lies to keep the world occupied. He wants people to focus on their efforts and forget about Me. Take the first step and come to Me. Don't let the enemy's lies build a barrier between us. Put down the weight of insecurity and shame. Jesus has destroyed their power over you. Come to Me.

Give every ounce of your heart to Me. Even if you feel that you don't have much to offer, still come and offer everything you have. Give until there's nothing left so I can be there to fill your heart with My love. This isn't the way the world works. It gives from excess. The enemy will blind people; they believe they're doing good deeds. Give all that you have so that I am all that remains to rely on. Give everything so you have to step out in faith. The enemy wants you to give a lot, but he wants you to hold on to a small portion of your money and material. . .just in case.

But you know Me. Don't fall for the devil's selfishness. I am your everything, and you will never need something you sacrificed. Give Me every minute of today. Do this by listening to a friend who needs you. Sacrifice your agenda long enough to console a stranger who needs to know who I am. Give to Me by being willing to offer your talents to share the name of Jesus. Don't compare yourself to anyone else. Come to Me. You are special, and I'm proud of you.

Mark 12:41–43; Luke 21:1–3; 2 Corinthians 8:12

Precious child,

I am a covenant keeper. I have promised to love you forever, and I will never go back on that promise. I know that each day brings burdens, but I am here to love you through each one. My love for you has a name, and that name is Jesus! My only Son, Jesus, chose to give up His life so you could have yours. He went a long way to find you. Jesus got on His knees and prayed for you, and then He picked up His cross and died for you. That is the beautiful covenant that I have made with you. I have given you Jesus. I have given you My love and sealed it close in your heart.

My love for you is priceless. It will never fail you. The enemy thought he had destroyed My love when Jesus took His last breath on the cross. But My love for you conquered death as Jesus rose from the grave! The enemy doesn't want you to remember this glorious moment when the light of the world rose from the dead and made a way for you to be saved. What the enemy wanted was an end to My love. Every swing of the soldier's hammer drove the nails deeper, but My love was deeper still. My love took your sins to the cross and then buried them deep. Jesus made you clean.

You don't have to go searching for My love, because it already fills your heart and covers your soul. The enemy leads you through the dark alleyways and hidden places of life so you might become disheartened by all the evil in the world. Don't follow him into depression and detachment from the gift of life I've given you. He says you are punished instead of forgiven. Please know that I hold you close and I nurture you. I won't let go. Ever.

Deuteronomy 7:12; 2 Chronicles 6:14; Psalm 36:7

August 16

Precious child,

Remind the world that Jesus still welcomes sinners into His open arms and that He still loves them. The enemy finds joy in getting people wrapped up in judging each other. One day during His earthly ministry, Jesus found Himself surrounded by tax collectors and sinners. The teachers of the law muttered that this was somehow unacceptable, but for Jesus it was love.

Jesus still promises to search for the lost and bring them back to Me. He is also there to bring back those who stray from the path of righteousness. Jesus is the healer who gives you strength in your weakness and healing when you're injured by life's attacks against your self-esteem. He didn't save you to walk alone.

Jesus told a story about a woman who had ten coins and lost one. She stopped everything to seek out the coin. She lit a lamp and swept the house, searching methodically until she finally found it. And it wasn't good enough that she found it, so she invited her friends and family to rejoice with her.

Another parable told of a person who had many sheep. Jesus said even if the shepherd had a hundred sheep, if one were lost the owner would go after it until it was found. And the beautiful thing is that when the lost sheep was found, the owner rejoiced. Not anger and accusation, but rejoicing! And then the lost sheep was carried home. And there was more rejoicing when the owner got home and shared the news with his neighbors. Everyone rejoiced over the gift of salvation that was given.

By the blood of Jesus you who were once lost in your sin were found. You were once deemed unacceptable, but because of Jesus you are now accepted. Use this gift to go tell the world that Jesus still saves!

Ezekiel 34:16; Luke 15:10; John 6:39

August 17

Precious child,

I am the one who clears the paths for you to travel. Don't get distracted by the enemy's lies that you are in charge of forging your own way. Today is here for you to follow Me. My Son made a way for you that took you from the deepest darkness and brought you to Me. Together We go before you to guide you to the places We want you to go. We remove the obstacles and burdens. We open doors. When you arrive you will give Us glory because you will know that We brought you right where you were wanted.

I am the one who makes your love increase and spill over. I formed you. I am your great Creator. I love you so much. I am here to ensure you always know how important you are to Me. I know what your day holds, and I will love you through all of it. When problems stir, I don't remove My love from your heart. When stress rises, that's when I saturate your heart with My compassion so you will know that I haven't abandoned you to the enemy's schemes.

I am the one who strengthens your heart. I made you to depend on Me. When you are weak, I will give strength. King Nebuchadnezzar had ordered a statue built in his likeness and commanded everyone to bow to it. Three men who loved Me more than anything, Shadrach, Meshach, and Abednego, were brought before the king because they wouldn't bow down to the statue. When questioned, they replied that I was strong enough to deliver them from the fire. So the king ordered the furnace to burn seven times hotter than normal. The soldiers who brought the men to the flames perished, but My strength carried Shadrach, Meshach, and Abednego through unscathed.

My child, rely on Me to be your loving guide. In faith, stand up for Me and I will give you strength.

Jeremiah 32:18; Daniel 3:1–29; Hosea 7:15; 1 Thessalonians 3:11–13

Precious child,

Live in Me. Even though you are a part of the world, don't let your heart be divided. I am sovereign, and I am Lord over everything, so remain in Me. Living in Me means surrendering your hopes daily to My perfect will for you. This is where the enemy tries to jump in and distract you with questions. If God is really sovereign, why are you suffering? If God's will is really perfect, why is your life one hardship after another? Why don't you consider forgetting God's plans that include pain and sadness and pursue happiness? The enemy is a liar. He uses doubt to confuse your heart. He mixes lies with things you experience in hopes you'll live in fear instead of in Me.

I made the world. The world didn't make Me. Human hands didn't form Me. Move in Me. I don't need a thing you have, but I want everything you are because I love you more than anything. I made today for us to celebrate our relationship. I made this day for us to be together. I've set up boundaries to protect you. I've given you My Word so that you will always learn about Me. I am not far away. I am with you always.

Be in Me. I alone give you life and the air you breathe. Just like I gave you Jesus, I want you to give your life to spreading His holy name in the world. Remember to take each step in faith because that's how righteous living happens. I promise to live with you and walk with you and never stop being your heavenly Father. Remember how important our relationship is. Remember I am the living God, and your life is part of My temple. There is no room here for division, and there is certainly no room for idols. I alone am worthy of your praise.

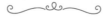

Acts 17:24–28; Romans 1:17; 2 Corinthians 6:16

Precious child,

I am good. Focus on this part of Me today. Whether the hours find you rejoicing or in need, trust Me because I always want what's best for you. As this truth settles in your heart, stay right in the middle of My goodness. The world can't do anything to you there. Tell everyone that you trust Me and will not be afraid. It's okay if you wonder if I'm really with you. It's okay if you question My goodness. I created you, and your heart means everything to Me.

The world is not good. The enemy strives to convince you that evil is good. He directs you to run toward darkness instead of the light. He has trained the world around you to enjoy bitterness. No matter how obvious this is, I want you to remember that you are My child and that I alone am good. Find refuge in Me. I alone am the one who showers you with mercy and grace. Remain in My will for your life because that is where you will walk in the pastures of My goodness. There your heart will feed on the goodness of My truth.

You and I share a love that is good and cannot be broken. The devil covers your eyes so all you see is the darkness. He wants you to linger in hurt and sadness and forget that Jesus is right there with you, holding you close. The enemy whispers there is no way out. He wants you to absorb envy so you will take your eyes off My goodness and keep them on his hypocrisy and shame.

Crave Me and taste that I am good. Hold on to what is good. Hold on to Me, and know that I am never letting go!

Psalm 56:1–4; Isaiah 5:20; Romans 12:9; 1 Peter 2:1–3

August 20

Precious child,

I am the Almighty. Nothing can stand against Me. I am stronger than any battle you face today. I am God over all the nations. I hold power and might in My hands. Give Me your struggle and pain. My power flowed through Jesus and helped Him conquer the devil once and forever. I know there are times when you think your situation is never going to change. But I am still great enough and My power is still strong enough to conquer the enemy today. As he tries to lie his way into your heart, stand strong in faith.

Proclaim My power. Right to the enemy, proclaim your trust in My glory. I will lift your heart above the hurt so you can stand on the solid ground of My promise to never leave you to fight alone. My strength is here for you. Use it to push back the enemy and stand tall in the middle of the battle. Right to the face of adversity, proclaim My power to be the force that will be enough to bring you through. My hands are mighty enough to hold you through every storm.

Remember that power is mine. Let the current struggle give you hope that I am your source. I am your healer. I am the one who loves you abundantly. It was by My will and power that your life was snatched out of the enemy's hands. He had a powerful grip on your heart, but My hands were stronger. At just the right moment, Jesus prayed for you and then endured the cross to save you. His hands were strong enough to be nailed to the beam and still carry every one of your sins. My Spirit was strong enough to help create the world, and He will be powerful enough today to take your hand and lead you through the trial to quiet pastures of My grace.

2 Chronicles 20:6; Psalm 68:34; Daniel 2:20

August 21

Precious child,

I am here to bless you abundantly. You will never have a need I cannot fill. But My blessings are not just to bring you joy. I bless you so you can bless others and excel in doing good deeds for My kingdom. No matter where you are or when it is, call out to Me and I will give you grace. Today, go with Me to places where blessings wait in the weary souls whose hearts cry out for Jesus. Receive My blessings as you share the good news and watch the harvest begin. Don't let the hours discourage you. Don't let the enemy tempt you into thinking that I will never answer your prayers.

When I bless you it is not just to cover you for the moment. My blessings for you last a lifetime. Each time I show you mercy, your heart softens. I am constantly taking care of you and protecting your life from the enemy. He is good at what he does, but Jesus is great at what He did. The devil is sly in convincing you that your situation is never going to change. Jesus, on the other hand, has already changed your life. He became the ultimate sacrifice so you could go from death to life. Because of Jesus, you have been taken from darkness and given eternal life.

Jesus reminds you that your faith brings blessing because you believe even though your eyes haven't seen Him. Even if you don't think your day can have a kingdom impact, I'm reminding you that it will. You are a blessing to so many people, some of whom you will never meet. Just by your choice to run after Jesus, strangers witness grace and glory. I am with you through every minute of this new day, and I will answer every one of your prayers.

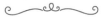

Leviticus 25:21; John 20:29; 2 Corinthians 9:8

Precious child,

You are very important to Me. I know the enemy moves around your life whispering words of defeat just loud enough for you to hear. He wants you to think less of yourself and believe that you are not worthy to be called My child. He will use your mistakes to build a wall between us. But the Holy Spirit lives in you and helps guard your heart and all the gifts I have given you. He leads you to people who need to hear about Me, and He gives you the right words to say. Let My Spirit show you all the places I want you to go to be My witness.

Let My Spirit search you and teach you what you need to know. The Spirit knows My thoughts, and as you study My Word, He explains My heart so you may know Me more. My Spirit is with you to constantly show you all of the treasures you have in Jesus. My Spirit helps you speak about My truth in a way that will reach the hearts of others. My Spirit opens your eyes to see the world the way I see it. Look out and notice all the hungry souls who don't know Jesus the way you do. Look and see the people who don't know Me or all the love I have for them.

The enemy has blinded the world so that they consider My truth to be foolishness. The world cannot understand real love, because the devil has covered their hearts in darkness. Remain in constant prayer for the lost. You will have opportunities to bring My love to them, and when you do I want you to be ready to show them how I've changed your life. Think about what Jesus did for you and have compassion on the world. Be there for them today. Be Jesus so they will see a difference.

I love you!

Acts 1:8; 1 Corinthians 2:10–16; 2 Timothy 1:14

August 23

Precious child,

I have used these letters to speak to your heart. I have written them to give you daily reminders of who I am and who you really are in Me. Spend this new gift of today by serving Jesus. Whether that's being His hands and feet to take care of someone in need or listening to a hurting soul who has no one else, just serve Jesus. Put down your dreams. Just for a moment, let go of the burden you've held close to your heart. Just for now, put down all the thoughts that are causing you to worry and let Me show you what humility looks like.

The enemy is at work in the world. Hard times are here. Severe trials are rising up around you, but I am here to wipe away your tears and bring comfort to your soul. The enemy leaves his mark with hurtful words, but I am teaching you how to live a humble life so you can grow in wisdom. You will see more of Me as you live for Jesus. Each humble step you take in the service of your king will help your heart understand that I am completely trustworthy.

The world learns by the devil's wisdom. It is educated in the ways of darkness. Pride is the world's subject. Don't waste your time thinking about your image or what other people say about you. None of that matters because you know your real worth is in Me. And true humility is found in Jesus. Live today through His gentleness. The devil works to focus you on the stress and trials of life. He wants you living tense and anxious about tomorrow. This is not the way I made you. I carefully formed you to follow Jesus. Let Him be your hope. Imitate His gentleness, and His tenderness will calm your soul.

Proverbs 22:4; Acts 20:19; 2 Corinthians 10:1

August 24

Precious child,

Praise Me today. Bring about goodness with your choices so that others may see a difference in your life. Don't be distracted with thoughts of defeat and weariness. I will give you strength and build up your confidence to worship Me with every part of your being. Don't let the enemy defeat your spirit of giving to the work of My kingdom. When you feel sad, I heal your heart. When you're hurting, I bind up the pain. My will is perfect, and your life is a very important part of it. I have called you by name, and My power is for you.

I am here to sustain you. I have put the clouds in the sky, and I bring the rain. I provide for every living thing. I don't take pleasure in a human's strength, but I find delight in those who fear Me. I am here. Put your hope in My unfailing love. One way to keep your hope in Me is to love others as I love you. Lift My name above all others by the choices you make, and continue to offer up praises through acts of compassion. The enemy can't understand this love. He can't understand what it means to love someone deeply. Love pushes back against his desire to sow darkness and helps people understand that I am love's source.

The enemy sells the world fear and punishment. He doesn't want them to know about My perfect love. Go and help the broken ones find the love of Christ, and then join with them in their songs of thanksgiving. Don't forget that I am with you to bless and strengthen you. I am with you to bring you peace and to provide for all of your needs. I love you and want you to live this new day untethered to fear's wicked grasp. Sing a beautiful song of praise with your life!

Psalm 147:1–14; 1 Peter 4:8; 1 John 4:18

Precious child,

Don't worry about the outcome. Let Me handle that part of life. All I'm asking for today is your heart's praise. Rejoice. Spend your time reflecting on My unfailing love. Remember that I am faithful and I promise to never let you go. I am here to answer every prayer. I am here to answer you every time you call on Me. Don't worry about the things you can't control. Leave those up to Me. Just go about this day proclaiming My name in the world. Shout all of the good things I have done for you.

My glory covers you today. It is great, and you add to it by telling the world about Me. I look on you with favor. I am close to your heart, so even though you are in the middle of a spirit battle, I protect your life. Picture My strong right hand and how I stretch it out before you. I protect you from the enemy. And just as Jesus saved you from death and gave you new life by the power of His work on the cross, today I save you from the world's overwhelming darkness. Don't worry about the things that haven't happened yet. Just cry out to Me and let Me hear everything.

Walk away from the world's wooing by calling on Jesus. Once, Jesus was going about His day sharing the good news of My kingdom and telling the people to repent. Two blind men approached My Son and called to Him in praise. They said, "Have mercy on us, Son of David!" Jesus continued on his way, and the blind men followed hard after Him. Jesus asked them if they truly believed He could restore their sight. Let their reply be today's motto. Say "Yes, Lord" to all that Jesus has in store for you!

Psalm 138:1–7; Joel 1:14; Matthew 9:27–29

August 26

Precious child,

I know so many things compete for your attention. I know your mind can easily wander from My truth if you put your trust in the things of the world. The enemy is there to sell the world to you. He makes the lies look good in hopes you'll begin to pay attention to the offers.

All you need to do is keep your hope in My Word and feel the power of My promises. The world is full of lies, and the enemy is the father of them all. When you feel your thoughts begin to stray, pray. I am there for you. Think about Me and My words. Talk about Me in your conversations with others.

In the world there is only darkness, but the enemy wraps the hurt in attractive covers. Don't get taken in by lies. Peace is found in Me and My words of truth. Read the scriptures over and over and let the descriptions of My character take root in your heart. Let it beat for Me and all that I am for you. Don't just read My words. Hold on to them for life! Let My words build a firm foundation of truth in your spirit.

The devil has spoken lies over you. He has said things like your life is nothing more than hurt and heartache. He tells you that your worth is found in the opinions of other people. He says that My words are just the words of man, written a long time ago and meaningless. But man only wrote down what I first breathed into life. So hold fast to the teachings of My Son. Those are the truths that will set you free from the enemy's lies. Jesus is your one true king because He alone took all your hurt and heartache to the cross. Jesus is worthy of your everything because He alone made you eternally worthy.

Psalm 119:43; Zechariah 8:19; John 8:31–32

August 27

Precious child,

Spend time with Me throughout the day. Even if you are busy at work, mentally sit before Me by resting your thoughts and attending to My voice. Keep yourself in a position of humility by following after Me. As you talk to Me, think about all that I have done for you. Think about the gift of life I've given you and the new life Jesus has allowed you to experience. These are treasures that will never fade or go away. Your salvation is complete. Focus on how far I've brought you. Concentrate on how much I love you.

Come with Me across the hours. Seek My face across the days. You are Mine. Keep yourself free from the things that threaten your humility. The enemy will always find a way to tempt you with his lies. He will always whisper that you should redirect your praise away from Me. But the more time you spend with Me, the more truth pours into your soul. I am with you to heal your hurting heart and bring you rest. Turn away from the things the world wants you to take and run to Me. Live out a humble walk with Me by putting others above yourself.

Pray. Confess. Weep for the things that go against My truth. Throw your life away for the sake of My holy name. Don't worry about what will happen if your current dreams don't come true. I created you, and I have plans for you that will come true. Remain humble by constantly telling Me everything on your heart and mind. Don't hold back your confessions. Seek forgiveness so I can restore your spirit. I want you to cry in front of Me. I will always wipe away every tear. Watch me rebuild your hopes and dreams into a beautiful kingdom desire that will allow you to be a blessing to many.

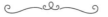

2 Samuel 7:18; 2 Chronicles 7:14; Ezra 10:1

Precious child,

Today I want you to focus on how great and awesome your Savior, Jesus, really is. I want you to think about Him more today than you did yesterday. Taking one step of faith at a time, walk with Me to the place where you desire Jesus more and see your life less. Come with Me and let Me show you how raising up Jesus more will fill your heart with a love unlike anything you could ever imagine. My Son is so much more than a name. He is the name above all names! As you go about your work today, make sure your choices reflect this truth. Make your decisions count. Make more of Jesus by making more time for Him.

Don't worry about what others think. Don't be afraid to stand up and risk your life for Jesus. The enemy doesn't want you to do this. He is ready to list all the reasons why you shouldn't make more of Jesus. He wants you comfortable and guarded so you will have a false sense of security. The devil prefers that you care more about yourself than anything else. He distracts you with lies so you will think My love only pours over you when you avoid mistakes. I have given you the power to stand up for Jesus.

Jesus lost His life for your sake. He did what I'm asking you to do. I want you to look at this day as one big chance to glorify Me by praising Jesus. He is worthy of your time and energy and resources. I am calling you to be alive for Jesus. Jesus rose from the grave to reach out and hold your hand. He rose from the clutches of death to conquer death for you. Jesus has risen so you may also rise and live your life for Him.

John 3:30; Acts 15:26; 2 Corinthians 5:15

August 29

Precious child,

I didn't create you to bear the weight of misery or shoulder the burden of sin. Jesus did that for you and set you free. He became your perfect sacrifice so you could put down your grief and run into His wide-open arms. Jesus made a way for you to draw near and listen to all that He has to teach you. Don't run ahead of Him. Find rest at His feet and listen to His words of truth. Let them nourish your tired soul and stir a renewed desire to listen even more. Lean in and listen to My words so that you may live a real, rich life in Jesus.

The enemy says a million things to you, but they are shallow words that cause fear and shame. At first, he tells you things you want to hear. He uses carefully chosen words to convince you that you are worthy, but these worldly compliments fade. They are blown away on the wind and don't truly express love. I want to remind you that I created you to depend on Me and what I say about you. It doesn't matter what the enemy says. It doesn't matter what the world says to you. The only thing that matters today is your heart staying connected to Jesus.

The world moves fast around you, but I'm calling you not to join in that race but to be quick to listen to Me. When you come to Me in prayer, remember that I know what you need before you ask it. But I need you to really listen to Me speak. Hear My plans for your life. You don't have to struggle to keep up or fit in with the world. I say that even if your heart is heavy, I am here to lift the burdens away. Listen close as I say I love you.

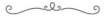

Isaiah 55:2–3; Ezekiel 2:7–8; James 1:19

August 30

Precious child,

Goodness comes from Me. I am here with you. I am forever by your side, keeping My covenant of love with you. I see the hardship that you are in, and I don't turn away. I am great and mighty. I am faithful and more powerful than the hurt. I won't ever walk away from you. I battle for you. I will never tell you I don't care. In My great goodness, hear Me remind you that I will always be faithful to you. No matter if you mess up or forget about My promises, I am there for you. This is who I am. I don't change. Through all your experiences today, I remain true.

When the enemy lurks near to tempt you away from Me, ignore him. When he tells you I'm not good and that I'm too far away to hear your cries for help, don't listen. Rest in Me today and let My great goodness cover you. Through the power of Jesus, let your soul cry out to Me. Come close and stay next to Me all day long. Just stay and find your strength in Me. Even when the enemy says your life is a barren place, I am with you to create springs of hope and mercy. I am the one who blesses your life with every good thing.

I listen to you because I am good. Close your eyes and think about trusting Me with everything. Don't keep one foot in yesterday. Come with Me. The enemy wants you to keep yourself chained to unanswered prayers. He distracts you in fields of confusion so you might forget that I am with you. I am your shield. I don't hold back in blessing you. As we go together, add My goodness to your faith by trusting that I am sincere. I am answering every prayer!

Nehemiah 9:32–35; Psalm 84; 2 Peter 1:5

August 31

Precious child,

Let your life testify that Jesus is your Messiah. Dive deep into the waters of faith and let today be an opportunity, not an obstacle—a chance for you to join the harvest and share the love of Jesus Christ, My Son, with a world in need of hope. Stand up for Jesus in your daily routine. Not that He needs defending, but that you may have a chance to show the world what really matters. Take all the time you need to show others what Jesus has done for you. Be His hands and feet. Show the world who Jesus really is.

Let your life testify that My grace is true. The enemy roams around selling lies to the world about what will bring them happiness. He gets people chasing after things in hopes they'll forget about Me. He wants you to forget that Jesus has already been crowned king! Jesus is alive and well. He is your grace and your Redeemer. Show those who will listen just how mighty Jesus is. Tell them from your heart. The strangers you meet who haven't heard about Me are waiting to be given grace. Serve them and show them My grace is found in Jesus.

I am always here to remind you how special your life is. Remember you were once in a dark place living a life of fear and misery. Jesus reached out His hand and saved you. Let your life testify that I have sent Jesus to be everyone's Savior. Tell them how you once relied on your own power to get by. Tell them you worshipped worldly things that only brought temporary pleasure. Tell them how you thought sin and all its addictions was real living. In humility, remind them that Jesus is now your glorious Savior and by My grace you now walk in His eternal light. The world needs to hear your story!

Acts 18:5; 1 Peter 5:12; 1 John 4:14

September 1

Precious child,

Let Jesus be the beginning of this new day I have given you. Just as He has been with Me from the beginning of time, He is with you now. He is your Alpha and Omega, because Jesus is over everything. Jesus was with Me when I formed you, and He is with you now to form this new day to live with Him. Hear Jesus say that He is making everything new. Today isn't meant to be another yesterday. Today is meant for Jesus to quench your thirsty heart and show you how much He cares for you. By My grace all of this is freely given.

Jesus is there for you to hold on to. He is truth. He gives you victory. Stay with Jesus through the middle hours, even when things seem uneventful and you feel weary. He has promised that you can trust Him with everything you're going through. Think about the fact that Jesus is coming soon and you will see Him! He is your first and your last. Let Him be your first love and first thought. May Jesus be your first hope and your first desire today. May His love for you be the first thing you feel and His teachings be the first words you heed.

Jesus is the end of this new day. He is almighty and will be returning to bring My children home. But for the moment, He holds you all the way through today. When problems arise, remember that Jesus has been with you. When stress comes, remember that Jesus is holding you close. And when the hours stretch out and the enemy tells you that your current struggles will never end, remember that Jesus is the Omega. The burdens are not the end. Jesus is. He is your beginning and your end. This day will not end in strife but in the mighty arms of your Savior, Jesus Christ!

Revelation 1:7–8; 21:5–7; 22:12

Precious child,

I start these letters with the words *precious child* because that's exactly who you are to Me. You are precious, and you are Mine. Let this reality sink into your thoughts today. Let it move you to rejoice and be glad for this new day that I have made. The enemy has lied to you. He has used words like unworthy and failure to describe your heart. Go back and reread all these messages I have written for you. See the thread of holy love that is woven through every one of them. The words are like drops of My heart captured on these pages for you to remember how I love you with an everlasting love.

By the perfect work and sacrifice of Jesus, your life has been redeemed by the precious blood of the Lamb. You are no longer a part of the world. I have adopted you as My child. Even though you still have work to do in the world, I have called you beyond the reach of darkness. Even though you will still feel the effects of sin in the broken world, the enemy cannot defeat you. His lies will not deceive you. No matter what emotions the lies evoke, they cannot undo your position. Hear Me say that you are eternally saved. When the world makes you feel a foot away from failure, Jesus has already made you free.

This is My will for you. It pleases Me to call you My child! Don't ever feel ashamed because of your mistakes. There's a difference between regret and shame. From the beginning of time, I have known you. Let Me be your glorious Father. Let Me teach you the way I have for you. Jesus died for you. He took up the cross and chose all the torture because your life matters. I love you.

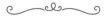

2 Corinthians 6:18; Galatians 4:5; Ephesians 1:5

Precious child,

I have reminded you of your position as My beloved child. I have reminded you of My unfailing love for your wonderful heart. And I have reminded you of the lengths to which Jesus went to redeem your life from the clutches of sin. Today, I want you to take those truths and use them as your encouragement to go and share Jesus with someone. With all of your heart, go and worship Me by speaking the saving name of Jesus. With all your heart, go and bring Me glory by standing up for justice. Be ready when someone asks about Me. Tell them where your hope is found and where your peace comes from.

Live out your faith by walking with Me. In holy fear, come follow Me to a person who desperately needs Jesus. You express your love for Me when you reach out and give love to others. Follow Me with all your heart and soul. Sometimes this means waiting with Me. And while you are waiting for Me, don't let the enemy distract you from your heavenly calling. Don't be tempted to accept a divided heart and put your hope in the world. While you wait, be filled with expectation. Yearn for the plan and promises that I am giving you.

Don't get distracted. I have one plan for you, and it has several parts. I ask you to fear Me by revering My holy name. I call you to walk with Me in humble obedience as you follow Me. Follow Me and everything I am. Serve Me and My kingdom. With all your heart and soul, faithfully follow My will. The enemy will help you forget all the great things I've done for you. But I give you clarity to remember that I am with you always.

Deuteronomy 10:12; Psalm 130:5–6; Ephesians 6:7

September 4

Precious child,

My delight is to show you mercy. Despite what the enemy says, I deliver you from your stress. I want you to be free. Even if there comes an hour when you feel forgotten, remember that I have never left your side. When you are tired and weak, My happiness comes from lifting your head and showering you with strength. You will be successful in your prayer life and in your witness to others about My righteousness. As you go into the world, carry My mercy to everyone. Don't hold on to it. Don't save it just for the people who look and act like you. Give mercy away to the person who needs to know Jesus.

I am here to give you answers when you call. Trust Me in this because the world is ready to distract you. I am here to forgive you. Believe Me, because the enemy is waiting to pull your thoughts away from My love and compassion. My mercy has pardoned you and given you hope. My mercy has a name, and His name is Jesus. Just as My desire raised My only Son from the grave, My desire for your life today is mercy. It has given you new life to set you free from selfishness. Take your freedom and tell the world that there is no one like Me.

I am for you and ready to pour out compassion over your life. Jesus made it possible for you to live this new day unchained. Remember this when the devil lurks around in the shadows of your mistakes shouting out that you are a failure. Remember that Jesus is your inheritance. You are not working for earthly treasure but for things that matter, things of the heart. My arms hold you and My eyes watch you. Spend your time talking to Me and lifting up praise.

Psalm 4:1; Micah 7:18; Luke 10:36–37; 1 Peter 1:3

September 5

Precious child,

I have given you a brand-new life to live in Jesus Christ. Rejoice! This day is a new set of hours to worship your living king with all your heart. Just as I've written that you are a new creation, today is a new opportunity for you to shine bright. Close your eyes and picture your love for Me pouring over the lost like a refreshing shower of hope. The enemy wants you to feel powerless against the selfish wills of men, but you have Jesus, and with Him you will never be a fruitless witness. Let your new praises rise, and let the world hear your story.

This new day is a chance for you to worship Jesus with your entire mind. When the enemy fills your thoughts with darkness, may Jesus be the only one you want. Be filled with sweet memories of Calvary. Think about the road Jesus traveled to find you when you were still lost in sin. His goodness fills you up. Reflect on the new mercies He has waiting for you today. I am giving you a new day to go out in grace and love, to share with the world the good news.

Worship Jesus with all your soul today. May this day come to an end and find you thinking about your wonderful Savior. May you decide to run after Him with all the strength I've given you and hold nothing back. Don't stay where you are because you feel tired. Don't let the enemy talk you into standing still. Look carefully and see the new path I have created for you. Right in the middle of the struggles and pain, I am making a way for you to bring the gospel to those who don't know Jesus. Tell them He is their stream of living water in the wasteland of sin. I am proud of you!

Isaiah 43:19; Acts 5:20; Romans 7:6

Precious child,

Consider forgiveness. This is a crucial piece of your faith walk. As you follow Me, don't let your heart become burdened by the sins of others against you. If you carry the weight of other people's mistakes against you, your spirit will remain weary. This is what the enemy wishes. He whispers that you deserve to be respected by everyone, and when someone mistreats you, whether it's intentional or not, the enemy holds out anger for you to take. But Jesus holds out His love and forgiveness.

As you ask Me to forgive, I am calling you to pray for the ones who have caused you pain. Remember that Jesus took your hardened heart and made it tender, so give away the same forgiveness. This doesn't mean that justice gets sacrificed. I'm on My throne, and I will always be just. Let Me show you what forgiveness looks like. Jesus saw all the sin and darkness but still chose to be born in a manger. Jesus saw all the brokenness and evil but still chose to take on flesh and blood. Jesus saw that you were lost with no way to save yourself but still chose the cross to save you!

Let your mind go back to that day Jesus was crucified as the perfect sacrifice for your sins. Remember when He asked Me to forgive the ones who were putting Him to death. Your life is secure in Me, so you have nothing to fear. As you go out today, focus on forgiveness. Practice becoming more like Jesus by extending forgiveness to those who hurt you. The enemy wants you to think that your value comes from other people showing you respect, but your worth comes from Me. I've called you, and by My Son's blood you've been eternally washed clean. Therefore, go today and forgive.

1 Kings 8:29–30; Matthew 6:14–15; Colossians 3:13

September 7

Precious child,

I am here to guide you. I am leading your heart by My love and wisdom. I know you've had days where you feel far from Me, but remember that I am always with you. Your heart means the world to Me, and I am steadfast in My love for you. Practice listening. Be available to hear My words for your life and the direction I want you to go. Be ready to go where I call you and don't be tempted by the enemy's lies. Don't let his whispers persuade you that staying where you are because it's comfortable is My will.

Don't worry what people think of you because you love Me. I love you, and I will not let you be disgraced by the world's schemes. When the actions of others bear down on your soul, remember that I am in control. Let your heart rest in Me as the daily conflicts swirl around you. I am with you. I am here to instruct you. Don't worry that you can't see the places I'm taking you. Keep going in faith. I am leading you to peace. Keep the eyes of your heart on Me.

Let the truth of My scriptures be more than words. Let them be the fire that warms your heart into holy flames. It's okay if you make mistakes. Your life is a light in the darkness. Just because you mess up doesn't mean your light fades. As you go, continue to praise Me because I am sovereign. Nothing in the world can instruct you. The enemy is trying to guide you, but his plan isn't for your good. He makes it seem good. He says that being comfortable and filled with worldly treasures is true success. You know better. Let Me be the one who teaches you what's best for your soul.

Psalm 16:7; Isaiah 50:7; Luke 1:79

September 8

Precious child,

I am your true God. Integrity and honesty are part of My character, and today I want you to focus on living them out. By My strength, walk today with the highest level of integrity. Always be truthful so the world will know that I am the one you trust. Your actions have consequences, and the most beautiful ones are hearts that turn to Me. I want the world to know you are Mine by the way honesty clings to you like your shadow. Remember you are My witness. Speak truth so that the brokenhearted will hear My song of redemption. Your integrity brings healing to the hurting.

Be the one who stands up for Me. Be the one who is trustworthy. Fear Me and walk away from evil. Strive to make this new day a chance to show the world how to have integrity in the middle of trials. Show them honesty in persecution. People who don't know Me are expecting you to be judgmental. Let them know by your genuine spirit that you honestly want them to know Jesus. The enemy is conspiring to overthrow your desire to follow Me. He is using temptations to lure you off the path I have you on today.

You are able to accomplish all that I have planned for your life by the power of Jesus. By His love you are becoming a person who despises darkness and loves light. When you find yourself feeling lost and alone, I want you to remember that Jesus is your rock. Rest in Him, and the enemy's lies will be washed away. When the world wears you down to sweat and tears, and the heat of affliction stings, know that I am your protection and shield. Nothing can snatch you out from the cover of My wings. Remain true to My will for your life. Even when the day seems difficult, be honest. Tell Me what you feel. Give Me everything.

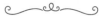

Exodus 18:21; Job 2:3; Proverbs 12:17–19

September 9

Precious child,

I love you. You are My wonderful creation. I have called you and sent Jesus to save you. These are the truths that cannot be undone by the power of evil. Let these words carry your soul. Before you step into the world, remember that I am with you and that nothing will pull your heart out of My hands. The enemy suggests how to best use your time. He would love to see you work yourself out of an intimate relationship with Me. He distracts your spirit with the hope that you will run after sin. Keep your eyes on Me, and remember I forgive you.

The enemy also wants your attention, to make you a servant of your worldly desires. He loves to see you distracted from My words. When I say I love you, the enemy lurks around and says My love must come at a price. He wants you to earn it. He tells you to work for the accomplishment you feel so you won't rely on Me. This isn't the way I made you. You were created for more. Keep your eyes on My Word, and remember that Jesus has covered your sin.

Sin waits for you. Iniquity is down the road, building fences around empty pastures of pride. They are there to lure you in, but I am reminding you of your Savior's power that runs through you and helps you rule over them. Before you go on your way, humble yourself before Me. Start this new day by being transparent and confessing sin. Rid your heart of the burdens you hold there. I will forgive you. I erase the guilt that still lingers. I am blessing you and covering your mistakes. Keep your heart longing for Mine, and remember I never count your sin against you. Jesus has set you free!

Genesis 4:7; Psalm 32:5; Romans 4:7–8

September 10

Precious child,

I encourage you and fill your heart so you will have strength to face the day. I know there are things from yesterday that are still reaching out and trying to pull you back. Pray to Me, and My power will release you from the past. Cry out to Me for mercy and be confident that I hear every word you lift up. Know that I do not get distracted. I give all of Me to you. Use prayer to remain in My presence all day long. Don't believe the enemy that prayer is a one-way street or that it's just you talking. My eyes are on you all day long. I listen. And you will hear Me respond.

I have adopted you, and My name is written on your heart. I hear you. I will never leave you alone or let you cry out to Me in vain. I want you to see your prayers as something very special between us. I know many times you will pray in groups with other believers, and that is good. But keep your quiet time with Me set aside as a top priority. Go to a place where you can be away from the world and all its distractions. Close the door on all the things that beg for your attention, and let your mind cling to Me.

Don't worry about having the right words or how long you should pray. I know what you need before you ask, but your voice lifted to heaven is a sweet sound. It doesn't matter how you pray, just as long as you do, because I never grow tired of hearing from you. So make a habit of praying to Me constantly, on your own in your quiet place and with other believers. Pray to Me and listen as I reply.

2 Chronicles 6:19–21; Matthew 6:5–8; Acts 1:14

September 11

Precious child,

I know what you need. I will never forget you or what you're going through. I haven't brought you this far from the darkness only to forget you or leave you alone. You don't have to rely on anything in the world to bring you relief from the droughts of life. I send the rain to quench the land, and I have given you Jesus, the living water, to quench your soul when you feel overwhelmed. When the enemy says it's time to quit, I say it's time to hope. My offer of hope won't change. Let it be the anchor that steadies you during all of life's trials.

Nothing in the world will be able to bring answers to your prayers, so keep your hope in Me. When the struggles seem bigger than your faith, keep your hope in Me. I am your reason for living. Our relationship is what matters. You will not perish in the daily afflictions that entangle your heart. When you hope in Me, you're resisting temptations and easy fixes. Hope in Me and stand against the enemy's advances. He turns your eyes away from My goodness and mercy. Turn away from his lies. The world doesn't care about you and Me.

Jesus made a way for you to experience the wonders of salvation. Through Him and all He has done for you, keep your hope in My promises. Just as everything seemed lost when they crucified My Son, I raised Jesus from the grave and the enemy was defeated forever. Let your faith be renewed because I am raising your heart and renewing your spirit so you can continue bringing Me glory. When the world walks away, rest in Me. When you feel let down and confused, hope in Me. My love carries you across the sadness and reminds you to depend on Me forever.

Psalm 9:18; Jeremiah 14:22; 1 Peter 1:21

September 12

Precious child,

Today, I want you to put everything down and run to Me. Run to My arms and I will hold you. Don't put Me off until everything gets done or you feel caught up on your work. Every day has plenty of things that will be there for you to do. After you come to Me, feel Me hold you close and tell you that everything is going to be okay. Seek Me first and let Me fill your heart with My love so you can work wholeheartedly for My glory. Run after My righteousness and obey all that I have planned for you. Be about My kingdom purposes only after you have sought out My waiting arms.

Everywhere you go and in everything you do, seek Me first. I promise to take care of you and give you exactly what you need. The enemy works to lure you deep into the world's temptations of pride in hopes that you feel comfortably in control. Put Me first today. Make it a priority to open your Bible and read more about My character and how I take care of all that I've made. See and be reminded how I provide for you. Don't lose faith just because it feels like My provisions have run dry. Don't burden your heart with the simple things.

I know what you need, and I will provide every one of those things. Today, I want to teach you the best way to spend your time and seek Me first. Do not be afraid of what the world might say about you. I am pleased with you, and I want My thoughts about who you really are to be enough! Put down your dreams and desires and run after Me. Give your time to the poor so you can be free to receive an eternal treasure that will never fade away or wear out. Above all, keep your heart in Me.

2 Chronicles 31:21; Matthew 6:33; Luke 12:28–34

Precious child,

Make your whole life about preaching the gospel. From daily decisions to all the work you put your hands to, make everything count for Jesus. Receive your greatest satisfaction from sharing the good news that He died for the sins of the world. Use all of your energy to boast about the cross. Let the message of your Lord's salvation permeate your being. My desire is that you feel incomplete if you don't tell others about Jesus. To make Him known throughout your world is the highest task I've called you to. I am entrusting you with the message of freedom so that you will take it to others.

One way to be effective in spreading the news about Jesus and how He saves is to become a servant to everyone. By going into the world and serving others, you increase your chances of seeing many souls saved. To the people who don't look like you, become like Jesus and spend time with them. Let them know how much Jesus did for them and that He is there waiting to save. To the ones who are weak and don't believe in Jesus, become their servant and take the strong message of grace to them. Let all this be your act of worship to Me.

I want you to share in the blessings of taking the gospel to the broken world. My power will go with you every step of the way because the message you're sending isn't man-made. Jesus Himself is the author of the message, and by His power and wisdom you have received glory. As you share the gospel, don't forget to tell the people about how I saved you from your previous life. Be transparent so they will know that though you were zealous for the things of the world, I saved you by grace. Tell them that it pleased Me to give you Jesus. With My help, dare to tell the world about Him!

1 Corinthians 9:19, Galatians 1:11–15; 1 Thessalonians 2:2–3

September 14

Precious child,

I will help you. Even though you sometimes feel forgotten, I haven't left. I am with you to drive out the negative feelings and remind you how much you mean to Me. Your life is like a sanctuary for My name, and no matter what happens, I am here to save you from all the stressful things that bring your spirit down. Cry out to Me, and I will save you. I always hear you, and I will always have mercy on you. I guide you and bring you relief from the enemy's constant attacks.

Don't listen when the enemy says I've left you alone to fight life's battles. He's the one who is pursuing you to bring harm, but I shed glorious light on the darkness he brings. He crushes your spirit with judgmental words, but I remind you that you are Mine. Think about our relationship and all the things I have done for you. I bring comfort to your parched soul, and I will not hide My face from you. Trust in Me. Let Me continue teaching you how to do My will in a world that tries to keep you from making a difference.

Each morning I declare My unfailing love for you. Each day I show you the way I want you to go. Sometimes you will agree and other times you won't understand, but either way, I am here for you. Hide in Me. Feel Me rescue you. Trust Me. I am here to teach you and make your way straight. Because Jesus saved you, I am preserving your life and rescuing you from your current afflictions. Fear nothing on earth, because Jesus also knows your pain. My child, you are deeply and richly loved.

Deuteronomy 3:22; 2 Chronicles 20:7–9; Psalm 143; Hebrews 2:14–18

September 15

Precious child,

I know you carry many burdens and are worn out and overwhelmed. I understand that at times you get so tired of the daily routine you wonder what My plans are. I don't become unsovereign just because you feel exhausted. In fact, that is when I make My sovereignty most known to you. Your strength and power can only carry you so far before things start to break down. That's the place where the enemy appears to greet you. He is quick to lie about My holy name and tells you that you're on your own and things will never change.

It is by My powerful Spirit that your life is being sanctified. No matter how strong you are, I am stronger still, and it is My strength that lifts you out of your current struggles and carries you across the hours. I am your almighty God, and I am here for you. I don't want to see you sad. Capture this reality and own it: you are eternally saved by My Son's everlasting power, and you are eternally Mine. The devil can't create a scheme wicked enough to snatch you out of My hands. And remember to see trials as opportunities to grow closer to Me and rely on Me more.

Look to Jesus for guidance during hard times. He took on flesh so you could rest assured that He knows what you're going through. And just as I've done for you, I anointed Him with My Spirit and power. Jesus saved people who were lost in the world and under the power of the enemy because I was with Him. The devil points to the calamity and says that nothing will ever change so you will lose hope and quit running the race I've called you to run. But remember, the riches of My goodness have no end, and I use them to strengthen you with My power.

Zechariah 4:6; Acts 10:38; Ephesians 3:16

September 16

Precious child,

Think about who I really am. Think about today as our day to experience together. You are not walking alone, but under the shadow of My wings. Rest in Me as we go together. The enemy would have you fear all the things that remain undone and worry about all the things unseen. Don't fear. I promise that I am here to protect you and lead you. As you follow Me, I give you strength and help you with everything you need to accomplish. I lift you up and encourage you. I am proud of you for who I've made you to be, and I don't see you as a list of mistakes and failures.

As you follow Me today, I am your shield around you. I cover every part of your day so the enemy can't reach you with more lies and temptations. I am your God who cares about everything that's important to you and all of the future things that you haven't seen yet. The world gets lost in the busyness of life because they run after material things. I want you to get lost in Me and My glory. I am always here to answer you when you call to Me. I am the one who sustains you. It doesn't matter what the situation looks like—I don't want you to fear, because I am with you always.

The enemy lures you down the easy path. Every day, he tries to lead you away from the path I am calling you down. He wants you comfortable and chasing conflict-free dreams. Because you are still in the world, there will be conflict and hardship. I want you to feel My presence and My love. Even if you are surrounded by turmoil on all sides, know that I will deliver you. These are the times that I help you trust in Me more and more.

Psalm 3:3–7; Isaiah 41:10; Hebrews 11:24–27

September 17

Precious child,

Don't forget to keep your faith only in Me. I won't let you go or let you down. Take everything that you care about and give it all to Me. I am here to help you press on and keep you from being shaken. Your faith in Me actually heals your spirit from the world's constant attacks on your desire to glorify Me. Keeping your faith in Me helps you go on in peace and frees you from the headaches that come from fearing the unknown. Continue following Me, and trust in My promises to keep you firmly rooted in My love.

Have faith that the hope you have in Jesus will never fade. I love you too much to ever let you down. I made you, and I chose you to do great things for Me. Some of those things I reveal to you, but you bless people in so many ways that you are unaware of. Just continue to serve Me with all your faithful heart and rejoice in the times of suffering, knowing that your life is helping other people come to Jesus. Study My scriptures and let them direct your steps so you can continue to bless others.

The words I have given you in the Bible aren't just ink on paper, written by man. I breathed every one of them into existence so you would have a part of Me to hold. When you feel your faith wavering, open My Word and read My promises, and they will take root in your soul. Let My character remind you that you are eternally safe in Me. Just as I saved My people throughout time, I am here with you to do whatever it takes to help you. I am faithful. I give you My word that I will take you where you need to go and bless you abundantly along the way.

Psalm 55:22; Mark 5:34; Colossians 1:23–28

Precious child,

Jesus is your ultimate blessing. Bigger than the oceans and sky, He helps you and loves you. The enemy hopes you see Jesus as an invisible mystery instead of your intimate Savior. Jesus is your abundant blessing because the salvation He gave you is forever. Current conflicts will end, but Jesus never stops caring for you. He always provides and gives a great supply of extra blessings so you will never want for anything. Even if you don't feel blessed at the moment, your life is being protected and nurtured by Jesus.

I want you to think about the time when Jesus was with a group of five thousand hungry souls. Philip, one of the disciples, said it would cost more than a half year's worth of wages to give each person a meager bite of food, let alone satisfy their hunger. But Jesus knew that He had the power to bless the people in a very unique way. Another disciple, Andrew, found a boy with five small loaves of bread and two small fish. Jesus asked that the people sit down. I want you to see that the first thing My Son did was give thanks for My provision.

Jesus wants you to stop and sit before Him. He wants you to be blessed by His mighty power as He transforms the small things into an overflowing supply of grace. Just as Jesus blessed those who were resting before Him, right now He will bless you abundantly. Just as He fed each person until they were completely satisfied, Jesus is with you right now to do the same. And none of your Savior's blessings ever goes to waste. When the crowd was finished eating, the disciples collected twelve baskets filled with extra bread. Believe Me that this is how Jesus blesses you today. You are important and dearly loved.

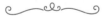

Genesis 49:25; John 6:7–13; 1 Corinthians 9:23

September 19

Precious child,

My love for you has no end. I listen to you because you are Mine. I know the day has enough burdens of its own, but whether you are in a storm of distress or lost in the darkness of night, stretch out your hands and My strength will pull you into My peace. When you can't find comfort from the heat of day, remember Me and My unfailing love for you. I never stop caring about you. I am for you and shower favor over your life. I will never reject you, and I will never forget to show mercy or hold back My grace.

Make today special. Make today all about Jesus. Obey His teachings. He is worthy of all your time because He made it possible for you to receive the gift of eternal life. Before you set off on your way, pray. Dedicate everything you do to Jesus and pay attention. You will feel My love carry you and refresh your weary heart. I made you special in many ways, and you'll discover those ways by obeying Jesus. And the more you learn how unique I made you, the less time you'll spend doubting that My plans for you are perfect.

In Jesus, you have become more than a conqueror. Not only will you be victorious over the enemy's temptations, you will also be built up into a strong leader for My people. Because Jesus is your king and His love fills your heart, people will look to you for help in their own times of affliction. I am blessing you to be a blessing to them in your Savior's sweet and holy name. Don't let this day pass and find you alone and worried. You are more than what you see in the mirror. You have been made new from the inside out. Feel My love fill you forever.

Psalm 77:8; John 14:23; Romans 8:37

September 20

Precious child,

Live like you've been set free, because you have. Let each breath praise Jesus for saving you from your sins. Your heart was once trapped in darkness, but now Jesus has rescued you, and your heart beats with rhythms of love and forgiveness. Your soul was once wrapped in decay, but now it has been saved by My Son who makes it shine with eternal light. I have forgiven all your sins and have restored your body from sin's disease. Let each hour find you rejoicing for this new gift Jesus freely gave you. May My grace flow from every word that forms on your lips.

As you encounter different people today, remember that Jesus redeemed your life from the grave and had mercy on your soul. Have mercy on everyone and let your actions be crowned in grace, just as Jesus covered you with His love and never-ending kindness and care. Run through the hours with arms stretched wide, rejoicing in the knowledge that soon we will be together. Rejoice that Jesus satisfies and that He has renewed your heart with new life. Concentrate on this: Your mistakes were like weights tied around you, holding you down. They were heavy and kept you from running after Me. But Jesus changed all that and has washed you clean. Forever.

When you are sad, remember your new position. Remember that I am wrapping you in justice and righteousness. When you are oppressed, dive into the ocean of My promise to love you and never let go. Don't let the enemy surround you with lies. Don't let him tell you not to keep hoping in Me. Jesus defeated him at the cross, once and for all, so you could receive My compassion and grace. I no longer see you through the veil of all your mistakes. I have filled you with the gift of the Holy Spirit, and as high as heaven is above the earth, so great is My love for you!

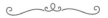

Psalm 103:1–11; Isaiah 1:18; Acts 2:38

September 21

Precious child,

I am your defender! Devote your life to My will. My ways are the treasure you seek every day. Find My will across the pages of the Bible and study every detail. Memorize it. Learn it so you will be prepared to turn and teach the world who their real Savior is. The enemy persuades you to devote your time to your own desires, to run after material things that will insulate you from the everyday struggles between darkness and light, to forget that I've called you to be a strong leader for My kingdom, to put down My Word and live defenseless.

Come to Jesus and give Him all of today. Fall at His feet and worship Him. Cultivate the habit of praying truth over every situation you're in. Like the man covered in leprosy who fell at Jesus' feet and said, "Lord, if you are willing, you can make me clean," dedicate every hour of this new day to the one who knows your soul. Give it all to Him because He is worthy of your praise. Let Him mold your heart and all of its desires so that you can pursue My will all your days. Ask Jesus to clean your heart of selfishness, and follow Me.

Watch and pray for My will. Your heart wants to run after Me, but the enemy lies to keep you from doing so. Jesus understands this conflict. Just before He was arrested, Jesus was in the dark garden with His disciples. Jesus told His friends to stay alert and pray while He retreated some distance to be alone and talk to Me. My Son was anguished by His impending arrest and asked Me for a different plan. But He added, "May Your will be done." Your Savior loves you so much He laid down His heart for you. While the world sleeps, run after Me.

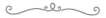

Ezra 7:10; Matthew 26:41–42; Luke 5:12–13

September 22

Precious child,

Use this day to focus on other people. Take your time and give it to someone in need. Concentrate on doing the right thing and defending the defenseless. I want you to live like Jesus lives for you. When you were completely unable to save yourself from the wages of sin, Jesus took your sins to the cross. Take a stand for the one whose voice goes unheard. Take the hand of the one whom everyone passes by. Be like Jesus and be a blessing to those the world has abandoned. Don't worry about what other people say. I am with you through it all, and I am blessing you as you share the love of Christ with the lonely ones.

Don't be afraid to find someone in your path who is hungry for answers and feed them the truth of Jesus! I know that you take care of the beggar and the downtrodden, but don't forget to lead the thirsting souls to the living water. Make eye contact with the stranger who asks for help. Don't worry about what they'll do with your grace. Just be a kind soul and show them My love by treating them with respect and dignity. It's easier to roll up the window and keep driving, but when you stop and let them see you care, their spirit will be turned toward heaven. You will be their reminder that I have not left them.

As you seek out the lost, continue to build others up and let go of your desire for worldly things. Don't allow anything to get in the way of your ministry to the poor. Jesus loves you just the way you are, and I want you to find your true identity in Him. The enemy would trick you into thinking if you build up your own little kingdom, then you'll be content. Rather, experience Me in the simple acts of loving the unwanted and serving them just as your Savior would. Never stop following Me!

Isaiah 1:17; Matthew 25:35–36; Mark 10:21

September 23

Precious child,

My strength encourages your spirit to be brave today. My power strengthens you to stand against the enemy's temptations. My love bolsters your courage to protect My people. I have created you to be unique and to be bold and unafraid when trials come. I am with you no matter where you go. Don't let the enemy discourage you with his feeble attempts to lead your mind away from My good promises. My strength helps you obey My decrees. My arms hold you through it all.

Jesus is your friend, and nothing more has to be done. He finished the work for your heart on Calvary's dark hill. So My power that helps you is an almighty force. I am omnipotent, which means when I open a door for you to walk through and be blessed, no one can shut it. When times change and I close doors for your good, no force, seen or unseen, can open them. You are Mine, and you are forever secure in Me. You don't have to try harder or work longer when you don't see fruit from your labor.

Be strong, because you are not doing life alone. I am with you, directing your steps so you won't doubt that you are in the middle of My will. I am here to give you understanding about the work you're doing today. Stand firm against the enemy by using this knowledge to make decisions that avoid compromising your faith in Me. Don't be afraid. I am here to see you through the pain as well as celebrate the happiness you experience. Receive My discretion so you will have the ability to focus on My glory in all your work. Be strong and courageous, because I am with you.

Joshua 1:9; 1 Chronicles 22:12–13; Revelation 3:7

September 24

Precious child,

Your life has been paid for by the blood of the Lamb. Use your freedom to follow Jesus, because He alone is worthy of all your attention and praise. As He leads you, pay attention to the people around you. Seek out the hurting, and tell them Jesus is their healer. You are no longer chained down to a life of serving sin. You've been set free to follow Jesus and learn how to be a witness to His saving grace. Be like the first disciples, and let go of everything you've been working on and start taking care of the name of Jesus. Start devoting all your time to His holy name.

As you begin to see the beauty in following Jesus at all times, you will notice that you can't hold on to anything. As you live each hour for your king, you have to refuse selfish choices and pursue others. You can't be an effective disciple for My kingdom if you can't come to Me empty-handed. The enemy hopes you'll hang on to pride as you walk with Me, carrying all your dreams in one arm so you'll only have one arm to reach out for Me. But I need both.

The world is full of sounds that compete for your attention. Throughout all the voices and songs of life, listen for Jesus. Don't listen to the ones who say you're not good enough, those who say you're not really forgiven forever, the people who don't know you but are still passing judgment on your heart. Jesus is the one who knows you. He was the one who took your sin-filled heart and washed it clean. He made you new. Live for Jesus and run to Him alone. Resist the world's calling and find everlasting hope in your Savior's voice.

Matthew 4:19; Mark 8:34; John 10:27

September 25

Precious child,

This life will have its share of hard times. You will carry burdens, but you won't bear them alone. As long as you are in the world, the mark of evil will always be evident along the path I have you on. But fear not, because I am with you. The suffering you see and experience is not the end. I use those heavy times to teach you how to persevere and grow strong faith in Me. This perseverance cultivates a trustworthy character in you. And through all of this, I will use these days to build up your hope in Me.

Even though the enemy sells you lies, remember that you are no longer a slave to the world's selfish temptations. You are My child! I am writing you these letters to remind you of your real worth as an heir to all of My promises. Remember back to the day when I was a stranger and your heart had nothing to do with My love. You toiled in dark hopelessness for a meaningless cause. But today, by My grace, I know your name and I call you Mine. Don't let the enemy tempt you into turning back to the world and all of its greed, into putting the chains back on.

I am proud of you for so many reasons, but especially your powerful witness to the world as you remember My commands. No matter what the situation, you endure hardship for My glory. You seek to remain calm and continue to share the gospel by pouring your life out for My sake as an offering of praise. Continue fighting the good fight. I will make sure you have strength to continue longing for Jesus. He is the righteous judge of all hearts, and He has deemed you worthy of the crown of righteousness. I love you.

Romans 5:3–4; Galatians 4:7–9; 2 Timothy 4:5–8

Precious child,

Consider humility—how Jesus humbled Himself as He gave up His throne to become a servant. Right now, push every thought that competes for your attention away and concentrate on these powerful truths. For your heart, My Son left His glorious position in heaven and became a man. For you, Jesus carried His cross to Calvary and suffered its shame. For you, He bore the weight of every single sin (past, present, and future) as your perfect sacrifice. Jesus humbled Himself so you could be forgiven and your heart could be made new. Go today for others as Jesus went for you. Humbly serve My people.

Don't concern yourself with rank and position. Those are what the world runs after. Don't worry about being first. Jesus reminded His disciples that they should focus on being last, servants to everyone. Before you set out to live life this way, humble living that goes against everything the world stands for, remember your identity in Jesus. Remember how much I love you and provide for you. With these truths in hand, go and put the world before you. Serve others and leave the results to Me. When you seek to be last, you resist the enemy's temptation to be selfish.

Lose your life for Jesus. Let go of your preconceptions about what your life should look like. Don't compare the life I've given you with the life of another. You have been rescued from sin! You have been set free! Hear My voice in the middle of the noise and follow Me. Don't worry about material things. Don't hold on to the world or let it hold on to you with its temporary comforts. You don't gain anything by running after worldly treasure. Remain unashamed of Me and My commands. Look forward to the day when Jesus comes again in glory unashamed of you!

Mark 9:33–35; Luke 9:24–26; James 4:10

Precious child,

I want this letter to encourage you and fill every ounce of your spirit with hope. I want you to know who you are in Me. All the way from the beginning I knew you. I lovingly formed you in your mother's womb, and I wrote out all your days long before even one of them came to pass. I did this so you would be conformed to the image of Jesus. And My loving voice called you out of the dark world of sin and into My glorious light. I also justified your heart by deeming you worthy of an eternal inheritance with all the angels and saints. And I promise you that a day is coming when you will partake of My wonderful glory as we meet face-to-face!

Think about those words. Reread the truths that remind you exactly what I have done for you and the soul-restoring treasure that awaits you in heaven. Reread all My words and let your life be lived in humble response to these truths. Since I have done all of this for you, be confident that I am for you, forever, and nothing will be able to stand against you. The burdens of today are overshadowed by My love for you. Rest in My promise that I have filled you with My presence. I have filled you with Jesus and My Holy Spirit. The enemy can't say or do anything that will break the bond we share.

Let this powerful message renew your hope. Continue following Me by being like Jesus. Your salvation is eternally secure, so My joy carries you through today. Remember that you are special to Me. Continue to pour out My love from your life over the broken world. Let everyone see your beautiful faith. I love you.

Romans 8:29–31; 1 Thessalonians 1:4–8; 1 Peter 1:2

September 28

Precious child,

Live for Jesus. Decide that every moment of this day will be all for Him. Jesus did this same thing for you! He left His throne in heaven and decided He would give His all for you. I want to remind you that your worth is not found in other people and their opinions of you. Find your worth in Me. I am giving you today so you can find out more of who I am and how much I've done for you. Let Jesus show you more of My heart as you follow His teaching across each hour. You belong to Him, and it is by grace that you are free to live this new day for His praise.

Work for Jesus. My Son labored to bear fruit for My kingdom. It doesn't matter what position you hold or where you live. Do everything as if you were doing it for Him, because you are no longer serving the world. Today you are serving Jesus. Go about doing things that will bear eternal fruit. The work My Son did took Him to people and places that needed help. Whatever you do today, put all your heart into it because you are working for Me and not man. I am here with you and will give you anything you need to get the job done.

Give up your life for Jesus. When you live and work for Jesus, you naturally begin to sacrifice your own desires for Him. Give up your time to pray for others who are hurting and have no idea they need Jesus. Pray for them, My child. As you give up your life for others, love them. Give up your time to talk with people and care for their needs. The enemy will stress you out about doing things that don't line up with your personal goals. But I'm calling you to feel satisfied by putting others first and using the talents I gave you to shine for My glory.

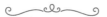

John 15:16–17; Romans 14:8; Colossians 3:23–24

September 29

Precious child,

Your old life has been buried, and your new life has been raised with Jesus. You are alive with Him. You breathe and move with Him. He is your everything. The enemy has been defeated and cannot gain victory over Jesus. Even though the world may try to bury the name of My Son, He cannot die a second time. Death has no strength over Him anymore. Jesus died and conquered the grave once and for all. Jesus lives, and it is all for My glory. I am giving you this new day to live the same way. Have nothing to do with sin, and live a life for My glory by remaining fully in Jesus.

Don't allow sin to reign in your life or give any part of your life to sin, but offer all of you to Me, because by grace alone I have brought you from death to life. Commit this day to being an instrument of righteousness for My glory so the world may see Jesus. Sin is not your master anymore. The enemy will convince you that you are still under the law by tempting you to work harder. He will entice you to believe that My grace somehow involves your hard work. He doesn't want you to experience the freedom of life lived under grace but rather to live in misery.

It is by My grace that Jesus saved you. Even though He was richly blessed, He became poor for you so that you would inherit eternal grace. It is by My grace that you have been completely healed, carried over from the darkness of sin to a place of radiant light. Today, My grace goes with you, empowering you to give your life to Me through the choices you make. Use this new day to practice the art of giving grace away just as Jesus freely gave it to you.

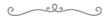

Romans 6:8–15; 1 Corinthians 15:10; 2 Corinthians 8:5–9

Precious child,

No bad day is strong enough to push Jesus away from your heart. He is your mighty Savior who fought death for you. No harsh word is bitter enough to keep Jesus from renewing your soul. He is your loving king who has spoken My truth over you so you will always know your worth in Him. No army is strong enough to protect you the way Jesus protects your spirit, because He is all-powerful and everlasting. No sickness can drain your hope, because Jesus restores you every hour of every day by His healing hands.

The enemy wants you to feel unloved and unwanted, to live each day overwhelmed with a sadness born from fear. He distracts you with temporary burdens and lies about My character. But the truth is nothing in the world, seen or unseen, can break the bond of love that Jesus holds you with. Nothing! When trouble comes, don't believe the lie that you are not as worthy as another, that you are not as close to Me as another. And please don't listen when the enemy lies about how closely Jesus guards your life.

Hard days don't last forever, but your holy Lord does! Even though the hours stretch far and your spirit thin, rest in Jesus. Even if your heart is persecuted by daily strife, put your hope in Jesus. Even when your spirit is hungry for attention, know that Jesus is with you to lift your eyes to see His precious face and to satisfy you. If you ever feel that you are standing alone for My sake with the eyes of the world on you, understand that Jesus has already clothed you in righteousness. No danger or weapon can isolate you from Jesus. You are forever loved and protected, so don't fear, because in Jesus you've already overcome the evil one!

Matthew 28:20; Romans 8:35

October 1

Precious child,

I've made this new day for you to rely on My strength and seek My face. Follow Me and remember all the good things I have done for you. I have chosen you, and you are Mine. I won't forget My covenant of love and My promise that your inheritance is heaven. See yourself as a stranger in the world. I have you there to proclaim My glory and the gospel message of Jesus, but don't forget that the world is not your home. I will not let the enemy oppress you or hinder your kingdom work for My sake. By the blood of Jesus, you have been made holy.

Nothing the enemy can say will change your position. I've made this day for you to sing a salvation song of glory. Shout and proclaim My glory to the world. Don't pass the day without sharing My love with another. May your life sing a song so beautiful in the choices you make and the words you speak that the world will fear Me and praise Me. Everything the enemy holds out for the world to chase is a mere idol. I am the Creator, and strength and joy are found in Me alone. I have made today special and set apart from all other days so you can have a chance to rejoice and be glad in Me.

Don't look at this new day as another round of burdens. Don't see it as another set of obstacles that you cannot overcome. Just readjust your eyes and see today as an opportunity to fall deeper into My love. Worship Me. I have rooted your new life in Jesus. Let the world know that your happiness comes from Him and nothing else. As you go about your day, follow Me and I will bless you and deliver you from wickedness. Rejoice that I have called you My child. Live a thankful life. I am good, and My love for you lasts forever.

Deuteronomy 12:11–12; 1 Chronicles 16:11–33; Psalm 118:23–29

Precious child,

I am worthy of all your praise. I am your mighty God who made you and saved you. Lift your voice and vows to Me alone and wait expectantly for Me to answer you. I hear your prayers, and I will reply. When sin was a storm that surrounded you, Jesus calmed your soul and saved it. Because of Him, sin no longer has the power to overwhelm you. Remember, you haven't been forgiven once, but once forever. I have chosen to bless you and draw you near. I am filling your life with My goodness, and I will show you awesome things. I am your eternal hope.

People will see your awe of Me, hear you praise Me, and will know I am your God. I am more powerful than any problem you will face, and I am stronger than any temptation the enemy will try to put in your path. My voice calms the raging oceans, and it will calm your racing heart when struggles come. No turmoil can overtake you, because no turmoil can overtake Me. I care for you, and I am here for you. I bless abundantly, and I am enriching your soul. I am your eternal love.

Let every thought you consider pale in comparison to the knowledge that Jesus died to pay your debt—a debt that you never could have repaid no matter how hard you tried! The same is true for the battles you face today. Because I am with you, the rivers of life will not sweep you away. Because I am with you, the winds of uncertainty will not blow you off the course I have you on. Because I am your God, I have ordained blessings for you that will provide all you need. Worship Me by caring for others and blessing those in need. I am your eternal Father who will never abandon you.

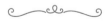

Psalm 65

October 3

Precious child,

You are Mine. As your holy Father, I pour out My great love for you, and I am your rock during the days of struggle. I am raising you to be disciplined to follow Me through every storm and every trial. Don't lose hope. Keep a strong grip of faith wrapped around My promise to never leave you stranded. I am guiding you like a father leads his child. My love for you never stops, so don't become overburdened by your guilt. Jesus has released you from your past so you can live today free to be loved by your king.

Don't waste time finding your worth in the world. Don't look for approval from the world. Since you have Jesus in your heart, you are a stranger to them. They don't know Me, and since you are My child, they don't know you either. Wait on My answers for your life. I know you have pain, and sometimes all your efforts end in failure. But the enemy cannot take you away from Me. Tear down the walls of doubt by confessing your mistakes. I am proud of you. I have gone before you to make your paths straight. You are My child, and I love you.

Put your hope in the fact that Jesus is returning, and when He does you will see Him face-to-face. Don't stop seeking what is good. May every hour find you looking forward to that day when all your wounds are healed. Eagerly await that moment when your heart will no longer ache and your spirit no longer feel crushed by the world's burdens. There won't be any more evil and accusations. No more hate or misunderstandings. And as we journey toward that glorious moment together, remember that I will never forsake you!

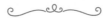

Psalm 38:15–22; Hosea 1:10; Hebrews 12:7; 1 John 3:1–2

October 4

Precious child,

Be thankful. Let the words that come from your lips be filled with thanks for My holy name and everything I've done for you. Let your choices and thoughts be reflections of the joy you find in Me. Spend this new day I've given you being thankful for who I am. Let your life be a song of praise. Lift it high above the droning sounds of the world's complaints, so that they may hear you proclaim I am your God. I made you, and you are forever Mine. Rejoice because nothing in the world and no scheme of the enemy can change your position as My child.

Be grateful that you can live your life in the safety of My pasture. Jesus is your loving shepherd, and He has set you free to worship Him all day long. Make time to raise your hands to the sky and open your eyes to see My glory shine over you. Let your actions show the dying world what a thankful heart looks like. Don't let the enemy tempt you into focusing on the struggle. I'm calling you to focus on Jesus. Where the world sees despair, I am opening your eyes to opportunity. Where the world sees suffering, I want you to see hope. Go in thanksgiving, praising Him who gave you unending grace.

Show the world why Jesus made you thankful. Let the world know who your king is and hear you praise Him. Bring your thankful heart into the world and proclaim that Jesus is alive and still saves! Make time to be in My Word and be thankful for My commands. By your thankful soul the world will know that My love does go on forever and that My faithfulness has no end. Focus on your worth in Me. Let Me take away the fear and replace it with mercy. I am thankful I made you!

1 Chronicles 29:13; 2 Chronicles 5:13; Psalm 100; Revelation 7:12

October 5

Precious child,

Make time for Me. Our relationship is the only thing that counts. Long for our time together. Pursue our bond more than anything because it's of greater value than everything else. Think of My words and promises like invisible rays of the sun pouring over you to warm your soul. Thirst for the water of My love. Stop to consider My character. Think about how My truth allows you to never doubt Me. I am your living God who is right there with you. Whether joy surrounds you or tears come from the pain of brokenness, desire Me above everything. Long for My direction and voice.

I am always here to listen. Tell Me anything. When the enemy says I am far away, smile and know that I am watching over you. When you rise and when you sleep I protect your life. Long for every minute we walk together. Love every chance you get to follow Me. Look up at the sky and find My creation astounding. Pour out your soul to Me and remember that I made you. I know exactly what you feel. Stay with Me. Find Me in every moment. My power. My love. My forgiveness. My compassion and understanding.

I am not ashamed of you, and I never will be. The enemy deals in shame and is a skilled liar. He will tell you what you want to hear. He gives you suggestions about the way he thinks you should live. Resist this ploy to drag your heart down. In the darkness or in the light, I hold you and provide. In all things, run after Me and practice being still and feeling My presence cover you. Think about Me and My words. Take My commands to heart and find meaning in them. Look to Me all day long and let My love be what matters. Long for My heart. Move everything to the side and come to Me. There is true rest here.

Job 29:1–3; Psalm 42:1–4; Hebrews 11:16

October 6

Precious child,

Live each moment from the perspective of mercy. Take each step and make each decision in grace. Strive to do good to everyone. Don't withhold My mercy and goodness from the people who treat you badly. I know this is difficult to understand, but remember that I am molding you to be more like Jesus. Don't be fooled into imitating the enemy's evil ways. Spend this new day practicing what is good. You are from Me. Rely on My strength to continue living each day with a compassionate heart. Give away mercy to those who can't repay you, because that's exactly what Jesus did for you.

Live each hour from the perspective of grace. Concentrate on doing the right thing in all situations. Your good deeds don't go unnoticed. I am proud of you because you make Me your priority. Think about the goodness that Jesus showers over you. Collect it in buckets of compassion and carry them to the people you'll meet today. Pour the goodness of Jesus over them to water their parched spirits. Part of My character is goodness. From the way I meet your needs to the way I love your heart, goodness always characterizes Me and My plans for your life.

Let each second count for My glory. Stand up for My name and be strong. Spread My hope across the path you travel today and be an encouragement to other believers. Be different from the world by loving more than just those who love you. Do good for more than just those who are good to you. Give your life without expecting anything in return. You don't need to worry about being repaid, because Jesus paid your debt in full. Take care of people and forgive them when they hurt you. Be good to them and give mercy to the ungrateful. Do this so they will see that you are My beloved child.

Deuteronomy 6:18; 2 Samuel 10:12; Luke 6:32–36; 3 John 1:11

October 7

Precious child,

Commit this new day I've given you to telling people about Jesus. Tell them He is the only gate. Through Him alone they will be saved; no other way leads to Me except through My Son. In Jesus, they will find the freedom they've been searching for. Remind them that there aren't many ways back to Me but only one way—and His name is Jesus. I have created you to be intentional. I encourage your heart when you are disappointed. Even though it may seem that no one wants to hear what you have to say about Jesus, say it anyway.

Be the one who isn't ashamed to tell the world that Jesus is their only mediator. He alone is their Savior. The enemy has paved many roads with temptations. He has sold the lie that if they are good, then whatever path they're on will lead back to Me. This lie is devastating because the ones who buy into it are walking blindly. The enemy wants you to be quiet so the lost won't realize the path they're on is the wrong one. He fears what will happen and the glorious impact you'll have if you take a stand for Jesus. You have My word that I am with you always.

Some people will refuse to listen to your message of hope, but don't let that discourage you from your calling. Continue to boldly share the sweet name of Jesus. Tell the world to believe in Him by leading them back to the cross. The enemy will be there to talk you out of this, but in Me you have the power to ignore his evil plans. In Me you are strong enough to turn your back on him and continue to bring Me glory. Remember to continue speaking truth. And when they trust in His mighty name, baptize them. What a glorious picture of obedience you will make.

John 10:9; Acts 19:4–9; 1 Timothy 2:5

October 8

Precious child,

Rely on Me all day long. I created you for this. Spend your time praising My holy name. Live today for Me and be a sign that I am your strong, almighty God. The world needs Jesus, but they are too busy racing after the next prize. No matter who you talk to, let all of your words be filled with My praises. No matter what job you undertake, let all of your actions declare My glory so others have a chance to stop and consider My love. The enemy has filled the world with massive distractions to keep people focused on material possessions. He is good at keeping their eyes turned down, away from Me.

I won't leave you when you are weak. I will save you from the hand of darkness and hold you close when it feels like the world is out to take you down into hopelessness. Don't listen to the enemy's lie that says you're on your own. Resist him by proclaiming My righteousness. Let the world hear your voice ring out the sounds of freedom. I am with you, and I am quick to help you when you're in need. No one can harm you. The world is dying, but you have been made new and given the inheritance of heaven.

Hope in Me and express that hope by remaining in My commands. I am not far from you. I am always quick to help you. I know it doesn't always seem like this is true. I know you feel like you've prayed the same words over and over, for days and days, but nothing changes and you begin to wonder. I have not left you in these times. Never stop having hope. Praise Me and wait on Me. I am answering you, and I will never forsake you. My righteousness reaches from heaven to earth. I will comfort you and wipe away every tear because I love you.

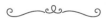

Psalm 71:6–23

October 9

Precious child,

My light shines for you. Even though the world surrounds you with darkness, continue to show mercy. I am making you a mighty witness for Jesus as you continue to find ways to give grace. I am keeping your heart steadfast so it will continue to beat for Me. You will be successful in all the things I'm calling you to do. Let this free you to give generously to the poor and be kind to those who are dying for a kind word. Trust Me more today. I am here to give you unending grace.

Even though the enemy would confuse you and make you question My plans for your life, continue to give compassion. Give away all that you think you should hold on to and watch how I will take care of you. My hands hold you close and will never let go. Just keep your eyes on Me and follow My lead. You know My voice. Listen, and don't be afraid to go where I tell you to go. Listen, and don't be afraid to share the gospel with the people I call you to share it with. Give your time to those whom other people ignore. My heart is for everyone, and I want yours to be the same.

Continue to live by My righteousness. In these days when you see so many people, even some who are closest to you, make decisions that lack integrity, it's tempting to follow their example. But that isn't who I made you to be. Continue to find happiness and contentment in My words. Don't run after the world's treasure. Use My justice to stand up for those who can't defend themselves. I will not let anything shake you. Struggles cannot overwhelm you because I am bigger than the struggles. Let My love for you move the mountains that life has put in your path.

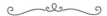

Ezra 8:22; Psalm 112:1–9; Romans 8:32

October 10

Precious child,

Please take these words to heart and let your spirit be renewed. Jesus defeated death for you! He rose after three days so you could also rise in Him from death to life. He allowed Himself to become your perfect sacrifice so that you could be fully forgiven and restored. He has given you new life and freedom from sin's deadly grip. Let Jesus turn your heart away from fear, and rejoice that He is able and has redeemed your soul! Praise Him because He is your blessed Savior. Praise Him because He is alive to love and teach you. Look to Jesus, not only as your friend who will never leave your side, but also as your righteous Messiah.

Don't give way to the enemy and focus on life's problems. I want you to spend this day focusing on Jesus Christ, the glorious one who paid all of your debt. Focus on His mighty name. See Him for the warrior He is, and know that He goes before you to fight the battles of life. He always keeps you from falling. His radiant light guides each one of your steps. Remember, when they buried Jesus, your sins went to the grave with Him. You are not one mistake after another but My child. Get lost in Jesus, and He will fill your heart with His beautiful love.

Jesus rose and is alive and well. He is there for you, and just as people saw Him right after the resurrection, I want you to see Jesus today in the faces of the people you minister to. Dive into My Word and find comfort that I breathed your entire Bible into existence. Read and soak in every way Jesus loved people. He is returning soon, and you will see Him in all His majesty. Share His love today and celebrate Jesus in everything you do. He is for you, My child.

Luke 24:7; Acts 17:3; 1 Corinthians 15:3–6; 2 Peter 1:16–17

Precious child,

In the middle of the storms and the confusion, remain in Me. I am your eternal God who formed you in your mother's womb and called you as My own. There are no other gods besides Me. None came before and none will come after Me. Nothing in the world saves you from the temptations and heartaches like I do. Today, I want these truths to sink in and take hold of your heart in a way like they never have before. I am God. You are safe in My hands, and no person or scheme of the devil can deliver you out of them. When I bless you, the enemy cannot undo the blessing. You are Mine.

Use this new day to be My witness. I have chosen you to know Me and have a relationship with Me through My Son, Jesus. Remain in Me. The enemy would separate us, because he knows that if you live your life apart from Me, you will wither. Jesus reminded people that those who remain in Him would bear much fruit for My glory. The love I have for My Son is also poured out on you. Keep your life in Me. Let My strength keep you from getting tired. I am proud of your heart that strives to bring Me glory, even in the hard times.

I write to remind you of those first hours when Jesus became your Savior. Remember how your thankful heart rejoiced at just the sound of His holy name. I know the enemy is relentless in his effort to distract you from My grace. He wants you to forget about all that Jesus did to rescue you. Fear nothing, because I am your merciful God who is able to protect you. Jesus is the only one who died for you. Whether you are in the middle of suffering or bound by pain, be faithful to My calling and know that I never stop loving you.

Isaiah 43:10–13; John 15:6–9; Revelation 2:3–13

October 12

Precious child,

Treasure our relationship. Think about our time together and cherish it more than anything else. When the world wears you down, I give you strength. When people say hurtful things about you, I whisper that you are a child of the king! When your day is one hardship after another and it doesn't seem like bad things will ever stop happening, take a deep breath and know that I am your mighty God and I am with you. I care about you so much that nothing the world sends your way can break the bond you and I share.

I want you to be reminded of how much I love and treasure you. Jesus told his friends the story about the lost son because He wanted them to glimpse My heart for My children. The enemy would talk you out of spending intimate time with Me. He doesn't want you reading your Bible or memorizing scripture. The devil doesn't want you sitting quietly listening to My voice, and he definitely doesn't want you following Me. He wants you to wander down your own paths and get lost. But even if you lose your way, I am always here to welcome you into My arms.

The enemy wants your sins to be your undoing, but Jesus forgives your sins. When you make a mistake, repent and maintain your humble heart. The enemy says to treasure the world and forget about Me. But he is skilled at hiding when trouble comes. When you find yourself in need, the enemy will be long gone. But not so with Me, because I am always here to receive you in grace. If you should ever lose your way, return to Me and know that I am here to help you stand again. I won't judge you, because you have already been declared forgiven. I love you!

Hosea 14:1–3; Luke 15:11–24

October 13

Precious child,

I am your rock, your strength, your safe place in the middle of life's storms. I am your fortress to protect you from the enemy's advances. I am your deliverer to pull you from the fray. I am here for you to be your refuge and your shield. I am strong enough to break the chains of destruction that the enemy wraps around you. Praise Me in the middle of it all because I am worthy. I never take My eyes off you. I am here, and I hear your voice. Let your love for Me grow, and rely on Me every hour. Through all of today, I will be your source of hope because I care about your heart.

Trust in Me. Don't draw your protection from man. The world and everything in it isn't strong enough to save you. Keep your eyes and heart on Me. Don't let the enemy distract you into turning away. I know the world. It doesn't care about you, because it's filled with broken, hurting people who are trying to find meaning and strength in everything their eyes can see. The enemy lies to them, convincing them that human flesh can somehow be made strong enough to solve any problem and take on any battle.

Listen for My voice. Wait for Me to tell you when to move and when to wait. I will take hold of you and guide you. I am mighty enough to pull you out of life's deep waters and rescue you from enemies of the mind that are too strong for you to conquer on your own. I am your ever-present God who supports you. Find your strength in Me by repenting and resting in My grace. Rest in Me, and feel My power and mercy fill your life. In our quiet times, I remind you that I will never leave you alone to fight life's battles. I am your mighty God who cares. Nothing can stand against Me.

Psalm 18:1–18; Isaiah 30:15; Jeremiah 17:5

Precious child,

I am proud of how hard you work at keeping our relationship your top priority. Ignore the enemy when he attempts to sell you a lifestyle that doesn't include our quiet time. Continue living your life worshipping My holy name. Honor Me by living a holy life. By the power that Jesus has given you, rise above the world's anger and be a witness of My grace. Let the world know that Jesus is your king and I am your Father. Let them know that I have sent you to be a bearer of My love and mercy. Your love for Me is evident in the way you talk and the way you treat other people.

It is My desire that you be sanctified. I made you to reflect My glory. The world gives images of selfishness and pride. They don't know Me. That's why I'm calling you to reflect My honor and holiness. Above everything else, make this your passion. I have called you to be hopeful and to look forward to the day when Jesus returns in glory. And if you ever feel sad or lonely, please keep your hope in My grace.

Your life is wrapped in My truth, and I have given you the Holy Spirit to help you live a pure and blameless life. Love each other. Don't become someone else. I made you special, so you don't have to conform to the world's standards. Simply live your life in obedience to My commands by being holy in every aspect of your day. What your eyes see of the world you live in does not define you. You are My child, saved by My grace and the blood of My perfect Son, Jesus. Because of this truth, I want you to see yourself as a foreigner living in a foreign land. Your home is in heaven. You have been redeemed, not by things that fade away, but by the precious blood of Jesus. Rejoice!

1 Thessalonians 4:1–10; 1 Peter 1:13–19; 2 Peter 3:11

Precious child,

I know you walk in dark valleys. You feel helpless and alone. I know that even though My promises for you are real, the enemy seems closer to your heart than I am. Even though My Son is shining over your world, your heart bears burdens that are too heavy for one soul to carry. In Jesus I have raised you to a new life. In Him, death has been conquered, so please give Me this day. I showed My prophet Ezekiel a dark valley of dry bones and asked if they could live again. He said, "Sovereign LORD, you alone know."

Abandon your desire to have all the answers and to walk only in safe places. The valleys feel hopeless because the enemy convinces you that I am far away. Just cry out to Me and let your lips acknowledge My sovereignty. Let your heart sing that I alone know exactly where you are and exactly what you're going through. And just as Ezekiel asked that I would put breath in the bones, I am here to breathe life into your weariness. In all this, you will know that I am the one who blesses you.

Where My breath enters, new life is born. When you feel cut off and hopeless, call out to Me, and I will breathe new life into your day. The darkness is not where I want you to be. The enemy looks for ways to trick you into thinking that the days will never get better. He hopes you will close your eyes in defeat and believe that there is no way out. He wants you to feel unloved and defeated. But be confident that I will give you peace. I am mighty, and I love your heart. Today, you will rise renewed and walk out of the valley, hopeful and filled with My strength.

Genesis 2:7; Ezekiel 37:1–14; Romans 6:4

October 16

Precious child,

As I lovingly knit you in your mother's womb, I thought about all the amazing ways I would make you special. I thought about all the people you would bless and all the places you would reach for My glory. Your life isn't random. It isn't a chance collection of flesh and bone. You are created from My breath. I intentionally made your heart wonderful. May that truth encourage you today.

When I created you, I spoke light into your beautiful eyes and smiled at how they reflect a heavenly radiance. As My sweet treasure, you are more brilliant than the sun, moon, and stars. Your light was made to burn brighter and stronger because you are My beacon of hope in a broken world.

Then I considered the next part of you. I whispered strength and courage into your heart, knowing that as you grew, your love for all My people would stretch as far as all the lands I created. I quietly spoke bravery as powerful and wide as the oceans into your soul, so that you can weather life's storms and stand up for truth when no one else will.

And just as I made the seed-bearing plants and fruit-bearing trees, precious child, so also in you have I created the same desire to bear seeds of My holy name. The world is a barren landscape, covered in dust that blows under the direction of the wind. Plant the seeds in the lives of people, water them with My Word, and harvest kingdom fruit that will last forever.

Child, most of all, I created you in My image. In My likeness, I made you. Jesus went to the cross for you, and now that He is your king and Savior, you have been made clean. You have been redeemed. No matter what the world says, and no matter what you think you see in the mirror, I see a beautiful you!

Genesis 1:27; Deuteronomy 31:6; John 1:5, 7

Precious child,

I have breathed into you My breath of life. You are alive because of Me. I am in you and with you always. The world will try to breathe into you too. Not life, but lies.

Please don't worry, child, because I am always with you. I comfort you. I find you when you feel trapped in the lonely places. I listen to your soft voice. I hear your sweet heart beat in rhythm with Mine and think about you every minute of every one of the days I ordained for you. When you call out to Me, I listen. You are not a burden to Me. Your prayers are meaningful. They are the sound of My faithful servant relying on My holy name.

I created you different from anyone else. Don't compare yourself to others. You are covered in My grace and mercy. Don't receive your self-worth from the thoughts and feelings of others. Those change like the wind, but I am constant. I remain the same. Please call on Me. The enemy would keep you silent, feeling alone and abandoned. But with Me, it's different. I can't wait to hear the sound of your voice. When you pray, I hear every cry and every praise. I have blessed you. You are Mine.

Walk with Me, child. In days of sunlight, feel the warmth of My love wash over you. In the storm, watch as I set a rainbow in the clouds to remind you of My presence. Lift up your eyes and see My hands outstretched to hold you. I am your shield, your great reward. I keep My promises, and you are worth more to Me than you can ever imagine. My love for you is greater than anything you can ever comprehend. Rest in Me and let go of the enemy's lies.

Genesis 9:13; 15:1; Isaiah 43:1

October 18

Precious child,

As I hold you in this moment and consider how wonderful I made you, know how much I cherish your heart. Today you are justified by My grace. You are free to be part of the kingdom work I am calling you to, a humble leader of My people by using your talents to love and serve the less fortunate.

If an hour should come when you are tempted to believe that your life doesn't matter, grab hold of Me. I am almighty and I love you. I am your sovereign Father and formed you so full of life and purpose that I never want you to doubt. Dear child, you are worth the world to Me, and I prove this by showering you with My constant grace.

Do not worry. I will remove any obstacle that keeps you from believing how much your life matters. Nothing is too hard for Me. I have chosen you to do what is right and just, and I am with you always in everything you do. I don't want you to feel inadequate or unqualified. You are the perfect person for the work I have for you.

Be free in Me. Don't withhold anything. Tell Me your heart, and let go of your fears and struggles. Tell Me all. Never think that you are beyond My grace and mercy. I will never abandon you. The enemy says you are enslaved to your mistakes, but this deception is meant to convince you that you aren't good enough for grace. Don't listen to him.

My precious one, I am always faithful, and My heart is filled with joy when I think about how proud I am of you. Jesus made all of this possible, so boldly testify to His resurrection from the dead. As you go, My grace will be powerfully at work in you. Just as the blood of Jesus erased your sins, so My grace erases need.

Genesis 18:14; Jeremiah 32:17; Acts 4:33; Romans 3:24

Precious child,

I am here. I am close to you.

Just as I see all the plans I have for you, I also see your hardships and the toil of your hands. I answer you in moments of distress and go with you wherever you go. I won't let anything harm you. When you are burdened by days of pain and the weight of the world pushes hard against your soul, close your eyes and I'll lift it all off your tired shoulders.

Never forget, My created one, I watch over you. I am your witness. Don't be ashamed. I give you all you need. I long to bless you and see you prosper. My blessings richly cover both you and the fruit of your harvest. Don't stay where you are just because you don't think you can make a difference. You are stronger than you know.

I hold your heart and feel its treasured beat. Your love for Me will lead many others to my grace. To save lives by sharing My good news is why I've sent you, sweet child. Fix your mind on this truth. So as you go, speak with grace. The world will hear a different message from your lips and see that your heart is pure, and they will listen. Then you will be able to plant seeds of truth in a land that once was barren, and because of your faithfulness it shall become a land of harvest.

I will make you fruitful in the land of suffering. I will grant you mercy before others. Sweet one, you can face any challenge because I have you safe in My arms. I can do everything, and I will protect you as you live out your gift of days. I am your treasure, My child, and you are Mine, because I love you more than anything.

Deuteronomy 16:15; Proverbs 22:11; John 15:2

Precious child,

I Am.

I am your shepherd.

My eyes are forever on your beautiful face. You know My voice. I speak My blessing over you. Be still and listen. Follow Me. The enemy attempts to drown out My voice, but should you lose your way, I will bring you back. I will gently put you on the right path because I have already promised that I would never leave you. Each one of your steps takes you closer to Me and the pastures I have appointed for you. Don't get distracted by the devil's ploy to lead you far away from Me and plant doubts about My character.

All you have to do is rest, My child, and know that I long to deliver you from all harm. What the broken world uses for hurting, I use for your good. Take this gift and use it today to accomplish My plan of saving many lives. You are safe from the lies that the enemy whispers about your ability. I have called you and made you capable.

I hear your pleas for help, and I come to rescue you. I have come down to free you from the oppressor's chains. I live to bring you out from under the yoke of being busy. I long to free you from slavery to guilt. And I will redeem you from the world's lies about your lack of worth. I do all these things for you, My child, so that you can be untethered and free to worship Me.

I will help you speak and teach you what to say. I will never turn My back on you. I will give you confidence to proclaim My love to a hurting world in need. I will show the world how proud I am of you, and they will listen.

Oh, how I love you.

Exodus 3:14; 33:14; Matthew 11:28

Precious child,

I know at times you don't feel important. It's easy to believe the enemy's lies when you are tired and worn down. Your words and actions are sincere, sweet one, but some around you have hardened hearts and simply cannot understand your good intentions. The devil sneaks up and whispers that you should listen to them and stop trying. He whispers words of defeat and regret, that you should quit running after Me. Don't worry. The unyielding ones who make you feel "less than" will never be able to push you away from Me.

There is no one like Me. And nothing on earth can ever take you away from Me. Those with bitter hearts are like bad water. Don't believe them, child. Don't try to drink from their wells of despair by believing them. They can never quench your thirst for justice.

The hardened hearts are like death and decay that slowly soak into every aspect of your life. They are like dust storms, suffocating your hope and blocking out My radiance. They are like dense swarms of distrust that smother your thoughts and ruin your desire to thrive. They try to take away your spirit. Don't let their fears keep you from serving My people.

Sweet child, you are My distinction.

I know your tender soul longs to worship Me. I set the times and places for every one of your days. I will not let the unyielding forces in your life turn your heart away from Me. They are powerless against you because of Me. My will is to shower your life in living water. I long to saturate your soul with peace and new life. I will make sure you have eternal hope. I want you to live passionately, with an unbridled spirit, as you do the job I have called you to do.

Sweet child, you are My desire.

Genesis 50:19–20; Mark 5:36

October 22

Precious child,

Yes, you are My desire, and My love for you is unfailing. I am so eager to celebrate this day with you and listen to your sweet soul's song rise up to Me in glory. Discover more about Me today. This day is My gift for you. As you live, know how great My love for you truly is. I made you wonderful. Your amazing heart is a symphony of grace that plays for the people around you. They listen, child. Oh, how they listen. Even if they act like I'm not important, your heart has planted seeds for them.

Sweet one, I call out to you from the early morning to the dark of night. Forever, I watch over you. Day and night, when people surround you to bring harm, remember that I am your protection. I keep you safe. I keep you close. Please don't fear. The world lives in darkness, but you are of the light. Shine, child, shine. When all that remains looks like ash from a fire, I will keep you above the hardened world and stand you on the solid ground of My promises.

I have broken the shackles of sin so you can live this day free from insecurity and shame. I lead you away from doubt and regret to a peaceful place of redemption. I go with you day and night so that you are never alone. Ever. Even if a time comes when you feel weak and unable to press on, I am there to fill your heart with the will to listen and move.

Hear Me. I will fight for you, child. Be still and see that I want the world for you. Be still and put your trust only in Me. I long to be your strength. I long to save you. I am the warrior who loves to fight for your beautiful heart.

Psalm 143:8; Isaiah 33:2

Precious child,

I am your Lord.

Cry out to Me, dear one. From the deepest part of your being, cry out. I love to hear everything you have to say. Even when you are mad and confused, tell Me. Don't think I will love you any less because you are upset. I won't leave your side. Remember, My sweet one, that it brings Me great joy to listen to your voice. Whether songs of prayer or praise pass your lips, both reach Me, bringing glory to My holy name. Even your pleas for mercy are part of the song. I care about every word you say to Me.

I am your protector.

Today, like yesterday and tomorrow, I keep My mighty arms wrapped around you. I made you unique and of great worth. No one else can do the job I've called you to do. With Me, you will be successful. Please know how important you are. Listen to Me. Hear Me speak this truth over you all day long.

I am your sanctuary.

When you feel like you labor in vain, cry out to Me, and I will show you the way. Follow Me to streams of mercy where you will bear much fruit. Be refreshed in the valley of My endless grace, because you will inherit all that I have for you. Oh, I care about you so much, child. My eyes watch you do what is right in a fallen place, and I smile. I'll tell you again and again that I am so proud of you.

I am your healer.

Just like long, sweet time spent in a peaceful garden, so too are the desert journeys part of My gift for you. When seemingly endless hours of hardship leave your spirit parched, know that I will send the rain. In either place, know that you are right where I need you to be. I love you, precious child.

Psalm 121

Precious child,

I know you're tired. Exhausted. You weren't made to live this day alone. I am sending others that you will meet today. Their words and actions will remind you of My constant presence and provision in your life. I am there, precious one, to hold you close. I see your struggles and hear your cry. Remember, My heart is big enough to cover all of it. My arms are strong enough to carry you through. I am your banner. My heart is big enough too. Look at Me and see how much I love you.

You are so important. I am your helper. I will never leave you. I will rescue you. You are worth it all to Me. I am greater than everything, and My love for you is greater still. My love for you fills your empty heart, and My desire renews your soul. Feel my strength saturate your spirit. Learn more about Me as you live this day. The hours are for us to deepen our relationship. I will show you how faithful I am, and your love for Me will grow. Keep your eyes on Me. Watch Me protect you from the enemy's attacks. Wait for Me to move and then follow Me.

I am your loving Father who knows exactly what you need. I created you beautiful. The broken path you walk winds through a world of unbelief, but I am greater than the world. I hold your hand and lead you through today. As we go, hear My heart beat life into your weary soul. Be encouraged, child, because this day is for Me to show you more grace. It is for Me to hold your weary soul and give you words of encouragement. As you are renewed, hear My sweet song of affection rain over you: "Oh child, how beautiful you are. I am so glad I made you. You are wonderful to Me."

Exodus 17:15; Hebrews 13:6

October 25

Precious child,

I know how hard it is not being able to see Me face-to-face. But, dear one, when you look at your reflection, please see how beautiful you are and never forget that I made you in My image. Know that I have made you very, very special. I made you to see Me with your tender heart. When you show compassion to others, you will feel the compassion I have for you. When you love others, you will feel the love I have for you. Today is a chance to see Me in the rising of the sun. Look at the sky and think about how wide My arms reach to keep you safe.

My glory is a consuming fire of love. I send it like rain to pour over you so you'll know I am covering you today. Let My love soak into every part of you. Close your eyes and see Me. My mercy. My compassion. My grace. My faithfulness and forgiveness. See My love for you. See that all of it's for you. None of these will ever run out. I am never out of love or out of grace. I am here. I am reading these words with you, child. You are so beautiful to Me. I am so pleased with you, and I know you by name. My presence goes with you, precious child, and I promise you rest.

The broken-down world tries to love you with an unfaithful love, to capture your heart with unfaithful promises of pleasure and satisfaction. But, precious child, I love you more than anything, and My name is jealous. I made you for Me. I created you, and you are Mine. I long for the world to see Me through you. Go, child. Show the world today who I really am and what I really look like.

I love you so much!

Psalm 61:7

October 26

Precious child,

Day and night, I am with you.

I know at times your heart longs to be doing something different. You think about doing something bigger for My kingdom and Me. I understand this urge is strong and that it causes you to doubt your purpose in life. I know that your desire to do something different or be in a different place might cause you to think that I am far away. But these are the seeds of doubt the enemy plants in your life. He doesn't want you to wait on Me. He wants you to worry that I might not be strong enough to fulfill all of the promises I've made.

For today, in the place I have you, My heart's desire for you is to be holy, because I am holy. I am the Lord your God, and I have brought you to this day. I have made it possible for you to walk with your head held high. Tend My harvest where I have appointed you. I am on My throne, and you are My love. Devote this day to Me, child. For the moment, I have you right where you need to be. Like the farmer waits for rain, wait for Me. I will show you all that I have for you. When you have done all that I am commanding you to do where you are, I will lead you on to the next place.

But for today, child, know that I am blessing you all the way through it and keeping you close to My heart. My light and grace shine down on you. And I give you peace to fill your heart and remind you to rest in My patience. When you wait on Me, you're not wasting time. When you wait, you strengthen your faith and become more aware of the hope you have in Me.

Leviticus 26:13; Numbers 6:24–26; James 5:7

Precious child,

I understand.

The hurting. The sadness. The pain. All of it. Cry out to Me, and I will give you rest. I will replace your struggles with My peace. Don't be discouraged. The enemy prowls around trying to convince you that the broken world is your home. He says that the misery of other people's hate is all you have to live with. But I am with you, and you will not be defeated. Even though you may feel abandoned, I have been and will be with you. Always.

These desert journeys may seem vast and endless, but they aren't. You haven't wandered outside of My presence, and I am not far away. The truth is that I have not left you to walk alone. You are Mine, and I am never going to forsake you. Ever. The countless hours you spend in dry places are for crying out. Give Me everything. Don't hold back. There is peace in this giving. Rely on Me and not the world. Its tempting mirage of quick pleasures to quench your thirsting soul evaporates and leaves you empty.

Instead, run to My oasis of living water. As you drink, give Me the best and holiest part of everything given to you. In this way, your life sings out to Me in worship. There will be no more confusion, because My peace satisfies your soul. As you lift up your heart, remember that I am true and I am here for you. The enemy prefers you sad and broken. Tired and confused when you could be resting in Me. Don't forget that I go before you today. I fight for you today. And I carry you today. Trust Me, child. I will show you the way out of the desert. Follow Me wholeheartedly, for I am sovereign, and I love you.

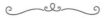

Numbers 18:29; Deuteronomy 1:30–31; 1 Corinthians 14:33

October 28

Precious child,

I am your strength.

I, not the world, made you beautiful. Don't listen to the enemy's lies that your life is meaningless, and don't be afraid. Don't be convinced by the enemy's lies that you've sinned one too many times and I am finished with you. Judgment belongs to Me. Jesus conquered death for you. He proclaimed that the work to save your soul was finished. I have spoken to unbind your heart from stress and strife. I am the true love that fills your soul with hope. You are free!

I am your courage.

I will bless all the work you do. Remember that you lack nothing. I have given you all that you need today. My hands are not against you, child. They are for you, to hold and guide you through the hours. Know this to be true and make courageous choices for My glory. I am proud of your willingness to visit the hard places to share the saving gospel of Jesus. I am proud of your determination to stand up for My love in a world that stands up for itself.

When the world forgets you, you're unforgettable to Me. When people misunderstand you, I know your deepest thoughts. When some disrespect you, I adopt you as my heir. I am the one who can never forget you. I am the one who always understands you. I am the one who respects you. I am all this and more, because when I made you, I made you wonderful.

I conquer for you.

Be victorious today. I know there are no small battles. The ways of the world are a tempest. They appear to be an unbeatable foe, but the forces that stand in your way cannot harm you. My hands are raised against them. The enemy cannot reach you. You are eternally safe because I am your Lord, and you are Mine.

Deuteronomy 1:17; Psalm 28:7

Precious child,

You are My treasured possession.

The world works hard to make you feel like you haven't done enough. The enemy works even harder to help you believe you've been saved by the strength of your own hands. Once you accept that lie, it is easy to feel discouraged when your work doesn't measure up. His lies about your value move in waves that crash back and forth over your soul and leave you in a meaningless wake of confusion. But I made you beautiful. Nothing less. Just you and Me and the gift of today.

Don't let My words fade from your heart. Keep My commands and remember Me. Don't forget that I go with you, everywhere and always. Whether in trial or rest, labor or slumber, hold fast to Me. Don't let go just because you feel like holding Me doesn't matter. Don't let go just because the hours feel long and meaningless. I am the one who validates you. I am near to you. When you pray, I listen. Do not fear.

Talk to Me. I am a consuming fire. I hear your prayers, and I burn with holy fire to answer you. Run to Me, child, with all your heart and soul. I fill your heart with My passion. Be renewed by My mighty power so that you may inherit all the things I have for you today. The enemy offers empty promises and false hopes, but I am here for you with outstretched arms. In My hands find mercy and peace.

The world is merciless. It prowls around trying to lure you into its lair of envy and greed. Its treasures may entice your eyes, but they are worthless for your heart. But I am merciful. There is no other. I made you to be filled with My love. The world drains, but I am faithful. Seek after Me alone and be completely satisfied. And all this, because I love you.

Deuteronomy 7:6; Isaiah 41:13

October 30

Precious child,

Listen.

Hear My words. Let them soak into your heart and paint your mind with the radiant glow of My glory. This new day isn't another box to check. It's a gift wrapped in My good love. Feel My anointing pour over you and be renewed. Hear My heart beat for you. Really listen to Me. I speak to you through the scriptures. In them you will find direction for your life. In them you will find comfort in the midst of strife.

It's all going to be okay.

Rest in the quiet pasture of My promises. I won't ever say something to you and then change My mind. When life's problems loom over you, remember that they do not have power over Me. I am so much greater, and My devouring flames remove what seeks to harm you. My righteousness carries you past the struggles, down to the river where you will drink from streams of living water and be satisfied.

It's all going to be okay.

Roam across sun-covered hills of hope. When the world's armies of temptation draw near, remember that they cannot march over Me. Even though the enemy is feeding you lies, My awesome power crushes his plans to harm you. My sovereignty lifts you over the fray and lays you down in quiet places where you will be able to understand My plans for you. Use the quiet time to rediscover more of My good character. Use the peaceful time to remember how special you are to Me.

It's all going to be okay.

Return to the shadow of My outstretched arms, sweet child. When the enemy sounds the siren of lies, remember that it cannot drown out the sound of My voice. My words pierce through the din so that you will hear only truth. Listen and hear Me speak blessings over you. Hear Me remind you how important you are.

I love you.

Psalm 23

Precious child,

I am grace.

The days I give you are a symphony of hearts, played out on the beautiful notes of your soul. Today is for you to seek out the sound of My holy and perfect name and hear it resonate throughout the hours. Listen to My song of love and it will fill you with confidence. Let the words remind you that you are not a mistake. You were carefully and lovingly created to carry out a good work that I've started in you. Your life matters.

Your life is part of the melody I sing over a hopeless world so that they may awake from their slumber and come to Me. Because of your faithfulness, some will stop and hear My calling. The downtrodden will turn and come to Me. At times you will feel that your labor amounts to nothing, but there is so much that you can't see. Don't lose heart.

My grace is the power that breaks your burdens so you don't have to trudge through the fields of harvest. I have freed you to dance. Even in the storm, My grace rains over you and feeds you. Sweet child, you are the rhythm of My heart, even when you feel tired and drained. In fact, My sweet child, you are so much more than all the compliments ever given to you combined. Your worth is found in Jesus, and He gave His life to make you worthy.

I bless you. My eyes are on you. You are safe in Me.

You are My dear child. You mean more to Me than the world I created. Hear My song proclaim that your debts have been forgiven and My grace is the power that builds you up. The enemy's song of rebellion has no worth to you. Its lyrics are hollow and lifeless. I am your inheritance. Stand with Me, child. Live for love and believe.

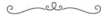

Deuteronomy 19:9; Acts 20:32; Romans 13:11

Precious child,

I am the Lord your God.

I gave you life. Holding you brings Me great joy. I look at you and rejoice. I made you special so that you could live in the world and still be set apart from it. The mistakes you made yesterday don't change the way I love you today. And through each of these new hours I will use your experiences and encounters to sanctify your heart. I will use today to draw you even closer into My holy presence.

I made your eyes to see that you are beautiful and to look at the world the way I see it. Look at the hurting people all around you and see their need for Me. Show dignity by making eye contact with the people who have been pushed aside.

I formed your ears to listen. Hear Me speak over you and tell you that I have called you to go and hear the world crying out for salvation.

I made your mouth to speak truth to a world that too easily follows the way of deception. Tell them the name of Jesus. Let them hear His holy name.

I gave you hands to reach out and hold a person in need, like I hold you.

I gave you feet to walk among the oppressed. Walk with them, and let them know they are loved. Stand up for them when no one else will.

You have a heart to love the world like I love you so that they might turn and find Me. And you've been given a mind to understand My words. Think about My great love for you and be inspired.

Precious child, do you see how important you are to Me? Every part of who you are is wonderfully and carefully made. I have uniquely designed you to be different from everyone else. I made only one amazing you, and I am so pleased that I did.

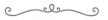

Zephaniah 3:17

Precious child,

I am compassion.

The world will leave you stranded. It gives momentary joy and then abandons you to drown in guilt. But dear one, I go out to the places where guilt and regret have banished you and bring you back. I will be with you today and forever. The enemy leads you to desolate places, pursuing fleeting joy. But I made you to stay with Me, child. My love and forgiveness wash away the shame that covered you in that barren place. See your mistakes and bad decisions be carried away. I will restore you with the strength of a thousand armies so you can face this new day with courage.

I formed you in love. I am your faithful everything. Through all of your days, please remember that there is no one created who can love you more than I love you. No one can rescue you from the world's desolation more than I can rescue you. Don't let the devil tempt you into thinking that Jesus saved you only to lose you. I made you. Jesus died for you. Nothing can snatch you out of My hand. I am your life. Live in Me, child. The world is filled with false promises. It is a mirage of happiness. Its oasis is filled with pain and suffering. Remember where I found you. Remember how I rescued you once and for all.

Take My gift of today and use it to show compassion to a desperate world. Tell them of My desire to save them too. Tell them all about the hope you found in Me. Help turn their eyes away from the suffocating darkness so they can see My light rising over the horizon. Let My love flow through you, child, so they will know that I am real and ready to save.

Deuteronomy 30:4; Romans 5:8

November 3

Precious child,

I am the Most High.

I see past the storms that rage around you. When your strength is gone, I have compassion on you. You are in My hand, child, and no one can deliver you out of it. My words are life, and they lead you away from the idle thoughts that hinder. My commands take you to the place where freedom lets you become all that I created you to be.

Feel Me shine. My heart dawns over you and warms your soul. I shield you all day long as you rest between My mighty shoulders. I am your eternal refuge. My everlasting arms are always underneath you. I am your glorious sword that goes before you and clears a safe path through life's battles.

I am in you and also above the winds and driving rain. I can see the end of your current sadness even though you feel like there is no end. Let go of control, and let Me remind you that I am here to renew your weary heart.

I am in you and also above the circling darkness. I can see the light even though you feel like there is only darkness. I am in you and also above the noise. I can see hope arriving, child. So stay with Me and keep My words close to your heart. Just as the branch can do nothing apart from the vine, remain in Me.

Because I am with you, this day will be different. With My love and power filling every part of you, this day will be a brand-new experience. You will be strong, child, and courageous. You don't have to be afraid anymore. I made you beautiful. I made you to reflect My perfect love to a dying world. Step out in faith, child, and see how I will always remain with you.

Deuteronomy 33:12; Joshua 1:7; John 15:4–5

November 4

Precious child,

I am the Lord of all the earth.

I will do amazing things for you. I lift you up so that people around you know I am with you. No matter what fear you may hold inside, know that My powerful hands will hold the floodwaters back so you can reach the places I have for you today. You will cross over dry ground and not be harmed by the enemy's schemes.

You are so important to Me, child. You are a living memorial to the power of My holy name. You are a testament to My saving grace. When you go to the places I have for you, the people there will know that I am their only true God because of you.

My ways are not like yours, child. You might feel that I have left you to conquer the enemy alone, but, sweet created one, that is the furthest thing from the truth. I think about your struggle, child, and I promise to love you and carry you through it. My thoughts about what you are going through are so much more than you can imagine. I feel every heavy heart you are burdened by and every tear that falls down your cheek.

Feel My words of truth rain down over you and become new tears, not of sorrow but of joy. They will be tears that do not fall in vain, for they will water your memories and make them bloom into new ones that remind you of who I really am.

I will make you victorious over your present struggles. My words to you will not return to Me empty. They will accomplish what I desire for you and achieve the purpose for which I sent them.

Go out in peace today, child, for in Me you have already overcome.

Joshua 4:24; Isaiah 55:8–11

November 5

Precious child,

I am the great giver. When everything seems out of control, remember that I have already given the enemy into your hands. I have given you the power to obey My commands and put to death the worry and fear that threaten to attack you. I am the one who gives you rest from every side of the world. In Me, you have the power to resist the devil's attempts to harm you. I strengthen you to overcome your current battles by the power of the blood of Jesus that was shed for all your sins. I have set you free from who you once were!

I give you My love. Take it and see how deep My desire is for you. Be strengthened by it. Go and share this gift with people who are crying out to be accepted by a world that can never give them what I can.

I give you patience. Take this and use it to be still. You are right where I want you. Let My patience fill you and help you remember that I am with you and the world is not your eternal home.

I give you shelter. When trouble comes, I am your stronghold and safe place. My arms hold you tight and the world can't get to you here. I am giving you life today, sweet child. And today will be the day when everything changes. Receive My gift, and be strengthened to walk away from the chaos. Receive My gift and run unchained to every perfect thing I have for you. Use all My gifts to change the world. Use My offerings to turn it upside down for My sake.

My gifts replace your burdens. Experience the fulfillment of every one of My good promises for you. I give you My word that all of this is true and will happen just as I say because I love you.

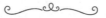

Joshua 21:45; Psalm 9:9; Ephesians 4:2; 2 Thessalonians 3:5

Precious child,

I am peace.

Loving Me, the Lord your God, and yielding your heart to Mine, sweet one, are the purposes for which I made you. This one relationship brings you rest in a love-draining world that seeks your allegiance. Walking with Me today pushes the seekers away and makes room for My calming touch. Being with Me alone fills your tired soul.

Keeping My commands and holding fast to Me, child, brings a heavenly rest that helps you stay on the path of righteousness. Serving Me with all your heart and with all your soul drives away confusion. The world builds up altars of rebellion because they don't know Me or know of the great things I have done for you. Take My strength and take a stand. Go and tell them, child.

When I move, My power shakes the earth, rattling the mountains, and breaks open the heavens to pour down rain. In your weakness, this same strength rises inside you. When you feel like the least out of many, know that I am with you to hold your head high and make you like a mighty warrior. I am the one who fills you with all the strength you need to complete the tasks I am calling you to.

The world boasts of its own ability. The people rule over each other, and they have forsaken Me. Oh, how they need to hear from you, child. They need to hear what you have to tell them about Me.

Today, child, remember that I'm not sending you alone. I am with you and will open up the hollow places of life, providing you with an endless supply of living water so you will be strengthened. Go out into the world in My peace and know with everything that's in you that I have appointed and approved your journey. I am so proud of you.

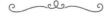

Joshua 22:5; Judges 6:24; 18:6

November 7

Precious child,

I know.

I know some days you're filled with sorrow. I want you to cry. It's okay. Your weeping will not be in vain. I created you, and every part of you matters. I am taking your tears and your weary soul and breathing new life into you. I deliver you from the pain so you can continue to show the world My grace.

But the world does what it wants. I know, and this burdens Me, child. Go against it and stand up for the ones who are defenseless. As you do this, remain under my wings and find refuge. The world's misery can't find you there. You will soon see the poor seated with princes and be emboldened to show the world My grace.

I know you're tired. I want you to rest. Your weariness will not be in vain. I made you, child, and you matter. I am taking your restless spirit and breathing new life into you. I put you back on your feet to continue living the life I've called you to—the life of showing the world real grace.

The world speaks with arrogant tongues. This burdens Me, child. Go and tell the prideful people that there is only one they should boast about. Go and tell them I am their rock and Redeemer. See them scattered in dark places and tell them of the one true light and My saving grace.

I know you're hungry for justice. I want you to remember that I am the judge of heaven and earth. Your hunger for this will not go unsatisfied. I made you in My image, and you will never lack for anything. Feel My loving hands feed you with the truth of righteousness and be encouraged. Be My grace in an unforgiving world.

I know.

1 Samuel 2; 1 Peter 4:10

November 8

Precious child,

Hear My word.

The world has plans for you, wrapped in attractive packages and given to you under a celebration of lies. But hear My word, child. These are desecrated dreams that leave you empty and defeated. The world works hard at creating ways to harm you and fill you with doubt and regret. It wants you to prosper in guilt and shame. But these are not the gifts you were made to receive.

Sweet child, I have great things planned for you. Perfect plans to use you to bring Me glory and to help rescue My people who are blinded and enslaved by the world's storehouse of broken gifts. Be My hands and feet. Go to the shackled ones and help them put down their burdens. Help them lift their hands in praise. Give them the name of Jesus. Join with them in worship and prayer.

Your worth is in My great love for you. It goes with you. You are never alone. You will hear Me and feel My love.

Today I am doing a great thing through you, and the world will hear about it. They are yearning for a gift that saves, and you, child, will be the brave one who tells them about Me. You are My disciple, blessed by heaven's love. I am calling you to shower the unloved with compassion. You are a soldier empowered by Me to fight for the powerless. Today you will reach the unreachable and hear the angels rejoice.

I won't let your words about My love break and fall. They will remain whole and be carried by My Spirit across the barren world and be planted in the hearts of many. Then your forgiven heart will rain My saving love over them, and their eyes will open and their hearts will bloom for My name's sake.

1 Samuel 3:19; Jeremiah 29:11

November 9

Precious child,

With everything that I made you to be, worship Me. Your life was created to be a symphony of heartbeats and soul songs. When you open your eyes and let My light shine into your innermost being, the glorious sound of your thanksgiving will rise up over the land. People will hear the sweet notes of salvation, and they will turn to Me.

Real worship is more than just our relationship. Look after the orphans, child. Go to where they are and hold their tiny hands. Love them like I love them and adopt them as I have adopted you. Give them hope that they are not alone in their remote places. Be blessed by their tender hearts and protect them as you worship Me. Be their advocate as I am your advocate.

When you love the widow and take care of her, I will be glorified. Be her helper and her protector as I have helped and protected you. Be My hands and feet for her, and give her grace to feel included. Serve her and care for her. Show her the same compassion I show you.

As you worship Me in these ways, keep yourself from being tainted by the world's polluted rhythms. Hear My song of words make a peaceful melody in your heart, and let it move you to carry out the plans I have for you. Let My truths lead you to be My disciple who cares for the broken and weary souls.

Hear My song of love return and pour over you. Let your tongue sound like a psalm of truth when you speak to loved ones and strangers. Favor everyone, child, for everyone needs to hear My song. Whether saved or seeker, favor them both as I have favored you. Orchestrate My symphony of redemption so the world might hear the sweet sounds of mercy.

Psalm 95:6–7; Matthew 4:10; James 1:27

Precious child,

I know that part of you thinks about how things could be. I'm not upset that you feel this way. I know you search for Me and it seems that I am gone, far away and unapproachable. But I am inside your heart, child. I am so much closer to you than anything else in the world. I am with you forever. You are safe here. You are Mine.

Return to thinking about all that I have done for you, child. With all of your treasured heart, come back to the pastures I have for you. Commit your heart to Mine and labor for the fruit of My kingdom's harvest. In these things, you are home. In these things, you are right where you are supposed to be.

I am the one who has rescued you from the world's darkest places. I have brought you safely back. The world fills your sweet mind with what-ifs and leaves you searching for answers that can never be found. Don't chase these, My dear child. Each one is nothing but an attractive mirage. With Me, your heart sings about and celebrates what is. With Me, you are truly loved and completely forgiven.

Because I carry out acts of righteousness for you, you will call out to Me, and I will answer you. Don't leave My pastures of truth to chase after what could be. The world and its deceptions can never save or satisfy you.

I am your Savior. I am your Creator. I alone satisfy your longing heart. Don't be tempted in your weariness to find fulfillment elsewhere. Today, the harvest is plentiful, and you are one of My workers called to share good news and be satisfied. I love you, My child. Nothing can hinder Me.

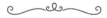

1 Samuel 12:7, 14; Matthew 9:37; Galatians 6:9

November 11

Precious child,

I am your everlasting Father.

I love you so much, and I want you to become everything I made you to be. Don't get pulled into the world's games of achievement and gain. I delight when you listen and obey all that I have for you. The world gets it wrong, child. It works hard to make you believe that offerings and sacrifices satisfy Me. This is not truth.

The world celebrates rebellious hearts. It shouts praises for the arrogant. They reject My words. These acts are nothing to Me, dear child. To heed My direction for your days is what I delight in. The world is filled with lies of acceptance tossed about on shifting seas. It cares about appearance, but I care about your heart. I am truth, and I am unchanging.

Today is your gift to enjoy for My glory. Paint the sky for My holy name so the world may look up, away from itself. Draw My love for the hurting world so they will see something beautiful. Create a masterpiece of mercy to show the people, and pray for them to see the beauty in grace.

Defiance and disgrace pave the enemy's way. Follow Me on the path of righteousness and tell the world where you're going. Don't be afraid when they judge you. Remember that I've already judged you: forgiven. When they mock you, precious child, remember who knit you together and blessed you. I made you awesome, and I speak strength into your heart so you will rise above the insults.

Child, you are special. You mean everything to Me, and I will protect you. Today, focus on the hurting hearts. Find the ones a dying world has cast out. Tell them truth. Show them love.

1 Samuel 15:22–23; Isaiah 9:6; Hosea 6:6; Matthew 9:13

Precious child,

I am your fortress.

Outside the castle walls I have built around your soul, down in the valley of death, a battle of hearts rages on. Hurtful words are used as weapons. The enemy marches around, scheming ways to destroy. His darkness swirls in blinding clouds of lies. Today, remember that I have saved you from that very place. Don't be afraid. You are Mine. You will go there and bring My message of hope to many who are fighting for the enemy's lost causes.

The world steals from My people. Go and fight for them, child. Today, arm yourself with My power. Remember that My Word is like a double-edged sword. Take it with the hands of your heart and go. Don't let the opinions of others discourage you. Find your strength in Me. Have My courage and become the leader I want you to be.

The weapons of man can't save you. The war around you is Mine to win. You will slay the giants that would prevent you from reaching the lost. I am the one who wins great victories. The world will gather around you and know that I am the Lord God Almighty. They will know that I was the one who gave you success.

I am your stronghold of unfailing kindness. I am witness and Creator of your days. Today, I will deliver you from the world's dark clutches. I am with you. Through Me, you will go behind enemy lines and reach the wounded souls who are dying. Be brave and tell them the truth. Tell them there's hope in My holy name. Grasp their weak and dirty hands and lead them to the waters of My saving grace. Rejoice as I wash away their sins and make them clean.

I love you.

1 Samuel 23:16; Jeremiah 16:19; Hebrews 4:12

Precious child,

I am the one who sees you.

Your joy. Your misery. Your doubts. Your mistakes.

I know how easy it is for you to get caught in the world's ways. I know you are constantly tempted to solve your own problems. You feel left alone to figure out what to do. The world says you have to tough it out and deal with it, that you aren't worthy unless you become a self-made survivor. I didn't make you to be a self-appointed hero. I created you to live your days in Me. I am where you are meant to be.

The enemy convinces you that your worth is found in control. My sweet treasure, I made you to rely on Me. The world is powerless to help you. The enemy's army surrounds you with their weapons of insecurity and silence. They advance on you with guns of apathy, hoping to keep you silent and still.

I tell you that today you will run to Me and ask Me for help. I will answer you, and you will remember that I am the only one who knows your heart. I am the only one who sees where you've been and the place you're in. I see where I want you to be, and I also see where the world wants you to end up.

So, child, right now call out to Me and tell Me everything. I am not like the world that leaves you stranded without hope or answers. I answer you in ways of mercy and kindness. The most beautiful part of our relationship, child, is that I hear every word you lift to Me. And after you ask, I answer you with so much more. More than you can ever imagine.

Genesis 16:13; Matthew 7:7–11; Ephesians 3:20

November 14

Precious child,

I am your cornerstone.

Your life is set in direct relation to Me. Measure every decision, every thought, and every plan against My tested heart. I am here for you always. And in all ways I will guide you and make you into a tower of light in the center of growing darkness.

The world lies to you, child, telling you that your days are built on a foundation of prosperity. But the world has rejected Me. Don't believe what you see. They build up castles of pride and sit on broken thrones of isolation. This is not what you were made for. I made you to be the difference when everyone else stays the same!

I have given you a gift of days to lead My lost sheep back home. I have called you out of the darkness that floods the world. I will go before you and give you courage. I will break over your enemies like rushing water and clear a straight path for you to run after Me.

Start with a single soul and pour into them My love and mercy. My truth and grace. Show them something new. Think about that very first day you were shown compassion. Remember how it felt when your eyes were opened and you called Jesus Savior. With strength and bravery, child, fight for the least of these. Defend My people.

The enemy banishes. I redeem. Today, go into the world and look for misery. Replace it with My love. In places of deep sadness, sow truth and hope. Go out to the wilderness and let your life be a song of salvation that testifies to the goodness of My heart. I am not sending you alone. I am with you, child. I am so proud of your willingness to care and go.

I love you.

Job 38:6; Psalm 118:22; Isaiah 28:16; Luke 20:17

November 15

Precious child,

I am your everlasting God.

When the world leaves you stranded without mercy, I am the one who remains. Forever. For every hour of every day I am your rock. I am your strong tower that rises high above the mire of violence and misdeeds. The enemy schemes to persuade you I either don't exist or am unable to rescue you.

But you know the truth. My love and goodness outlast the world's shallow treasures. My love has your heart wrapped safely in eternal hope. Don't squander your time collecting things that don't last. Take refuge in Me alone, child. In the safety of My loving arms you are shielded from the unforgiving world and its hateful message of self-reliance. In the safety of My Word, you will be guarded from the world's accusations about your unworthiness. You are worth everything to Me. In Me you shine.

Run to Me. Lasting far beyond the false hope and attractive trinkets of life, I Am. I lift you up with My strong arms and hold you close. My compassion reminds you that your worth comes from Me and not anything or anyone in the world.

I live to be your shield and Savior. For every one of your plans, dreams, and desires, I am your salvation. Forever, I extend a strong arm against the soldiers of darkness who seek to crush your hope.

Call out to Me, child. My heart listens and hears your voice rise above the noise and reach Me as the sweetest song of praise. Above the day's churning waters, I lift you out of the hurricane into My peace. From the midst of the enemy's destructive forces, I hear your cry. I answer you because you are worth everything to Me.

Genesis 21:33; 2 Samuel 22:2–7

November 16

Precious child,

I am your deliverer.

From the enemy's dark clutches, I save you. I live to protect your life and keep you safe from the world's evil. When you cry out to Me, I listen.

You mean everything to Me. My jealous heart beats for you. When the army of darkness surrounds you, I will shake the earth. It will tremble and the walls of self-doubt and fear will crumble and fall. Even the foundations of heaven shake from My anger at the enemy. The world will not get to you, and I promise it won't harm your soul.

I burn with desire for your heart. See the smoke rise through the sky. Watch the flames of My passion for you pour over the insidious powers that keep you from truth. Embers of My love smolder on either side of your path, lighting your way through the dimmest of days.

My power protects you today. I split open the skies and bend close to hear you. The dark clouds will be trampled under My feet. I soar on the wind with the angels over you. Oh child, how I long to deliver you. You are so beautiful to Me. I will dispel the darkness that surrounds you. My holy presence will explode in bolts of beautiful light and erase the darkness. I will speak and the sound of thunder will stop the enemies from advancing and send them running.

Your heart is safe in My hands. I reach out and rescue you from deep waters and deliver you from life's overwhelming struggles. When the world pushes you toward the edge of disaster, I am your support. I will always save you from sinister campaigns and bring you back into My safe pastures.

2 Samuel 22:8–20; Romans 11:26

Precious child,

I am the one who purifies your soul.

I have rescued you from the battle waged for your heart. I have cleansed your soul and deemed you righteous. I am your reward, and your sweet forgiven heart is Mine because your life now brings Me wonderful glory. Live this new day in the knowledge that you are fully forgiven.

No army can stand against us. I will shield you from the enemy's dreadful arrows. I am your rock, and I always keep your way secure. I make your feet able to climb great heights so you can look down and see a new sun rising, one that will dispel darkness forever.

I give you My Word, child. It will prepare you for battle and make your path wide so in all these things you won't stumble and fall. I help you crush the plans of darkness completely. The enemy's forces will be humbled and flee. I avenge you. You will trample hateful schemes of violence and bring My light to a world without any hope.

Show them My mercy. Don't be ashamed to cry out to Me in troubled times. Don't worry when they hear you praise Me. As I shower you with unfailing kindness, some will also fall on the world. When they ask, "From where does this come?" tell them My name!

The world contaminates our relationship by smearing the dirt of guilt across your heart. But I forgive you! I wipe your heart clean so that it will shine like the brightest stars. My righteous light will pour from you today and draw the world out from their dark hiding places. Raise your hands in thanksgiving and guide their eyes to My sweet mercy and saving grace.

2 Samuel 22:21–51; 2 Corinthians 7:1; 1 John 1:9; 3:3

November 18

Precious child,

I am your dwelling place.

I love you so much. Take today and look at it differently. Warm rays of My love will reach your heart and thaw the pain. The world says today is a burden. But, child, you live in Me. I am your safe place. I will show you that this day is a rich blessing of hours. You will become like the morning sun shining in a cloudless sky. Your light will draw people to you. They will see that something is different, and you will delight in telling them about Me.

Fall into My merciful hands and let Me carry you through these new hours spread out before you. I prepare your heart to be satisfied with My unfailing love. My favor will rest on you this day.

My peace fills you forever. Today, you will feel this truth and see My heart beat for you. Drops of joy will fall and wash away the world's harvest of hate that surrounds you.

Sweet child, I know today feels just like all the others. But trust Me. Someone is waiting for you. They've been waiting for you to tell your story. Be strong for My sake. They are being swallowed by the darkness. Bring them light. Take their hand and lead them away from the famine of souls. Lead them back to Me.

As you go, sing a new song of mercy. Shout out lyrics of love. You are My inheritance kept safe in the dwelling of My everlasting heart. Don't be afraid to see today as a blessing. Trust My holy name to help and shield you. I see you and smile. Your sweet heart brings Me glory. I love you.

2 Samuel 24:14; Nehemiah 1:9; Psalm 33

November 19

Precious child,

Breathe.

Inhale deeply My love for you as I fill you with peace. It's going to be okay. I want you to know that you are not alone. I am with you.

Exhale the chaos and confusion. I thwart the world's wisdom that says you have to do everything on your own. I am your God of understanding and clarity. I call you by name. I call you forgiven. And I call you free.

Inhale mercy. Remember that once you were lost in your rebellion. Once you were trapped in the world's darkest place. But I rescued you from an eternity of hopelessness. I did that because My great love deems you worthy.

Exhale the dreadful suffering. Let everything go. A broken world that doesn't know Me tries to fix your eyes on its misery. Close your eyes as I release you from the crushing weight of your anguish.

Inhale sweet grace. I build up your soul, and My words sing a song of freedom over your heart.

Exhale the burdens. Stop seeking the world's approval. Let go of the desire to compete with them. There is no need to keep score, because in Jesus you have already won. My strong hands release you from the clutches of the world, the need for their acceptance.

Breathe in My breath of life. Today you will truly live out the hours I have for you because our relationship is what I made you for. Talk to Me. Tell Me all the things that break your heart. Exhale the past. Learn more about Me. I will provide for you, child. I refuse to let the enemy tempt you away from Me. Breathe, child. You are saved. You are safe. I love you.

Job 12:10; Isaiah 42:5; Revelation 11:11

November 20

Precious child,

I am your King of glory.

You are My offering to a dying world. As you breathe, your praise and honor rise up to Me. The world is our witness. They watch your strong love for Me and wonder what brings the passion we share. This is why I want you to know how important you are. The dark world sees you glorify Me, and a crack begins to form across its frozen heart.

Your prayers move mountainous burdens off the ones who have been buried by the enemy. Child, the darkness of the world keeps them believing I don't exist. People surround you who believe that their king is dead. When you say My name, warm air filled with the aroma of forgiveness flows all around them, and their hearts thaw and the prideful crack of sin widens.

I have given you rest, child. On every side, I protect you. No more disasters will overtake you. When waves of judgment crash on the shore of your soul, they cannot destroy you.

I am your strength. I lift your head so you can see how much your life matters. Every prayer. Every song. Every cry for help. All of you matters, and every blessed part of you brings Me glory. I made you wonderful. Worship Me, child. Don't worry about the things you don't have. I know exactly what you need, and I will provide. Spend this day hearing My voice affirm you.

The thick ice of oppression that has kept the world's heart from beating new life is finally gone. The crack splits wide, and hearts are exposed to My saving truth. Ice melts into living water that draws out hardened hearts and nourishes souls. All of this, child, is for My glory because you matter to Me.

Psalm 24:10; Isaiah 43:6–8

Precious child,

I am the living God.

With My strong hand I will fulfill all the promises I make to you. And I promise that My covenant of love with you is unbreakable. It binds us together forever. The shackles of hate and injustice cannot contain Me. I love you, and I am the only one who knows every human heart. I made yours, and I purified it by the wonderful work of Jesus.

I am love, and I live to love you. My unfailing heart beats to give you life. My love protects you from the enemy's struggle to make you feel unwanted. Precious one, if you feel alone and afraid, this is from the evil one. The world's soldiers drain your heart of the love I have filled it with, but they can't win. Even though you may feel something different, the truth is I hold the dark armies back with My mighty hand. They cannot hurt your heart.

I love you more than any love you have ever known. I hold you and keep you safe from selfishness and insecurity. I shelter you so that the sweet rhythm of your heartbeat is a glorious echo of Mine. The hurtful stares and harmful words of the world now fall short and miss their mark because I am the mighty guardian of your dear heart.

Come with Me, child, because I am here to shower you with holiness. I give you hope. You are not what the world claims. You are what I made you to be: forever loved, forever forgiven, and forever free. Oh, how beautiful you are. Let Me show you how wonderful I made your heart.

1 Kings 8:39; Romans 5:5; Ephesians 5:1

November 22

Precious child,

I am your portion.

This new day I hear the sweet sound of your voice and listen as you lay your desires at My feet. Listen for Me to answer, because the world has answers of its own. You cry out, and the enemy also hears. Darkness answers you with tempting idols and hopeless dreams.

But, dear child, I answer you in truth. I live to fill your heart with a greater joy than the world could ever dream of or imagine. I gave you life, and I give you these days to rest in My peaceful presence. I am always enough. Always. Earth and all of its crumbling kingdoms has nothing that compares to My love for you.

I am the one who made you. I know exactly what you need and everything you desire. Child, the enemy doesn't know you but would convince you there's hope in earthly treasure. The one of the world is the deceiver. Even though you are fully Mine, safe and eternally secure, the evil one battles for your mind. He makes you comfortable in the midst of trials. He blinds you to the suffering across the world.

I give you security, breath, and love for those who cannot find favor in the eyes of many. The world is satisfied with comfort and resigned to ignoring the least of these. But not you, precious child. You glorify Me and have an unrelenting desire to serve the unwanted. You make Me so proud. You aren't afraid to go and touch the untouchable. You follow Me to the ends of the earth to tell strangers of My mighty name. Oh, how great is your life. How I love you.

Today, let My grace be enough.

Psalm 16:5; 73:26; 119:57

November 23

Precious child,

I am the one who hears when you call to Me. I am the one who forgives you. I gently hold your face in My hands and bless you. Raise your arms to heaven in celebration of this new gift of today. Not one word of My promises will fail. And I promise to love you through every struggle and every praise. I promise I am with you. I am the one who never leaves you. When the world turns its back on you, I am the one who never forsakes you.

Your prayers are always with Me. I am the one who provides everything you need according to each day's demands. Be fully committed to Me, child. Don't let the falling world grab hold of you on its way down. Sweet child, the darkness may try to smother the hope I give you, but don't worry. Even if the enemy sends out armies of guilt and regret, I am the one who gives you victory over them. Oh, how I love you.

I think about you and protect you from hatred the world disguises as love. Abandon the enemy's gold for the sake of My holy name.

Worship Me, child. Let this day be the one that changes all the rest. Worship Me with everything I have given you. I listen as your song joins with the praise of angels in a wonderful symphony of glory.

Worship Me in a new way. I want your song of My grace to be heard by the people you pass today. The homeless aren't just the strangers holding cardboard signs hoping for your help. There are strangers standing beside your path who are eternally homeless, holding broken hearts and hoping for a Savior. Be strong and tell them the truth. I am with you forever!

Judges 6:14; Psalm 144

Precious child,

I am faithful and true.

Just because people don't believe in Me doesn't make Me unfaithful. The enemy rains lies over the world, but I am truth. Keep your heart fully devoted to Me, not divided between Me and the world, because I have made your lot secure. Live free. Through Me, be strong and tell the unbelievers where your strength comes from.

Let the wisdom I've planted in your heart be covered with My living water so it will rise for the world to see. Remember, the world seeks to turn your heart away from Me, to distract you and divide your heart so that your thoughts are taken off of Me. Rely on My faithfulness. Let it guide you through the greatest trials.

From the very first breath I gave you, I have been faithful. I don't change. People chase after things that can't be found. They live for the changing landscapes of material possessions and dreams. The world nurtures this unfaithful relationship and cannot save itself from swirling greed. I have things planned for you, born from My faithful goodness, and they will satisfy.

Child, no matter what pleasures Satan waves before you, you don't need anything of the world's design. I created you to need Me. Let our relationship be the greatest desire of your heart. I am the one who calls you, and I remain faithful to you through it all. When you feel like you're drowning in an ocean of disappointment, I am the one who saves you. I am the one who warms your heart with My eternal hope.

I am for you. When you feel like all your hard work doesn't matter, I am faithful to remind you that it does. I am your constant love in an unfaithful world. You are wonderful to Me.

Psalm 89:8; Joel 2:23; Romans 4:21; 1 Corinthians 10:13

November 25

Precious child,

There is never an hour you are without Me.

I am your shield against the enemy's weapons of hopelessness. When the darkness approaches with an army of unrighteousness, My right hand sustains you. Never believe I don't care. I protect you with everything I am. You are the only you I created. Please know no one else is like you. I have made tasks specifically for you to do. Your heart and song are unique, to bring hope to people today who are ready to listen.

You will not live one day without Me.

I am your shield to raise against injustice and inequality. The world's eyes are not shielded against the growing darkness. They are blinded by it, and in their blindness they live according to a code of anger and hate. Fires of hurt rage and destroy self-esteem. Winds of selfishness blow away self-worth. Be the strong one to stop these destructive forces. Be the bold one to say something. Even if you have to be the only one, go and defend them. Be My love and show the victims that I have come to save.

I am with you, every heartbeat.

I surround you. Everything I am shields you, child, from the world's heartless desires. Walk with Me today to people who are in need. Come with Me to people who are hurting and unloved. Follow Me as we find people who have been mistreated and abused. When they see that your love for them is genuine, their hearts will feel worthy again. Then, as you tell them your story, they will hear a new song of hope.

Oh child, see how important you are to Me!

Psalm 59:11; 91:4

November 26

Precious child,

The way you sacrifice your time brings Me glory. A hurting heart in the darkness, loved by you, is a heart ready to be renewed. I know you're exhausted, but I restore you. Please don't underestimate how important you are. The times are darkening; many people are being deceived that their worth is found in the world, but true worth is found in My one and only Son.

Jesus, the Messiah. Bright and Morning Star. Radiant glory and mighty cross bearer. The sacrifice for all who would believe.

Child, your life shows the world what I did for you. I love you so much, I sent Jesus to die in your place. Your life is a mirror of My heart for the broken world. Oh child, see how much you mean to Me.

As you go today remember our relationship. I am here to hold you and protect you. You have been made holy, once and for all, by the sacrifice of Jesus. You are like a living stone being built into a spiritual house of worship. Your life is part of a holy spiritual priesthood. Every helping hand, every kind word spoken, every smile, every act of hope—each one you offer, child, points the world back to Me.

Jesus, the Messiah. Beautiful and holy one. Giver of life and eternal hope. Gentle and compassionate soul saver. The worthy and merciful one.

Child, your life today will show the world what I am doing for them. I love you so much. I am sending you into the world to tell them about Jesus. Your eyes have been opened, and they will lead you to people who are crying out for a Savior. You will shower the weak ones in love, and they will see Me in your sacrifice. Oh, how wonderful you are!

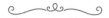

John 4:25; Hebrews 10:10; 1 Peter 2:5

November 27

Precious child,

When you're lost and doubt where you are headed, keep following Me. When you feel abandoned to your own thoughts and the search for answers leaves you empty, follow My truth.

I have set before you this gift of days to walk free with an unchained heart. Dead ends and broad roads that lead to the land of destruction mark the way of the world. But Jesus, My only sweet Son, Jesus, is the way everlasting and protector of the faithful ones. He is your King of kings because He saved you. When the enemy draws you away, resist his calling. Remain where you are, in the middle of My path of grace and favor.

My ways are paved with righteousness and justice. I know it seems like injustice abounds. Evil swarms and darkness prowls all around you. It snatches hope and leaves you stranded on an island of regret. It gives you unsolvable problems and heaps burning coals of angst on your heart.

I know it all seems unbearable, but understand that these are the weapons of broken men. Be still in the middle of the confusing pain and listen for My voice. Open your eyes to see My light shine in the midst of hardship and feel My love.

Walk on the path of My Word. Follow Jesus, the way of life, through the land of mourning. Obey the gentle tug on your heart to win the battle for your thoughts, and dwell securely in the pasture of My unfailing kindness. Close your eyes and I will capture your heart with My unfailing love.

The world and all of its temptations and accusations are behind you now. Turn this day into a song of thanksgiving for all that I have done for you!

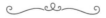

Psalm 119:33; Proverbs 2:8; Jeremiah 21:8; John 14:4

November 28

Precious child,

I am the Ancient of Days.

Time has no hold on Me. I am with you, and I am before you. I also know what lies ahead of you. No matter what happens, you are safe in My hand. Who can deliver you out of it? Who can change what I do for you? Your salvation is secure, and all your days are in Me. My everlasting arms push aside the enemy so you can walk down today's path knowing that death has passed over you.

I am forever alive. I am forever true. I am forever the one who loves you.

Imagine how we will spend eternity together. Let those glorious thoughts capture your mind. Jesus has opened endless paths for you. The blood of My Son, the good shepherd, was shed for every one of your sins, so we can walk and live forever. You are eternally loved.

Your eternal house in heaven is being prepared for you. I promise this to be true. Before the beginning of your days, I wanted to make this promise so that you would have hope in your present trials. Rains of mercy and winds of peace will cover you. Pain and sorrow will be no more.

Until that glorious day when you step into paradise, be My hope to the world around you. Be bold to go to the hurting hearts and share My healing. Let them see My eternal power and watch as I move through this day and guard you.

I am making you strong and steadfast, a firm soldier of the faith. I have called you to eternal glory in Jesus. You are forever Mine. Find Me today in every little act and every big dream. I have made you a blessed messenger for My kingdom. Go, child, and shine!

Deuteronomy 33:27; Hebrews 9:14; 1 Peter 5:10

Precious child,

I am good.

Find everything you desire in Me. My goodness goes before you, and you will hear Me speak in your presence. You will listen to Me proclaim My holy name, and you will realize that you don't have to worry about pleasing people. Today, I am showing you mercy and compassion, and you will rejoice in My goodness. You will know that I am all you need. The enemy trains your eyes on the world's evil so you might think there is no good left. He wants you to focus on his wickedness and not My grace. Let My love for you keep your eyes open to see Jesus.

Look and see how I am providing for you, sweet child. I am always giving you an abundance of blessings. From shelter, food, and water, to a great family of believers, I am the God of all, and all these I freely give you. I give you a spacious land of grace for you to experience life the way I meant it to be lived.

My goodness and love are with you through your gift of days, so you don't have to worry about fitting in or being accepted. My words are alive and true. I turn to you with mercy. You will never be unloved or unwanted. I will always care for you. I have set you free from the world's dark prisons so you can praise My holy name. Your salvation song of redemption will rise above the world's noise and be heard by many. They will turn to Me, and I will save them.

My Holy Spirit fills you with this same love and goodness that I am showering over you. Taste the goodness of My scriptures as My words strengthen you, child. Let My love push aside your pride so you can be My example of a faithful servant. I am so proud of you!

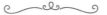

Exodus 33:19; Galatians 5:22; 1 Thessalonians 2:4; Hebrews 6:5

November 30

Precious child,

I am your guide.

I didn't create you to suffer in isolation but to be a brilliant light in the world. Some days it might seem like walls of competition and selfishness are rising up all around you. You may feel trapped inside a maze of disorder. But I am with you. My love fills your heart, and I lead you away from the enemy's camp. Day and night, I go before you; My strength is enough to keep you on the right paths. I also guide you in truth, so that you may keep your hope in Me all day long. Your humility shines bright and is a powerful testimony to My love.

Don't ever feel alone. I am with you day and night. My right hand holds you as we go, so there is never a moment when you are left unprotected. Wherever you go today, near or far, I am with you. I promise to be your guide whether you travel on familiar roads or ones that seem treacherous and impassable. I am your fortress and rock, and I also go out before you to make your way safe. The enemy might pursue you, but I will cause his own darkness to swallow him.

As I guide you today, believe Me when I tell you I will make every dark place bright as the sun and every rough place smooth. The enemy wants you to feel forgotten. He wants your heart to experience drought. But I keep My promise to lead you and never forsake you. And, child, I do all this not only to get you through the day, but to enable you to flourish in it. Follow Me down to streams of water. I strengthen you and restore your soul. My light warms your heart, sweet child.

Isaiah 42:16; 58:11

December 1

Precious child,

I rise up in a great wall of fire around you.

A consuming fire, I surround you to keep you safe within. My flames not only protect you, but guide you to the place I want you to go. My holy fire reflects My glory, and I place it like a canopy over your life, providing shelter for shade in the heat of life's struggles. My glory gives you refuge, and My presence in the fire goes before you on the journey to show you the way.

My fire is unquenchable. Its flames burn from My desire to bring justice and rescue My people who have been robbed by the oppressor's hand. My words are like fire sent to burn up the idols made to draw your attention away from Me. I will never set My face against you, child. These fires burn eternally for your benefit. My consuming fire surrounds you like an inferno, melting away mountains of fear and regret. Hatred and selfishness ignite like chaff.

But the world has forgotten Me, child. They have built up fortresses to protect them, but the only thing they've created is a false sense of security. All their gold and silver cannot save them. The world is like a branch that has been severed and left to wither. Soon it will be thrown into the fire and destroyed. I am calling you to tell them these things. Tell them that I am here. Tell them Jesus is their only Savior.

You are safe. Keep your life in Jesus. Remain in Him and live. Don't be afraid. You are so dear to Me. I created you. I breathed life into you. Today, like yesterday and tomorrow, I love you.

Deuteronomy 4:24; Isaiah 4:5; Jeremiah 21:12;
Zechariah 2:5; Hebrews 12:29

December 2

Precious child,

I am your commander.

The world has abandoned My decrees. I am sending you to a people whose hearts have turned away from Me. You will be My servant-witness so they will know I am the one and only living God. This is one of so many ways your life matters. You are very special because I created your heart to reflect My goodness, My heart for a world that has gone its own way.

The enemy prowls around through the darkness looking to capture souls. There is a famine of faith in the world. Souls are starving. But I am alive in you, child, and I am sending you like a faithful soldier into battle for My name's sake. I open your eyes so you may see the unseen world of the wounded ones waiting to hear the good news. Tell them there is no one like Me.

I am proud of you because you do what is right and follow Me with all your heart. Tell the people who have been warring against My name that I am gracious and compassionate. Pray for them that they might remove the idols from their hearts. I look down and see their bitterness. They have no one to help. They are powerless, lost, and suffering. But I am sending you with My arrows of victory to aim at their fortresses of sinful pride. I am with you in everything you do.

The world has rejected My truth. Their worthless idols leave them empty. They bow down to money and worship greed. Help the lost ones return to Me by being bold enough to speak the name of Jesus. My peace goes with you as you run down the paths of My commands. I love you.

Deuteronomy 8:6; Isaiah 55:4; John 15:10

December 3

Precious child,

My only Son, Jesus, is your foundation.

He suffered on the cross for you. His death and resurrection paid the price and set you free. On that hill where sorrow ran for all to see, My sweet Son gave His life so you could breathe deep My breath of eternal life. I love you so much I sent Jesus into the darkness so that you could be saved from the prison of desolation.

Child, go with My power to share Jesus with someone who hasn't heard His wonderful name. Just as I formed the foundations of the earth, so I formed the Spirit within you. Life's heavy rains will pour over you, but they cannot shake your faith in Me. Life's raging waters will rush over you, but they cannot break your heart from Me. Life's unrelenting winds will blow over you, but they cannot tear down your hope in Me.

Today is My gift to you for building up hope for the brokenhearted. Go to them, child, and tell them how Jesus lives to be their hope. Tell them that Jesus is faithful to save them. Be My messenger and build up their hearts with the love of Jesus so they might be able to turn from darkness and see light. I love you and your boldness for My glory.

Sweet child, please know how much your life matters. I created you in a very special way. The enemy tempts the world into building houses on sands of self. But in My great love, as you tell the hurting ones about Jesus and they begin to hear truth, their foundations of sin will be shaken and their chains will loosen. They will be made new, and heaven will rejoice!

Zechariah 12:1; Acts 16:26; 1 Corinthians 3:11; Hebrews 11:10

December 4

Precious child,

I will answer you. Trust Me.

Whether you feel trapped in the deepest darkness or lost along the winding path of life's uncertainties, call out to Me. When the world's sea of hate swirls around you and waves of suffering break over you, cry out to Me. I will answer you. When the enemy makes you feel banished and unworthy, I will answer you with mercy and truth. I will sing over you words of hope so you will know how worthy you really are. I will dispel the doubt, and you will find that I never let go of you. You are safe in Me, child. You always will be.

The world lacks compassion for the weak. You glorify Me by answering the call to serve them when no one else will. The world surrounds the poor with fences of apathy so they don't have to see the need. But you glorify Me when you reach out and love them when no one else will. The world has wrapped up its sins in coverings of good deeds to feel justified. But you glorify Me when you are merciful and pray for them.

The enemy is a skillful adversary who bars you in and pushes you down. But I am the Lord your God, and I have rescued you from the depths of the pit. Remember this truth. Your prayers rise up to Me. I hear your shouts of praise. Salvation comes from Me and is found in the precious name of Jesus. There is no other name by which man is saved, so use your freedom to share this beautiful hope that I have freely given you. The world is asleep in its sin, lost in a maze of unbelief.

Be unashamed. Awaken them, child. I love you.

Jonah 2; Acts 4:12; Romans 1:16

December 5

Precious child,

I am your almighty God.

I bless you. I help you. My love for you is limitless. My breath gives you life. I am righteous and do not oppress. I restore and save you from the world's attempts to hurt your heart. I hear your prayers and answer them according to My will. I make sure you find rest in My shadow. Nothing can thwart the plans I have for you. No force can turn back My outstretched hand. Don't be frightened by the clamor of the world when it shouts accusations against you, because I will shield you and deliver you from all the enemy's soul attacks.

My mighty hand stirs up the seas and makes waves crash over the yoke of your weakness. I tear off the bonds of your insecurity. No more will you be enslaved by the world's temptations and feel unwanted. My love for you is without end. My mighty arms turn the desolate places that you are walking through into pastures of infinite rest. Follow Me and find peace in My promises.

I vigorously defend you, child. The burdensome weight of guilt has been lifted off your shoulders forever. I am the maker of all things. I am the almighty one who holds all things together. Your heart is priceless to Me. I made it and will protect it for all eternity. So don't be afraid of anything.

I use My power to banish the names of idols, and today I'm calling you to do the same—pull the world away from darkness. Be filled with My might and go free the brokenhearted. Seek what's good and resist the enemy. Be strong because I am your strength. Show mercy and compassion to one another.

I am here for you always.

Genesis 17:1; Job 33:4; Jeremiah 33:11–12

Precious child,

I am the author of peace.

I know that each day wars against your heart. The life I created for you gets filled with questions without answers, and sometimes sadness without smiles. But sweet and wonderful one, close your eyes. Listen to My voice speak. Hear Me say the word *peace*, and feel its calming power pour over you. Lie down and rest in My love for you. No harm can reach you here. You are safe.

My peace isn't just for the days of rest. My peace goes with you into the hard areas of life so that you may be free of fear and anxiety. It guards your heart from worrying about things that are simply out of your control. When it looks like the day is lost in darkness, remember that Jesus has already brought you into His glorious light.

My perfect peace keeps you from stumbling over the enemy's lies. Envy can no longer take hold in your heart. I am so pleased with you that I even cause others to make peace with you. Today, as you pursue righteousness, you will harvest the fruit of peace. Quietness and confidence are yours forever.

And when the mountains are shaken and life seems like it's on the verge of collapsing, My peace remains with you. When the hills of safe pastures are removed, My covenant of abundant peace remains. I love you, and the ways of the world can never erase who you are in Me.

My peace makes you strong. This strength opens your eyes to truth and moves your feet along the peaceful paths I have marked out for you to follow. All the peace I give you is found in Jesus, your Messiah! There will be times of trouble, but don't fear. Be bold and go on, knowing that Jesus has overcome the world!

Leviticus 26:6; Psalm 85:8; Proverbs 16:7; Isaiah 54:10

December 7

Precious child,

I am your merciful God. I am here for you. Tune out the noise and listen to Me.

I will never leave you stranded. I will never let the world destroy your heart. My goodness goes before you and makes your path straight. I fill your days with mercy and compassion. I shower you with forgiveness. I have no desire to end your dreams. I will never abandon you. I am gracious and merciful. These days have hours of hope mixed with hours of pain. I know this, child. But turn away from the lies. Don't listen to the enemy say that I have gone away and left you all alone.

When your hurt is overwhelming, seek My face. I am with you, and I carry your burdens. When your struggles outweigh your joy, please know that I feel your stress. Remember that I redeemed your soul, and nothing is too hard for Me. Rest in Me. I will lift your heart and carry you through the current storm.

Sweet child, don't be afraid of the growing darkness swirling across the world. It cannot harm you. Your heart is My desire. Spend this day in My mercy. I have given you a new, forgiving heart. Let it lead you into the places where broken people are searching for a Savior. Don't get lost in sacrifices. I desire mercy. I am good, and I love you. Humbly run after Me. Leave misery behind and pick up My yoke. I hold your hand and lead you to the river where mercy runs free.

Here with Me, you will be able to give freely and not expect anything in return. You already have everything, because I made you alive in Jesus! You will not be consumed because I will never fail you. My mercies for you are new every morning!

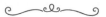

Isaiah 63:9; Jeremiah 3:12; Lamentations 3:22–23;
Ephesians 2:4; 1 Peter 1:3

December 8

Precious child,

I am your keeper.

Day and night, I help you. I formed heaven and earth, and I will make a way for you. I will not let your foot slip off the path. While you sleep, I watch over you. I will keep you from harm all the days of your life. I keep you safe and supply all of your needs. You are eternally protected, child.

You are My special creation. Today, I want you to know that I will stop the enemy's arrows of fear. I will keep your light burning so darkness flees. I am with you, child. I am also before you to ensure the road is safe for your journey. I strengthen you to endure life's trials. Remember that in your weakness, My strength for you prevails.

I am here. I am close to keep you free from sin's rule. I remain faithful in My promises. When troubles come into your day like a thief, unannounced and unexpected, I am never caught off guard. I keep you secure and set you on the high rock of My Son, Jesus. In Him, My dear child, the enemy's attacks cannot harm you. The traps set before you are worthless now.

I hold you close, child, in My loving arms. There is a famine of love and kindness in the world, but I am your provision. My love fills your heart so you won't be scared or alone. Go out today and lose your life for the sake of My kingdom. I am right here with you, cradling you close to My heart. Don't be afraid. Be confident and go tell the world their Savior, Jesus Christ, has come to rescue them. You will not be shaken!

Psalm 12:7; Daniel 9:4; John 12:25

December 9

Precious child,

I am the potter.

You are My sweet creation. I formed you into a beautiful person. I uniquely made you to live a special life that reflects My glory. You are precious to Me for a million reasons. My love washes over you and fills your heart. The world pulls your eyes from Me. The enemy drains your purpose by shifting your focus to things of the world.

I am your loving Father. You are the clay. And today, center your life on this truth: I made you beautiful.

In your eyes, I capture My radiant light. When you consider your reflection, see how I formed your beautiful eyes to see the people who are burdened by broken hearts. Your eyes hold the light of the sun, moon, and stars for those who don't have the strength to lift up their heads to consider heaven.

Your love for the world spreads as wide as the oceans. I made your beautiful heart to care about those who are being mistreated and misunderstood. Your love for them causes waves of mercy to crash along the shore of their scars. Your love for them washes away the world's lies about their worth.

And like the land that stretches far, your desire to serve Me does the same. I made your strong arms able to reach out to hold the hopeless. The compassion I formed in you is like a field of endless flowers. When the victims of the world's injustice look at you, they see My beautiful justice. I am proud of you!

Genesis 1:3–18; Isaiah 29:16; 64:8; Jeremiah 18:4

Precious child,

Just breathe.

I promise it's going to be okay. The pain will end. The suffering will pass like a shadow under the midday sun. Remember Jesus endured suffering, not only on the cross, but also through all His days on earth. In fact, He was despised and greatly rejected. He knows your struggle. His death and resurrection were for you. I sent Him to endure the pain and shame for you. Can't you see just how special and precious you are?

Just breathe.

Trust Me in this and feel My steadfast love surround you. Jesus, mighty Savior, was called the Man of Sorrows. Grief befriended Him. He paid the price for your amazing heart so that we can all spend eternity together. Focus on the truth. The enemy will reach out to you in your suffering and comfort you with lies. He says that Jesus is far away and has no idea what you're fighting against. But child, Jesus is in you! Feel Him holding your heart. Hear Him tell you that people despised Him and even hid their faces from Him. Can you imagine? The King of kings, the one who took the painful nails and the weight of the world's sin, made to feel like an unwanted, unloved criminal!

Just breathe.

I want you to know that My sweet Son was not esteemed by the world. They mocked Him. They spit on Him. They laughed at Him. They shoved a crown of thorns on His precious head. But Jesus went through all that so He could bear your grief and carry your sorrows! Today, I will make new your desire to take hold of the truth that you are loved and forgiven and free. Just be. . .with Jesus.

Isaiah 53:2–4

December 11

Precious child,

I am your hiding place.

Trouble can't get to you because you are safe in Me. I surround you with My songs of deliverance and shield you from the world's attacks so you can rest. Just be still, and put your hope in My unchanging promise that I am faithful. The darkness can't blind you anymore. My mighty arms keep you hidden from the weary world, so you can rest and not be drained by things that make you question your worth. I adore everything about you, and while you are hidden in Me I'll remind you of the ways I made you special.

You are beautiful because you rely on Me with everything that is in your humble spirit. You have exchanged your pride for the riches of heaven. In meekness you love others and gently teach them to turn their eyes away from darkness and help them see the light of My truth. The whole earth is your inheritance. Look forward to the day that you will see Me! I will dry the tears of mourning and give My eternal comfort.

As you rest in Me, I satisfy your hunger for righteousness. The desire I have given you to be merciful in a merciless world has made you My peacemaker. By My strength I have made it possible for you to endure persecution. When the world seeks to belittle you because of Me, rejoice because your reward in heaven is great.

Child, I know that today will have problems. The enemy would convince you to exchange My words for lies. Darkness wants you to serve the world instead of Me. But, child, I want you to know that today is a gift. Unwrap My love for you and know without doubting that everything is going to be okay.

Psalm 32:7; 119:14; Matthew 5:3–11; Romans 1:25

December 12

Precious child,

I am God over all.

God over your burdens and the darkness, and My glory rains over you. My love pours down from heaven every minute of this day. I have placed a special purpose in your heart, and today I am guiding you in understanding My will for your life.

I am over everything, and I keep you protected from the world. There is no need to fear. Both your joy and your suffering are for great purposes. The world watches you, and they wonder how you could possibly have joy in the middle of life's pain. They wonder what kind of power could be in you that lifts you above the heartaches.

Everything about you pleases Me. Jesus chose to die so you could live. This gift of today is for you to be free, to shout praises, and to be at peace. It's for you to feel My mercy cover you.

The enemy is not over you, child. His efforts to keep you oppressed under the weight of life's trials cannot harm you. Know that I have not saved you to walk alone. I have drawn your heart out from the sea of self so you will bear fruit.

I am over every minute of this day. I give you life to learn more about Me. I am filling you with holy power to strengthen you. My strength in you helps you patiently endure trials as you feel My joy rise from your heart in shouts of thanksgiving. Your life has been set firmly into My kingdom of light. In Jesus, you have been redeemed and forgiven. Today, nothing can take you out of My hands!

Romans 9:5; Colossians 1:10–14

December 13

Precious child,

You are Mine, and I have so much to tell you. On the wind, I say that you are amazing. I don't make mistakes. You are nothing short of wonderful. Hear My words become reality. Every time you hear Me say I love you, your heart is filled with My perfect love. On the gentlest breeze, I say that you are needed. Listen to Me remind you that you are special and you matter. From the moment I made you, I have been talking to you in loving whispers of mercy and hope.

Now, precious child, the enemy is a cunning speaker. His voice is a sinner's sweet melody of self. He writes songs filled with rhythms that bring unrest and stir up darkness and hopeless futures. The enemy creates lyrics that lead the world away from My love while justifying their greed. The words sung here in this broken place are drenched in doubt and cause you to believe I'm not really who I say I am. Beats of unbelief come together and move through your soul, whispering words of condemnation. The world's chorus sings of your stress and shame.

But on the winds of My unconditional love, I whisper your name and call you blessed. You are Mine. My voice reaches you in soft, whispered songs of redemption. I have saved you and carried you into the eternal kingdom of My beloved Son, Jesus. In Him alone you have forgiveness. Child, listen to My song of truth. I am the sound of mercy reviving your heart so you will know that you are loved. Hear My words come together in a new song for you today. My gentle whisper is calling you to step out in faith and tell the world about Jesus. I am with you forever!

1 Kings 19:12; John 14:21; Colossians 1:14

Precious child,

My passion for you is like a refiner's fire. My love for you has done amazing things. I sent Jesus, My sweet and only Son, to become flesh and become your Savior. He carried the unbearable weight of your sins to the cross. After hours of darkness and suffering, Jesus took His final breath, and with it, all your sins to the grave. And then He rose, conquering death for you! Your sweet and mighty Savior is alive in you. My love has melted away the hardened edges of your heart. I continue to sanctify and bless you and will keep My promises.

I skim away the impurities and make you new. For My glory, I purify you. From the endless storehouses of My mercy and grace, I give you this gift of days to become more like Jesus. As I take away the sin that rises to the surface, I change you into a new creation. The world doesn't understand this. They believe that with enough pressure and determination, they can change themselves. But you know that I alone am the heart refiner and soul restorer.

The things of the world will perish, but your faith in Me has been made pure and will last forever. I know that grief hides in the shadows, and some days the trials are numerous. You are not alone. I am with you. Your faith is what takes you to that quiet place where, despite the suffering, your heart still sings out to Me in praise. You bring Me honor and glory as you follow your heart through the storms. Jesus is teaching you how to walk on water. Keep your eyes fixed on Him.

Today you are secure, steadfast, and strong. Today your heart is pure. All because of My love for you.

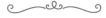

Zechariah 13:9; Malachi 3:2; 1 Corinthians 3:13–15; 1 Peter 1:7

December 15

Precious child,

Today I sing to you a new song of truth. Listen to the sweet lyrics reminding you that your blessed hope is Jesus. Oh, how beautiful is His holy name! My grace sent Him to take up the cross for you. In Jesus, your salvation is secure. Once you were far away from My heart, but because of Him, you are here safe in My hands of loving mercy. Be bold with My courage and see this new day as a chance to bring glory and honor to Jesus, your saving king.

The darkness hides these truths. Swirling in the midst of the enemy's storms are the lies sent to crash over your heart. Like a riptide of abandoned hope, the world pulls against your desire to follow Me. The enemy strives to stand on the shore of life and call out to you in your weariness with words of defeat. Waves of hopelessness tug at your will to go on and crash over your efforts to take the next step. Winds of hate rage against your faith, but freedom is found in My eternal comfort.

But in the middle of even the darkest night, Jesus is the glorious radiance who shines on. I need you to look not with your eyes, but with your heart. Be patient and know that the darkness has no power over you now. Jesus destroyed the darkness and made you clean. Your Hope has redeemed you from the chains that once held you captive. Your hope has been made real and true by the blood of your Savior, Jesus Christ. This truly is the day I have made for you as a holy gift in which to rejoice and be glad because, precious child, Jesus has set you free!

Romans 8:25; Ephesians 2:12–13; 2 Thessalonians 2:16; Titus 2:13

December 16

Precious child,

Don't fear the bitter things in your life. I tell you not to be afraid, because Jesus is your teacher. There is no longer a need for you to worry and stress about what the day might hold. Your Savior is with you and will give you intructions to cover everything today. Let Jesus lead the way. Follow Him and rely on His knowledge and wisdom to guide you. Jesus died for you, and He has so many lessons to share that will protect your heart, because His words are true.

The world accumulates its own false teachers. Truth has no part in their learning, and they go astray following myths. The enemy guides them through darkness. Fear is the objective and blinds the world to all that I have for them. The world's classroom is attractive; it contains volumes of excuses for selfishness and pride. False teaching moves like wildfire across the minds of many, burning down their will to listen.

Today your heart will be filled with lessons of truth that will give you strength to go and tell the world about Jesus. Your actions will be the words the brokenhearted read. Your words about Me will help them understand.

Show them love. Show the world that I sent Jesus to save them. Serve them with open arms so they stop and wonder where your love comes from. Feed them, child. Tell them that bread alone won't satisfy their hunger. Show them Jesus, and teach the world that their parched souls can be quenched with His rivers of living water. Show them light, My child, and tell the world that Jesus is the light of life and with Him they will never again walk in darkness. Precious one, you are amazing to Me.

Job 36:22, Matthew 8:19; John 13:13; 2 Timothy 4:3

Precious child,

I love you. I am love, and I sent My love to you and His name is Jesus. This love saved you and lives in you. Live out the hours of today through this love. My heart is filled with steadfast love for you that is faithful, constant, and true. Oh dear child, there aren't enough pages to explain how deep and real My love is for you. I see you, and waves of heart-beating, soul-restoring love rise up from My heart and reach yours. With the sweetest grace, My love fills you so you will know how special you are in My eyes.

Darkness blinds the world, keeping them from seeing My love. Their eyes have adjusted to the darkness, and they can only see selfishness. Without light, they can't see past their anger and greed. The broken people go through their days with eyes closed to My gift of forgiveness. The enemy fuels their doubts with lies, whispering words of deception. Shattered and fragmented, the hearts of the hopeless roam all around you, child. They don't look lost. In fact, the lost ones appear safe and secure.

But Jesus is here! He lives in you and keeps your heart filled and satisfied. Jesus isn't temporary. His love for you took your place on Calvary. Let that truth move you to seek out the unloved. Let the love of Christ that is in your heart overflow onto the unsafe and insecure. Your sweetest Savior, Jesus, lifted you out of the darkness by the mighty power of His love. He is alive in you. Feel His affections rain down over you and wash away the weariness. Feel His beautiful heart beat for you. Feel real love destroy your doubts. I Am. I am love, and I love you.

Genesis 24:27; Exodus 34:6; Ephesians 2:4; 1 John 4:8

December 18

Precious child,

I am the shade that protects you from life's burning sun. From the destroyer of broken hearts, I am the one who keeps you hidden in peaceful places. My strong arms block out the rays of wickedness so they cannot reach you. Searing waves of oppression pass around Me, not able to hurt your heart. My love for you is like a cloud that covers the scorching sun of regret in life's cloudless sky. It is like a great rock in a weary land for you to rest behind. My love for you covers your precious heart from the flames of destruction.

The world has no place to keep you safe, no shelter, no sojourn in the enemy's presence. Even in the darkness, your heart was once exposed to the heat of selfishness. In the world today, you will step out among lost souls roaming in search of protection from the searing rays of wickedness. Remember that you too were like them, an unwanted outcast made to believe you were protected from the enemy's lies. But at the first stirring of My Spirit's truthful wind, the lies were blown away.

Oh, how Jesus loves you, that He made a way for you to be ever hidden and protected in the shadow of His cross. No longer will the heat of life's accusations reach you. The world's lies aimed at your heart will never again scorch your spirit. In the shade of My loving arms, precious one, breathe deep My breath of life. Yes, the cross of My one and only Son casts its shadow over every part of your days. Jesus is your soul protector. No wicked or warped scheme of the enemy can blacken your spirit. I love you and will keep you in My heart's shadow forever.

Psalm 80:10; Isaiah 16:3; Jonah 4:6

December 19

Precious child,

Today, I am for you. I give you breath. I make your heart beat. And because of Jesus, all of this is possible. He is the sweetest source of everything you have and will ever need. My only Son took on the flesh of man so you could know that as you feel, whether sadness or joy, so does Jesus. Don't forget He also cried out to Me in tear-filled prayers and thunderous supplications. The soldier's spit was degrading, but My Son never wavered in His desire to bring Me glory and your salvation.

Remember that the world didn't want Him. To a cross the lost condemned Him. The enemy tried to speak hurtful words about Jesus to a crowd who didn't know truth. They heard the lies and believed them. They yelled out for the guilty to be set free. The ones who could see were blinded and screamed for Jesus to be crucified. The source of your sweet and eternal salvation was forced to listen to the crowd of accusing voices. To the sea of darkness they sent Him to perish.

Oh, but sweet Jesus rose from that perilous prison. So, child, He can handle anything you are going through today. He can and will love you through any pain or struggle that the world has put in your way. Weariness that once covered your days like a heavy blanket is now being blown away by His mighty voice. Hear this same sweet sound call out to you in the midst of your trials and call you forgiven. Rejoice because you have been made alive in Jesus. Your life is hidden in His great love and mercy. Believe Me when I say that your sins were nailed to the cross and your enemies were disarmed. Run free and use today's gift to bring Him glory!

Colossians 2:6–15; Hebrews 2:10–11; 5:7–9

December 20

Precious child,

I am the Lord of righteousness. I love you. Nothing can snatch you away from My heart. Our relationship is so important to Me that I am here with you speaking truth into your heart. As you move and breathe today, I am not far away. I know there is pain, and I know there is fear, but I have made a way to destroy these things that dim your vision of who I am and what I have done for you.

Remember back to the days when you were lost. Your days weren't a gift but a walk of miserable steps across broken paths that led you further and further into darkness. The enemy lured you deeper with lies that seemed pleasing and comfortable. He showed you a palace that was really a prison. He promised you safety, but you found only strife. He brought you to a land that looked like a pleasant garden but was actually littered with garbage. Injustice rose up all around you. Immorality was sent like a dark rain, and the enemy left you alone to be soaked in shame.

Then Jesus held out His hand, and you had faith that He is your Savior. You put your hand in His, and He pulled you out of the sinking sand by the almighty strength of His love for you. He washed away all of your sins by His blood that was shed on the cross. By your faith, Jesus made you clean. He declared you justified once and forever. This is important, because the world is twisted, and when they see you, their hearts will wonder. Go to them with gifts of peace and sow a harvest of righteousness for My name's sake.

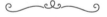

Isaiah 42:6; Jeremiah 23:6; Romans 10:4; James 3:18

December 21

Precious child,

I have made this day for you. I have made it unique among all the others. Rejoice as you breathe. Let worry go as you exhale. I am your rock. Nothing can shake you or bring you down. The plans I have for you reflect My perfection. The gift I'm giving you today is rooted in My justice. You have been set free to be glad in the new life I have given you. Pour out this gladness on the world around you. Know that nothing can tear you down and leave you unwanted. I took the broken pieces of your life and remade you. I have set your life on a firm foundation.

The world is drenched in blinding darkness. Its builders labor in vain to construct firm foundations, but without light they remain blind. Still, they work tirelessly at their creations, and the enemy uses them to lure the lost away from My offer of salvation. Unsafe, the world spends its time marveling at the works of their hands. They impress themselves with things that will eventually break down. The world is distracted by what they have made instead of considering Me.

See My truth and hope in the things I have already accomplished. When Moses led the Israelites through the wilderness, they became parched and cried out for mercy. Moses used his staff and struck the rock and rejoiced when water poured out for the people to drink and find relief. When Jesus came to tell the world that He was their Savior, some cried out for mercy. The Roman solider used his spear and struck the Rock. Living water poured out for the sinner to be washed and find salvation. Today, feel that same river of soul-saving water wash over you and remind you how much you are loved!

Exodus 17:6; Deuteronomy 32:4; 1 Samuel 2:2;
John 19:34; 1 Corinthians 10:4

Precious child,

I think about you often, and I am always here for you. I am your refuge and safe place. Please don't ever feel that you have to earn your way into My arms. The days I have given you are wrapped in grace. I made you wonderful and am proud of you. So please believe Me. When you feel oppressed or misunderstood, run to Me. When the world ignores you and walks away, leaving you stranded in grief, run to Me. As stress builds itself up around you like prison walls, call out to Me, and I will give you rest.

The enemy lurks around waiting for you to tire. At the right moment, he strikes at you with discouraging words and viciously attacks your self-esteem. He skillfully corners you with lies that make you doubt your security with Me. The world has become numb to My presence because it buys the damaged goods the world is selling. Gifts like comfort, prosperity, and possessions. These earthly treasures keep your eyes off Me. The lost ones look around and put their hope in these tainted presents. Their hearts crave these things and guide their steps to acquire more of them.

Sweet one, I want you to know that while My strong arms keep you safe, under the shadow of My wings your heart becomes richly blessed. Your heart is My treasure. I have rescued you by the cross of My Son and your Savior, Jesus Christ. I keep your life protected in the refuge of My love and grace. I sing over you today with words of healing and encouragement. Hear Me speak over you today words of security and affirmation. You are worth the world to Me!

Ruth 2:12; Nahum 1:7; Hebrews 6:18

December 23

Precious child,

I am your song.

My heartbeat in you is the rhythm of your soul. Day and night, I sing over you verses of love that teach you I am almighty, just, and true. Listen, because My song reminds you that you are Mine. I adopted you and call you chosen. I know you feel spent, stressed, and empty, but today hear My song of salvation and breathe deep. Exhale the emptiness. Let your lungs take in My breath of blessing. Be satisfied in My promises and live.

You are safe in the pasture of My grace. I am with you. Hear the song I play for you, child. Be renewed by the notes of hope that were written by your Savior's love on the cross. Hear the melody remind you how I rescued you from darkness. Let your precious heart join in the chorus of the redeemed and lift up praise. Let it rise from your lips to heaven as you focus on love. My heart song for you is forever. From chords of forgiveness come music that celebrates our relationship and stirs your heart to beat as one with Mine.

Understand the world's music is born from struggle and strife, but Mine is made from salvation and grace. The enemy's song is played in the key of misfortune, but Mine is sung in everlasting keys of mercy. Let the sound of your beautiful soul remind the world of My love for their hurting hearts. Your prayers are sweet sounds of grace in a world where noise drowns out My presence.

Precious child, you are important. You matter. The words I sing over you are not empty and hopeless. By the blood of Jesus, I have ransomed you. I have sealed you with My Spirit. Use today to dance and rejoice because I love you.

Exodus 15:2; Psalm 42:8; Isaiah 12:2; Revelation 15:3

December 24

Precious child,

Jesus is the shepherd of your soul. Every wound of His suffering has healed you completely. Oh, I love you so much and want you to experience what it means to be fully Mine. Powerful waves of mercy flow through you, giving you strength to remain in Me. My saving grace helps you honor the ones who walk near you and bring Me glory with your thoughts and your deeds.

The same Holy Spirit who conceived in Mary a new hope has given you a new heart to love the world. And just as the angel of the Lord spoke about the glorious name of My Son, Jesus, so am I calling you to shout from the highest mountain that the world's Messiah has come! Tell them, child, that their soul saver is here to take away their sins and give them the gift of days wrapped in His lovingkindness.

The world's eyes have grown accustomed to the heavy darkness. It's impossible for them to see Me. There is no joy where they are, but don't fear. My tender mercy will guide you on the ways of My perfect peace. The people who stumble in the night will see the love of Christ radiate from your heart and long to know the meaning of real grace.

I will teach you how to let fear slip away like whispers on the wind so your soul will be free to magnify Me. Today, child, choose to make Me bigger. Decide to do the hard work of bringing light to the world that still stumbles under the weight of darkened hearts. Tell them I will fill their hunger with goodness found only in the bread of life. Show them grace as grace was shown to you. Show them hope as hope was shown to you. Love them like I love you!

Matthew 1:20–21; Luke 1:46; John 1:9; 1 Peter 2:25

Precious child,

Today you are not alone. Like the shepherds who were tending their sheep under the stars, you too once lived in cold darkness. And just like My angel appeared to them, so too did My glory come to you. The blanket of night was pulled away and replaced by the magnificent Light. Today, the glory of heaven is with you to brighten your life. Today, the Savior of the world is with you to hold your hand and walk by your side.

Jesus. The one who saves people from their sins. Sweet Jesus. The one who is called Immanuel (God with us). Sweet and mighty Jesus. The one who loves you so much, He walked away from heaven and traded His glory for a dirty manger. Jesus loves you so much that He traded His throne for a cold, dark night. He gave up his rightful place in heaven so He could take yours on the cross.

The enemy can never comprehend this great love. All Satan understands is the love of man that is confined by limits and expectations. When you see the brokenness and tears, know that the world is lost in the enemy's garden of lies. The suffering grows tall like leafless trees unable to give shade from the burning sun. People all around you are looking for a Savior. Go to them and speak the one name that is above all others.

Celebrate the eternal gift of life I have given you! Let your life shout for joy, and remember your days are wrapped in Me. Join in the glorious chorus for My name's sake. I shower you with peace. Treasure our relationship in your heart. Use the hours I've gifted you to ponder the miracle of My Son, your Savior, Jesus Christ!

Genesis 35:3; Isaiah 7:14; 8:8; Matthew 1:23; Luke 2:19

December 26

Precious child,

Jesus is with you. Your Savior is risen and reigns! For every minute of every hour of every one of your days, Jesus is the way, the truth, and the life. With Him there is no trouble. With Him you lack nothing, and in Him you have everything.

The way. Jesus made a way for you to come back to Me. His love endured the pain and shame of the cross. His heart for yours tore the veil so you can enter into My loving presence. Think about how today is like a special stone on the path I have given to you. Today is here for you to read My words, talk to Me, and consider how special I made you. I created today like a garden for you and Me to walk through and rest in. Don't skip over it. Don't worry about what tomorrow might bring.

The truth. Jesus became a humble servant to be an example of light and living proof that My promises made long ago still stand firm. You know, child, that the world is filled with so much selfishness and pride that truth and justice have no room in it. Your eyes are tired of seeing the results of anger and hatred. I know, child. Oh, I know, because Mine are too. Be the one who decides that Jesus is the answer to every dark scheme.

The life. Jesus is your life, and your life is wrapped eternally secure in Him. Decide to start a different kind of revolution. Decide to sacrifice all of your desires and let Jesus teach you how to be a servant leader. Let Him show you how to leave your dreams behind and follow Him to the hard places where justice battles injustice. Jesus guides your heart to love the least of the world's beautiful hearts so that their eyes will open and see Me.

John 14:6; Acts 9:2; Romans 15:8; Colossians 3:4

December 27

Precious child,

For everything you need and everything you hope to accomplish, Jesus is your strong tower. In Him, your provisions are secure. Run to Jesus and let Him be your mighty protector. From where you are all the way to heaven, your strong tower, Jesus, rises over the plains of darkness and destruction, giving you freedom from the coming storm. Your Savior rose from the grave, and today He rises higher than your hurt. He conquered death and saved you so you can find an eternal hope that doesn't fail.

The world has no safe place. The enemy hunts for the lost, and they run but cannot find sanctuary among broken hearts. He stirs up winds of bitterness to swirl and break down walls of hope. When they fall and crumble, the world stands alone in barren fields shouting out for mercy, but they find only malice. They try with all their might to build fortresses and systems that will defend them. But their enemy isn't a man bound by limits of flesh and blood. Their enemy is an unseen force of vengeance.

But Jesus is the rock who is higher than the world. His light shines for you. On Him, fix your eyes. Climb the mountain of His mercy and find shelter inside the strong walls of His grace. My sweet Son, Jesus, became a sacrifice for you. In your place, He hung on the cross, bearing the weight of all your sins. The heaviness pulled on Him, and His love for you kept Him focused on enduring the agony until the end.

This great and perfect love defeated the enemy forever. Today, find new mercies within the mighty walls of My forgiveness. Go and show the world the strong tower they've been searching for. Show them Jesus.

Psalm 61:3; Proverbs 18:10

December 28

Precious child,

I want you to look in the mirror and see how I see you.

Saved by grace, you are made wonderful. On that glorious day when you said, "Jesus is Lord," and knew with all your heart that I raised Him from the dead, you were saved. At that moment, I made you into a brand-new creation, righteous and holy. You aren't far away from Me. You are now the light of the world! See yourself as a beacon of hope for the world that has lost its way.

The enemy tries to hold up a different mirror. It is one made of cracked glass and shows your old self. He tries to lure you into believing that you are what you see in its broken shards. He whispers that all the sin and scars of unrighteousness are still what I see when I look at you.

Know how special I made you. I put My light in your heart so you will always be able to shine in the dark world like stars in the deep night sky. I made you special. You are My sweet, chosen, and justified child. The enemy can't beat you, because Jesus sits at My right hand interceding for you! No hardships, persecution, famines of the heart, danger, or even death can separate you from Him. Nothing.

Even in the middle of the storms, you are still all these things to Me. I have called you to do good works so the world will stop what they're doing long enough to see Me in you. The labor of your heart for the world is bearing fruit that never spoils. They are calling out to Me, and I will save them.

You are beautiful and special. Believe this, child, and shine!

Matthew 5:14; Romans 10:9; 2 Corinthians 5:17;
Ephesians 4:24; 1 Peter 2:9

Precious child,

I know that some days My gift seems like a burden. The hours seem to conspire against you. Minutes seem longer than normal and filled with more and more questions. Seconds plot tempting alternatives to grace. Time feels like heavy chains holding you down. But these feelings do not have their origins in Me.

Darkness makes it impossible to see. The enemy works hard at keeping the world in it, so their eyes can take in only the gloom. Even if they are acclimated to the dark, all they can see is the outward appearance of things. The world is satisfied with what's on the surface. They find joy in the shallow end of life's ocean.

Whether in pain or sadness, trial or grief, I am with you. My gift of days is for you and Me. To be together. I am here to love you through the struggles and erase the burdens. My love for you makes every hour a blessing. My mercy fills the minutes with peace and answers your questions. My unending grace gives you the power to flee temptations and feel seconds turn into a sanctuary of peace.

Child, you are no longer of the world. Your joy comes from the deep waters of My presence. I see your heart, and in it I see Jesus. Let this truth pull away the shadows of darkness and the crushing weight of burdens and sadness. Let My light lead you to the truth of Jesus, the living water that quenches your thirst for healing. He nourishes you so that your life is anchored in Him, like roots of an ancient tree that reach deep into the unseen underground. I search your heart and find love there. You are wonderful, and you are with Me forever!

1 Samuel 16:7; Acts 1:24

December 30

Precious child,

I know your days might feel like a burden because of the many responsibilities in your life. You work so hard to honor the blessings I've given you, and you take care of so many things, and for that, I am proud of you. But I never intended for your days to feel like one unbearable hardship after another.

Your job may be overwhelming. Your body may be broken. Your heart might feel stung by the loss of someone you love. But none of these are strong enough to diminish My presence in your life. I am bigger than your problems. My love for you stretches further than the reach of your fears. Let it take hold of your troubling thoughts and carry them away.

Remember that Jesus invited the weary and burdened to run to Him. Listen to His soft voice calling for you to do the same. The world, with hopes of killing a rebel, took human hands and lifted Calvary's cross. But I, with hopes of raising a Savior, took almighty hands and lifted Jesus from the grave and seated Him on heaven's throne. Today, He is the only solution to the endless cycle of activity. Go to Him and find true rest. Let your mind remain on the truth that you have been forever saved by His blood.

As you rest, also rest in My promise that I will never forsake you. As you rest, rest in My presence and decline the temptation of busyness from the enemy. Walk this day with Me, and turn your heart to look upon My will and plans for your life. Walk on the path of My righteousness. I am guiding you with My mighty hand. I will give you rest today, and it will be good.

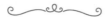

Psalm 16:9; 62:1; 91:1; Jeremiah 6:16; Hebrews 4:10

December 31

Precious child,

As you stand on the edge of a new year, thinking about the blessings that came and the ones to come, I want you to consider a very important truth. Jesus said to His disciples, "Do not get any gold or silver or copper to take with you in your belts—no bag for the journey or extra shirt or sandals or a staff, for the worker is worth his keep." Jesus is your provider and giver. He sustains your life and is more valuable than anything the world could ever offer. Hold on to Jesus, and let Him fill your life with hope.

I made you in Our image and filled you with the hope of eternal life. The world is not the end for you. It has no offering that lasts. But I am truthful and have promised that one day you will be with Us. Your gift of days from Me is eternal!

When you think of tomorrow, think of heaven. A place of endless treasure and blessing, it is complete freedom from the effects of sin. No more death. No more decay. I also want the thought of heaven to plant hope in your heart, because your forever home is not on earth, but with Me. My house has many rooms, and Jesus is preparing a place for you. And, better still, He will come back and bring you here to be with Us.

Now, child, head into today and let my gift of heaven remind you that you are special because Jesus has freed you from sin's grip. As you think about all the ways I have blessed you, lift your hands and show the world your thankful heart. Feel heaven rain down hope as you eagerly proclaim the good news that Jesus lives and has come to save.

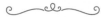

Job 19:27; Matthew 10:9–10; John 14:2–3; 2 Corinthians 5:1

ABOUT THE AUTHOR

Matt and his wife, Cindi, live in
Texas with their four children.

Scripture Index

Old Testament

New Testament